CRIMES OF TERROR

Crimes of Terror

THE LEGAL AND POLITICAL IMPLICATIONS OF FEDERAL TERRORISM PROSECUTIONS

Wadie E. Said

OXFORD
UNIVERSITY PRESS

Oxford University Press is a department of the University of Oxford.
It furthers the University's objective of excellence in research, scholarship,
and education by publishing worldwide.

Oxford is a registered trade mark of Oxford University Press in the UK and certain other countries.

Published in the United States of America by Oxford University Press
198 Madison Avenue, New York, NY 10016, United States of America.

© Oxford University Press 2015

First issued as an Oxford University Press paperback, 2018
ISBN 978-0-19-029681-0 ((paperback) : alk. paper)

Library of Congress Cataloging-in-Publication Data
Sa'id, Wadi', author.
    Crimes of terror : the legal and political implications of federal terrorism prosecutions / Wadie E. Said.
        pages cm
    Includes bibliographical references and index.
    ISBN 978-0-19-996949-4 ((hardback) : alk. paper)
1. Terrorism—Prevention—Law and legislation. 2. Terrorists—Legal status, laws, etc. 3. Prosecution.
4. Trials. 5. Sentences (Criminal procedure) 6. Imprisonment. 7. Espionage. I. Title.
    KZ7220.S235 2015
    345'.02317—dc23
                                                                    2014038580

Note to Readers
This publication is designed to provide accurate and authoritative information in regard to the subject matter
covered. It is based upon sources believed to be accurate and reliable and is intended to be current as of the time
it was written. It is sold with the understanding that the publisher is not engaged in rendering legal, accounting,
or other professional services. If legal advice or other expert assistance is required, the services of a competent
professional person should be sought. Also, to confirm that the information has not been affected or changed
by recent developments, traditional legal research techniques should be used, including checking primary
sources where appropriate.

(Based on the Declaration of Principles jointly adopted by a Committee of the
American Bar Association and a Committee of Publishers and Associations.)

To Jennifer and Edward

Contents

Preface to the Paperback Edition

THERE HAVE BEEN a number of developments worthy of note in the period since the initial publication of *Crimes of Terror*. While this preface to the paperback edition documents several of the most significant of these developments, it is important to note that none of them affect the book's central conclusion. That is, a kind of exceptional criminal justice system has emerged to cover those charged with crimes related to terrorism. So where the normal rules of law and procedure might impede the government's efforts in a prosecution, once there is an allegation that terrorism is involved, courts tend to relax those rules. And with the passage of time, it has become increasingly clear that terrorism really means Islamist terrorism, if the most recent tranche of prosecutions tells us anything.

At the outset, a quick note about what the investigation and prosecution of individuals charged with terrorism-related crimes can never bring about: absolute security. The deadly June 2016 attack on an Orlando nightclub produced hand-wringing over the fact that the FBI had previously investigated the shooter, Omar Mateen, and found that he had no actual ties to terrorists of any sort. Writing in the *Washington Post* after the shooting, Glenn Greenwald pointed out that the FBI had followed its procedures correctly in investigating Mateen, and that to expect it to continue to monitor him under those circumstances was antithetical to our sense of freedom in a democratic society. To retain any sense of liberty would require that we abandon the illusion that we can realize absolute security. He wrote: "Just because someone successfully carried out a violent mass attack does not prove that police powers were inadequate or that existing powers were misapplied. No minimally free society can prevent all violence. In the United States, we do not hold suspects for crimes they have not committed."[1]

This book highlights the government's preventive approach to terrorism prosecutions, which assumes that it can stop attacks before they occur and implies that the type of comprehensive security Greenwald criticizes is attainable. But absolute security is an illusory notion. After all, his article notes that, in other contexts, people recognize the risks that come with trying to completely do away with a well-understood hazard. The number of car-related deaths in the United States reaches many times more per year than the sum total of terrorism-related deaths since and including September 11, 2001. However, our society does not demand more restrictive measures to eliminate such fatalities "because we rationally assess that this fatality level—tragic and horrifying as it is—is the worthwhile cost paid in exchange for the benefits of efficient auto travel and affordable cars."[2] Likewise, the benefits of living in a free society are obvious. In the terrorism context, however, the idea of a tradeoff between security and liberty is constantly challenged and bends in favor of more security and less liberty; the idea of absolute security is certainly alluring.

The relaxing of the duty to give *Miranda* warnings in terrorism cases, documented in these pages,[3] is a case in point. This type of exceptional measure is framed as a correct and useful path to take, especially in comparison to the more extreme and ineffectual method that lurks just outside the picture, waiting to reassert itself, that of Guantanamo-style military detention. In a January 2017 article the *New York Times* extolled the government's interrogation of suspected al-Qaeda member, Ahmed Warsame, without providing him with *Miranda* warnings. reporters Adam Goldman and Benjamin Weiser point out that Warsame eventually incriminated himself and also provided important information that led to several other successful terrorism prosecutions and disrupted plots.[4] This breakthrough, the article notes, demonstrates the usefulness of terrorism prosecutions in federal court as opposed to the cumbersome and ineffectual military commissions model. After all, Warsame never would have cooperated had he been in military detention from the outset, or so the article argues. But as this book points out, the choice need not be between federal prosecutions that disregard the basic protections afforded criminal defendants, on the one hand, and a novel and opaque military justice formulation that

1 Glenn Greenwald, *The FBI Was Right Not to Arrest Omar Mateen Before the Shooting*, WASHINGTON POST, June 17, 2016.
2 *Id.*
3 *See* p. 80-84.
4 Adam Goldman and Benjamin Weiser, *How Civilian Prosecution Gave the U.S. a Key Informant*, N.Y. TIMES, Jan. 28, 2017, at A12.

seems to focus only on ensuring that those caught up in its wake are permanently incapacitated. Additionally, a functioning justice system that relies on treating individuals differently because of their classification as terrorists is itself a questionable proposition.

Consider then a few more noteworthy developments since the original publication of *Crimes of Terror* in May 2015. In keeping with the trend that terrorism suspects deserve greater punishment than ordinary criminal defendants, the maximum penalty an individual convicted of providing material support to a designated foreign terrorist organization (FTO) has been increased from fifteen years in prison to twenty years.[5] As Chapter Two documents in detail, the material support law has served as the government's chief statutory tool in prosecuting terrorism-related crimes. While material support prosecutions have raised a whole host of legal issues since the law's passage in 1996, the period between the initial publication of this book and the paperback has seen the law employed in a manner approaching the formulaic, with the target being the defendant accused of material support of the FTO known as the Islamic State in Iraq and Syria (ISIS). Over 100 people have been charged with materially supporting ISIS, and the majority of those prosecutions involved accusations that an individual tried to travel to the Middle East to fight with the group.[6] Very often the charges were driven by the use of an informant, who helped target and encourage the defendant, continuing and perpetuating the trend described in Chapter One.[7]

And in certain instances, the government's approach to investigating individuals based on their suspected links to terrorist groups has raised the bar of provocative tactics to new heights. In October 2015, journalist Aviva Stahl broke the story of how an undercover officer with the New York Police Department (NYPD) pretended to convert to Islam while posing as a student at Brooklyn College.[8] The same undercover officer, "Mel," had earlier been identified as thwarting the plot of two New York women to build and detonate a homemade bomb on behalf of ISIS.[9] If the bombing case eventually goes to trial, she will be allowed to testify with her

---

5   18 U.S.C. §2339B (2015).

6   Trevor Aaronson, *The New Targets*, THE INTERCEPT, April 20, 2017, https://theintercept.com/2017/04/20/fbi-stings-zero-in-on-isis-sympathizers-few-have-terrorist-links/; Karen Yourish and Josh Williams, *ISIS in America*, N.Y. TIMES, Feb. 4, 2016, https://www.nytimes.com/interactive/2016/02/04/us/isis-in-america.html.

7   Aaronson, *The New Targets, supra* note 6.

8   Aviva Stahl, *NYPD "Converted" to Islam to Spy on Brooklyn College Students*, GOTHAMIST, Oct. 29, 2015, https://www.nytimes.com/interactive/2016/02/04/us/isis-in-america.html.

9   Aviva Stahl, *Coming Soon: A Rare Look at How Terrorism Cases Are Made*, VILLAGE VOICE, May 23, 2017, https://www.villagevoice.com/2017/05/23 coming-soon-a-rare-look-at-how-terrorism-cases-are-made/.

identity obscured, possibly in a niqab, or full face covering.[10] The Supreme Court has long permitted deceptive tactics by the police in investigating crimes, as those tactics do not offend the Constitution.[11] Preying on an individual's religious beliefs by pretending to convert to their faith, while in deep violation on a personal level, is not forbidden by the Constitution. Indeed, the Court has ruled specifically that, in cases of police investigation, "the Fifth Amendment privilege is not concerned 'with moral and psychological pressures to confess emanating from sources other than official coercion.'"[12] So where the police have not employed violence or a threat to cause the suspect to act or confess, they probably acted legally in most cases, false religious conversion notwithstanding. Of course, one wonders how often law enforcement officials convert to faiths other than Islam in the context of a terrorism investigation.

While Chapter One details the use of informants to drive terrorism prosecutions, subsequent developments reveal the essentially limitless discretion FBI agents have in recruiting and cultivating those informants. With the oversight of a supervisor, an FBI agent can recruit a minor as an informant, and with prior approval from the Department of Justice, clergy, journalists, and lawyers can be recruited as well.[13] Despite the adoption of guidelines purporting to ban racial profiling in federal law enforcement, the FBI exploits loopholes to profile certain groups as presumptively terroristic.[14] As a result, the wide-scale mapping of communities continues apace, allowing the FBI to generate and retain information about populations, such as the American Muslim community, that it wishes to keep under surveillance. The standard for conducting investigations at the lowest level, which are known as assessments, is remarkably lenient, but allows for the use of varied and sophisticated investigatory tools that reveal a great deal about an individual.[15] The government's ability to conduct surveillance of suspect communities therefore remains formidable and essentially removed from oversight, thereby underscoring and amplifying the trends observed in Chapter One.

It should be noted that not all cases and developments the book documents are entirely negative. By way of example, Hamid Hayat, whose case is discussed in detail

---

10   *Id.* (noting how this proposal was made in open court by the trial judge)

11   Perkins v. Illinois, 496 U.S. 292 (1990) (allowing the introduction of a non-Mirandized murder confession made to an undercover officer while defendant was jailed on unrelated charges).

12   Berghuis v. Thompkins, 560 U.S. 370, 387 (2010)(internal citations omitted).

13   Trevor Aaronson, *The FBI Gives Itself Lots of Rope to Pull in Informants*, THE INTERCEPT, Jan. 31, 2017, https://theintercept.com/2017/01/31/the-fbi-gives-itself-lots-of-rope-to-pull-in-informants/.

14   Cora Currier, *Despite Anti-Profiling Rules, the FBI Uses Race and Religion When Deciding Who to Target*, THE INTERCEPT, Jan. 31, 2017, https://theintercept.com/2017/01/31/despite-anti-profiling-rules-the-fbi-uses-race-and-religion-when-deciding-who-to-target/.

15   Cora Currier, *Based on a Vague Trip*, The Feds Can Surveil Anyone, THE INTERCEPT, Jan. 31, 2017

in Chapter Three, has continued to chip away at his conviction for attending a terrorist training camp in Pakistan, winning the right in June 2017 to present evidence that his trial counsel's performance was defective, and that the government withheld significant exculpatory evidence from him.[16] That these developments occurred in a case where the informant's own mother referred to him as a "bagful of lies" is probably a sign that judges are willing to scrutinize the record in terrorism cases with a bit more rigor than before.[17] Even those convicted defendants assigned to the restrictive Communications Management Units (CMUs) have at least earned the right to challenge the basis for their confinement there by Bureau of Prisons' officials.[18]

Overall, no subsequent development has invalidated the book's documentation of a general terrorism exception to the normal rules and protections of criminal law and procedure. With its rationale rooted in prevention and proactive prosecution, terrorism prosecutions continue to hint at the possibility of absolute security. But such a quest is quixotic and ultimately harms the targeted communities, as well as rendering law enforcement's actions less subject to oversight and scrutiny. The cost to our liberties of the terrorism prosecution phenomenon should not be underestimated.

---

16 Abbie VanSickle, *Judge in Infamous "Sleeper Cell" Agrees to Hear New Evidence That Could Help Convicted Terrorist*, THE INTERCEPT, June 12, 2017, https://theintercept.com/2017/06/12/judge-in-infamous-sleeper-cell-case-agrees-to-hear-new-evidence-that-could-help-convicted-terrorist/.

17 Abbie VanSickle, *Small-Town Terrorists*, THE INTERCEPT, Nov. 19, 2016, https://theintercept.com/2016/11/19/infamous-post-911-california-sleeper-cell-case-continues-to-unravel/

18 Aref v. Lynch, 833 F.3d 242 (D.C. Cir. 2010).

Preface to the Hardcover Edition

IN EARLY 1999, during my last year of law school, my father showed me a communication he had received from David Bruck, one of the nation's leading capital defense lawyers. David had been appointed, along with Bob Tucker of the D.C. Federal Public Defender's office, to represent one of the defendants believed to be responsible for the August 1998 attack on the U.S. Embassy in Nairobi, Kenya, which resulted in well over a hundred deaths, many more injuries, and widespread property damage to the Embassy compound and surrounding area. Through a mutual friend, David had been referred to my father, who asked me directly: "Wadie, is this the type of thing you're interested in?" During my time living and studying in the Middle East, I had learned about the various Islamist groups operating within the region. While I had followed some of the coverage in the Arabic press about the shadowy Saudi figure, Osama Bin Laden—who appeared to be living in Afghanistan, having moved there from the Sudan after he was expelled from Saudi Arabia—I had not really paid much attention to the man or his message. Here was my first introduction to the al-Qaeda phenomenon, as its members had been accused of the bombing, and in a federal criminal case to boot, where the defendants faced the possibility of the death penalty for their actions. "Sure, I guess," was my somewhat nonchalant reply.

My father met with David, inviting me to join them, and proceeded to lay it on a bit thick. "I would love to help, but this is not the type of thing I know anything about or, to be honest, really care to involve myself with, but maybe Wadie could help you. He has studied Arabic extensively and is very much in the know about Islamist groups." David readily accepted, particularly as he and Bob were restricted in their abilities to communicate with their client and were forced to rely solely on a court-appointed interpreter. Having a voice on the defense side capable of speaking directly with the defendant in his native language was seen as a valuable tool the lawyers could use in developing their case. And from that point, I was introduced to the world of terrorism prosecutions through perhaps the most notorious of them all: a vast, constantly shifting and expanding action entitled *United States v. Bin Laden*. The case raised a whole host of interesting and complex legal issues. The defendants—at the time there were four—were facing the prospect of being put to death for their actions and were held in the most restrictive pretrial conditions then offered by the federal system. While still in Kenya, FBI agents had interrogated David and Bob's client at length and wanted to introduce those incriminating statements at any upcoming trial. The matter of the applicability of *Miranda* warnings abroad, as well as the accuracy of the translations by the Arabic translators working for the government, were quickly the subject of legal wrangling that was only resolved after several rounds of pleadings, hearings, and judicial opinions.

Though I remained involved very loosely with the defense team for about two years, even after the client had fired David and Bob and had them replaced with another court-appointed lawyer, I was not counsel in the case, and my role remained peripheral. Terrorism prosecutions at that time were a relative novelty and usually occurred only in situations involving spectacular attacks, like the Embassy bombing cases or the 1993 bombing of the World Trade Center. The attacks of September 11, 2001, quickly signaled that the government would start to avail itself of federal criminal laws as one method among many to pursue those it suspected of terrorist-related activity. In particular, the government made extensive use of one law, which criminalized the provision of something called "material support" to specially designated foreign terrorist organizations (FTOs), and whose passage in 1996 was controversial and contested by groups like the ACLU and the Arab-American Anti-Discrimination Committee. I found myself following several cases where the government levied extremely serious material support and other charges against defendants whose activity was unquestionably nonviolent. The idea of working on such cases appealed to me a great deal, certainly more than my tasks as a litigation associate at a large corporate law firm.

By chance, my resume made its way to Fletcher Peacock, then the Federal Public Defender for the Middle District of Florida, whose Tampa office had been appointed to represent Hatem Fariz, one of the defendants in the prosecution largely focused on Sami al-Arian, a former computer science professor at the University of South Florida (USF). Dr. al-Arian was a well-known figure in Palestinian and Muslim-American circles, largely due to his advocacy on behalf of his brother-in-law, Mazen al-Najjar. The latter had been detained for several years in the late 1990s on the basis of secret evidence the government steadfastly refused to divulge that purportedly showed his leading role within the Islamic Jihad Movement in Palestine, or Palestinian Islamic Jihad (PIJ) in the government's formulation. Dr. al-Arian's efforts were so successful that he managed to get wide bipartisan support for a draft bill to outlaw the use of secret evidence before Congress, a measure that stood on the verge of being passed at the time of the 9/11 attacks. He had also been the subject of a media campaign into his suspected links to the PIJ, which reached fever pitch for the first of several times in late 1995. At that point, Ramadan Shallah, one of the researchers al-Arian had sponsored at an Islamic studies think tank loosely affiliated with USF, had just left the United States and reemerged as the leader of the PIJ in Damascus, after Israeli agents assassinated the previous head, Fathi al-Shikaki, in Malta in October of that year.

While the firestorm over the think tank—the World and Islamic Studies Enterprise, or WISE—subsided in time, it did spawn investigations of Dr. al-Arian by both USF and those hostile to him in the local press. No criminal charges were ever filed against him at that time, and he resumed his activism on behalf of al-Najjar, although USF took a series of actions against him, despite his tenured status. Interestingly, his campaign against secret evidence garnered an early supporter in the then Governor of Texas, George W. Bush, running for President on the Republican ticket and searching for votes in the critically important state of Florida. Bush's pledge to outlaw the use of secret evidence by the government seems to have played a leading role in Florida's Muslim population voting for him en masse, which perhaps adds a further wrinkle to the contested and troubled history of the 2000 presidential elections in that state.

In any event, shortly after the 9/11 attacks, Dr. al-Arian appeared on media pundit Bill O'Reilly's show on the Fox News Network, presumably to speak out against the attacks in the name of the American Muslim community. However, during the show, O'Reilly attacked his guest, essentially accusing him of being a terrorist and calling on the Central Intelligence Agency to follow him wherever he went. Apparently, this interview went some way toward reigniting a federal grand jury investigation of Dr. al-Arian. In February 2003, Attorney General John Ashcroft announced—in a live televised press conference—al-Arian's indictment, along with several others, on various terrorism-related charges to the effect that the men made up the North American "cell" of the PIJ. The charges included a Racketeer Influenced and Corrupt Organizations Act (RICO) conspiracy count—on the theory that the PIJ constituted a criminal enterprise under that statute's provisions—a conspiracy to commit murder abroad count, and various material support counts, among several others. The indictment abounded with strange details; several of the individuals indicted were abroad and never extradited, including one, an academic named Bashir Nafi, who lived in Britain and held citizenship in the Republic of Ireland. Mazen al-Najjar was also named as a defendant, despite being held in immigration detention for much of the previous five years, before finally being deported in August 2002. How could it be that someone firmly in custody for several years was deported from the United States only six months before being indicted on serious terrorism charges? Either al-Najjar was a dangerous member of the PIJ leadership or he wasn't—the mere possibility that he was being investigated by a federal grand jury should have been enough to enjoin his removal from the country.

The case raised many questions, beginning with the timing of the indictment. The defendants had been in the United States for many years and were well aware of the negative publicity that WISE had generated for Dr. al-Arian. Could they really have been operating as some sort of American cell for a group on the State Department's list of FTOs since its inception in 1997, given the extensive scrutiny and criminalization of Islamist activity in the United States? None of the defendants were implicated in any way with any violent activity in the Middle East, except in the most roundabout and tenuous of ways. There was also the question of RICO, which is ordinarily used against organized crime. Was a group with overt and explicit political goals like the PIJ really comparable to the Mafia? The nature of the material support law remained open and in flux—did the government have to prove merely that the defendant knew he was providing material support to an FTO, regardless of motivation, or did it have to establish a specific intent to further the illegal goals of the FTO? Finally, there was the issue of the Foreign Intelligence Surveillance Act (FISA). The prosecution revealed that the FBI had been listening to the defendants and many others for well over a decade in some cases to the tune of approximately 27,000 hours of wiretapped phone calls and thousands of pages of intercepted facsimiles, most of which were in Arabic, and all pursuant to warrants issued under FISA. The government wanted to use the al-Arian prosecution as a vehicle to showcase the Patriot Act's innovation of officially bringing down "the wall" between the foreign intelligence and law enforcement wings of the FBI, thereby demonstrating the concomitant benefit to national security.

In any event, I ended up working on the case for around three years as a federal public defender. The prosecution included a six-month jury trial, dozens of witnesses, conflicts over translated material, and countless motions all throughout the prosecution, as well as many other issues too numerous to mention here. After all the extensive briefing and arguments my colleagues and I made on all of the above subjects, I often found myself studying the issues in dispute well after the court had ruled on them, usually in the government's favor.

One of the things I relished upon joining the academy was the opportunity to continue researching these topics in detail. But where I thought I might produce one or two law review articles on the material support ban or the role of *Miranda* warnings in terrorism-related interrogations before moving on to other areas of the law, the issues raised by terrorism prosecutions continue to evolve, consistently grabbing my attention. For instance, the government has begun making extensive use of informants primarily to spy on the Muslim community in the United States, and these operatives have been given wide latitude to suggest plots and employ provocative tactics to get their targets to sign on to those plots. The types of evidence the government has sought to introduce at trial seem to transcend normal matters of direct guilt or innocence and have focused more on thoughts and associations. There also exists a sentencing enhancement specifically for terrorism offenders, which treats them like career criminals, regardless of whether they have ever been convicted of a crime.

After the jury acquitted my client in the al-Arian prosecution of most of the charges against him—the other counts remained hung, with a strong majority of jurors in favor of acquittal—he pled guilty to one of the least serious charges and avoided that enhancement. However, his short stay as a minimum security inmate in a federal facility close to his family in Florida was interrupted by a transfer to a new unit in Indiana designed by the federal Bureau of Prisons to keep those sentenced in terrorism prosecutions apart and incommunicado from the outside world.

The above subjects struck me as legally controversial and merited greater study. All along the line, the terrorism component of the charges in any given case seemed to create exceptions to the normal rules generally applicable in criminal cases. So I continued to work on matters related to terrorism prosecutions long after I thought the topic had been exhausted. This book is the net result of all those efforts.

Of course, some of these arguments and details have appeared before, but much of this work is new and synthesizes and enhances the themes I have been exploring for more than a decade. I should point out the articles I have written on which I have drawn in this volume. They are: *Sentencing Terrorist Crimes*, 75 OHIO ST. L.J. 477 (2014); *Constructing the Threat and the Role of the Expert Witness: A Response to Aziz Rana's* Who Decides on Security?, 44 CONN. L. REV. 1545 (2012); *The Message and Means of the Modern Terrorist Prosecution*, 21 TRANSNAT'L L. & CONTEMP. PROBS. 175 (2012); Humanitarian Law Project *and the Supreme Court's Construction of Terrorism*, 2011 BYU L. REV. 1455 (2011); *The Material Support Prosecution and Foreign Policy*, 86 IND. L.J. 543 (2011); *The Terrorist Informant*, 85 WASH. L. REV. 687 (2010); *Coercing Voluntariness*, 85 IND. L.J. 1 (2010); and *The Exceptional Nature of Terrorism: The United States and Middle Eastern Legal Systems*, 32 HASTINGS INT'L & COMP. L. REV. 831 (2009). Hopefully, what follows adheres to and logically builds on my work to date.

* * *

There are many to whom I owe thanks and appreciation for their efforts in seeing this book make its way into print. I wish to thank Kevin Pendergast, my former editor at Oxford University Press, for seeking me out and encouraging me to submit a proposal on the topic of criminal terrorism prosecutions. My current editor, Blake Ratcliff, went above and beyond in helping me frame the arguments in this book and ensuring that the material is presented in the most accessible manner to both the specialist and general reader. A special thanks to Alden Domizio and the editorial team at Oxford for helping shepherd this book toward publication.

At the University of South Carolina, many of my colleagues were very generous with their time over the years in reading drafts of my work and discussing ideas with me, and their insights and advice has proven invaluable. In this regard, thanks are due to Derek Black, Josie Brown, Tommy Crocker, Josh Eagle, Lisa Eichhorn, Susan Kuo, Ben Means, Colin Miller, Eboni Nelson, Joel Samuels, and Joe Seiner. Associate Deans Danielle Holley-Walker and Jaclyn Cherry showed great understanding and support for this project during its pendency. Dean Rob Wilcox was very generous in allowing me the time and research assistance to write the manuscript, and he deserves great thanks. I acknowledge the great work of the administrative staff at South Carolina: Kimberley Bradshaw, Alyne Hallman, Inge Lewis, Felicia Stevenson, and Carol Young deserve many thanks for their help with my articles and this volume. I must single out Vanessa Byars for her incredible efforts in editing and proofreading my writing over the years and making sure all the citations referenced what they said and were in proper form. To her, I offer my sincere thanks and appreciation. Finally, my research assistants did an outstanding job on the numerous topics and phases covered in this book. I thank Wafa Abu Salim, Lloyd Flores, Jael Gilreath, Ryan Grover, and Steve Sutherland for all their help.

Many others also read my work in the last decade and offered excellent feedback and thoughts on the material, as well as steady encouragement. Heartfelt thanks are due to Amna Akbar, Asli Bali, George Bisharat, Jack Chin, Robert Ferguson, Suad Joseph, Ugo Mattei, Laura Nader, Aziz Rana, Song Richardson, Stephen Sheehi, and Chantal Thomas. I must also acknowledge and thank Raj Bhala, Marc Miller, Natsu Saito, Mark Sidel, Nirej Sekhon, Shirin Sinnar, Spearit, and Burns Weston for their help with my work at various stages of this project. A special note of thanks is owed to Sudha Setty for engaging with my work in its many incarnations over the years.

Lastly, I wish to recognize and express my deep appreciation to my friends and family for their support throughout my academic career to this point. In particular, my late father's work has greatly influenced and informed my own. My deepest thanks and gratitude to my wife, Jennifer, for her invaluable assistance in seeing my work make it into print, as well as reading all my drafts with a critical, yet supportive, eye. It is to her and our son, Edward, whom this book is dedicated. My hope is that, despite the somewhat grim subject, my contribution allows a greater understanding of what terrorism prosecutions represent and how a critical reflection on the phenomenon might constitute a small push on the way to a more just society. I should note, however, that no matter the great help and contribution of others to this volume, all of its errors and shortcomings are my own.

INTRODUCTION

IF THE AMERICAN government charged you with being a terrorist, would you rather face criminal charges in a federal court or be tried before a military commission? The answer to this question seems obvious at first blush. An Article III federal court, with the full panoply of constitutional protections for the criminal defendant, naturally suggests itself as the far better option. But an examination of the record of criminal terrorist prosecutions to date—particularly in the period after September 11, 2001—reveals a disturbing incursion on the procedural and substantive rights we associate with a federal criminal trial, such that the answer becomes more complicated. Problematic also is that the infringement on these rights, often in the name of national security, has consequences far beyond the administration of an individual terrorism trial. The exceptionalism a criminal prosecution of terrorist crimes engenders permeates the process from the formation of a case through to the (almost inevitable) sentence, affecting nearly all of its aspects. If someone is suspected of engaging in or supporting terrorism, then the government will argue that the normal rules should bend to accommodate extraordinary actions taken to defend national security. These actions include spying and the use of informants/provocateurs, which rely on specious theories about the nature of terrorism. Once the government charges someone in a terrorism prosecution, the government can avail itself of laws and evidence that tie a defendant to a concept of terrorism that is exceedingly broad, often with no link to any violence whatsoever. Finally, individuals convicted of crimes tied to terrorism can find themselves facing a much longer sentence than normal, owing to the existence of a special sentencing enhancement.

When faced with a government asserting national security as a justification, all too often the courts acquiesce.

The criminal terrorism prosecution is a phenomenon that wreaks havoc on the law from multiple angles. Any one prosecution can result in deviations or exceptions on several points, and in this volume, many cases are discussed repeatedly in separate chapters, as they offer new theories of criminal liability, admissibility of evidence, and sentencing practice, for example. Only now are we beginning to recognize, slowly and inexorably, the effect of the terrorism prosecution on ordinary criminal law and procedure, which has triggered the expansion of the government's powers at the expense of a defendant's rights. Although there is a growing, albeit small, recognition of the negative consequences of this phenomenon, prosecution in federal court is regarded by a diverse chorus of voices as an option far preferable to military commissions, due to both the regularity of the procedure and, more tellingly, the effectiveness of the result. Academics, prosecutors, senior government officials, and advocacy groups have all argued that prosecutions in federal court should replace trial by military commission, as it is the option most consistent with the rule of law. More specifically, the federal court prosecution, with all its attendant rights and clearly delineated procedures, is superior to a system that allows for indefinite detention pending charges before a military tribunal, whose rules and practices are continually shifting.

While this book does not challenge the valid criticisms of indefinite detention and trial before military commissions as currently constituted, it asks that the reader really and truly consider the costs imposed on criminal law and procedure by federal court prosecutions when juxtaposed with the statistically limited threat of an international terrorist attack in the United States. In other words, this critique seeks to go beyond the binary of the criminal trial versus the military tribunal model to examine what the more prevalent and regularized terrorism prosecution has wrought on the law.[1] Consider as an initial point that critical to most of those making the argument in favor of criminal prosecution is the fact that federal courts mete out harsh punishment and have a very high record of conviction. A 2010 commentary on the issue published by the Center for American Progress—an "independent nonpartisan educational institute dedicated to improving the lives of Americans through progressive ideas and action," whose board of directors includes former Senator Tom Daschle and former Secretary of State Madeleine Albright[2]—puts it directly: "The facts are clear: Criminal courts are a far tougher and more reliable forum for prosecuting terrorists than military commissions."[3] This is a theme echoed by prosecutors, who also tout the reliability and stern penalties promised by the criminal model.[4] Even the first chief prosecutor of the military tribunals, Morris Davis, has come out in favor of criminal prosecution, arguing that his experience with the tribunals demonstrates their ineffectiveness.[5]

In keeping with President Barack Obama's as yet unfulfilled promise to close the military detention facility in Guantanamo Bay, Cuba, Attorney General Eric Holder has been making a slow and steady effort to extol the federal courts' effectiveness as a forum to try terrorism suspects, with a focus on the fact that they produce convictions. In April 2014, at a press conference held on the occasion of the conviction of Osama Bin Laden's son-in-law Suleiman Abu Ghaith on terrorism charges, Holder called the criminal trial model "tried and tested," noting "we will continue to rely on it."[6] Senator Dianne Feinstein echoed these sentiments, calling federal court prosecution "not just a valid way to prosecute Al Qaeda terrorists, but a better and more reliable way."[7] The following month, upon the conviction of the British cleric Abu Hamza al-Masri on multiple terrorism counts, Holder went even further, stating: "With each efficiently delivered guilty verdict against a top Al Qaeda-linked figure, the debate over how to best seek justice in these cases is quietly being put to rest."[8] At the very least, the government's current position reduces the fear that it will rely on the threat of military tribunals to produce the most advantageous prosecutorial posture in a criminal action.[9] For now, Holder's policy choice of federal prosecution over military tribunals has been considered a success, based solely on the number of convictions generated in high-profile cases.[10]

On a different but related tack, the federal prosecution model has garnered support from leading academics and also advocacy groups, such as Human Rights First and the American Civil Liberties Union (ACLU), which tend to stress that criminal adjudication in American courtrooms best preserves the notion of the rule of law.[11] In light of the military/civilian either/or debate, academic criticism of the criminal model has been sparse, albeit increasing in frequency somewhat recently. In 2004, legal scholar Kim Lane Scheppele remarked that admission of the defendants' confessions in the trial of the perpetrators of the 1998 attacks on the U.S. Embassies in Nairobi and Dar es Salaam "should give human rights lawyers pause."[12] From a different angle, Yale Law professor James Forman, Jr., observed in 2009 that the harsh and "profound abnormality of our domestic criminal justice system" helped inspire the Guantanamo regime.[13] The critical landscape seemed sparse for a time, prompting scholars Jeanne Theoharis and Laura Rovner to lament in a 2012 law review article that few scholars had explored holistically the erosion of defendants' rights in federal prosecutions occurring in the shadow of the Guantanamo tribunals.[14]

In the realm of advocacy, criticism has been more pronounced, especially with respect to certain aspects of law enforcement's heavy-handed investigations of suspected terrorism and the chilling effect those investigations have had on the American Muslim community. A 2009 ACLU report documented the negative effect the government's counterterrorism strategies have had on Muslim charitable giving and the concomitant infringement on religious practice.[15] A 2011 report from the Center for Human Rights and Global Justice at New York University Law School examined the government's role in creating and manufacturing the threat posed by American Muslims targeted by law enforcement and informants.[16] Additionally, in 2013, a joint report issued under the auspices of CUNY Law School's CLEAR project highlighted the wide-ranging reach of the spying program the New York Police Department ran on the city's Muslim community.[17] The latest advocacy reports have taken on the criminal model in its entirety, with the July 2014 publication of the joint report by Human Rights Watch and Columbia Law School's Human Rights Institute detailing a series of human rights deprivations in federal terrorism prosecutions, and the May 2014 report by Project Salam and the National Coalition to Protect Civil Freedoms striking a similar chord.[18] This is of course not to discount the many excellent journalistic investigations of terrorism prosecutions that have been written over the past decade and a half, many of which are cited and discussed below.

However, the focus of this book is on the distorting effect the terrorism prosecution has had on American criminal law and procedure and how that distortion has disproportionately affected the Muslim community in the United States. To examine properly the institution of the terrorism prosecution, we must understand two critical points that make terrorism prosecutions different from most ordinary criminal cases. First, the emphasis is on preventing acts of terrorism before they occur, according to the Department of Justice (DOJ). In the wake of the attacks of September 11, 2001, the DOJ explicitly adopted this preventive mindset, which has continued to guide terrorism investigations and prosecutions since then.[19] This contrasts directly with the pre-9/11 approach, which centered on punishing individuals implicated in politically motivated violent acts that had already occurred. That is not to say that the pre-9/11 cases did not offer much by way of legal innovation, but a prerequisite for prosecution was an act of violence and a link to the United States.[20] A focus on prevention ensures that violence need not occur before the government can charge someone with terrorism-related crimes. Many of the prosecutions examined in this volume across the various chapters should be read with this preventive posture in mind, as it raises real questions about an individual's dangerousness if the government has to rely on a suspect's political or religious activity and/or statements to bring terrorism charges before any violence has taken place. Overall, the nature of the terrorism threat—which the government has identified as chiefly a Muslim threat—has been exaggerated, something to which the preventive paradigm has contributed significantly, as between 2001 and 2010 some "94.2% of the all the terrorism-related convictions [recorded by the DOJ] have been either preventive prosecution cases or cases that involved elements of preventive prosecution."[21] Indeed, in many if not most instances, the government played a central role in suggesting the plot, a fact that raises questions not merely about an individual defendant's dangerousness but also about the national security-driven need for the erosion of rights courts repeatedly have approved.

The second major innovation concerns the use of 18 U.S.C. § 2339B, the criminal ban on providing material support to a designated foreign terrorism organization (FTO). While the statute's origins, structure, and litigation history serve as the subject of an entire chapter, it is important to bear in mind that the material support ban constitutes the government's chief statutory tool underpinning many of the cases discussed in this volume. When Congress passed the law in 1996, it focused on the supposed problem of terrorist groups raising money for violence under the cover of humanitarian activity. Whether or not that concern was exaggerated at the time, the concept of material support centered squarely on tangible contributions of money, weapons, and equipment that aid directly in an FTO's violent mission. As envisioned, the statute allowed for the prosecution of individuals contributing to an FTO's efforts several steps removed from violent activity, thereby broadening the concept of terrorism and whom it taints by association. Specifically, even individuals motivated by purely charitable or altruistic concerns were not spared the law's predations, and several were sentenced to long prison terms. The years since the passage of the ban have seen the courts further widen the concept of material support, to the point where, in 2010, the Supreme Court declared constitutional the statute's criminalization of the provision of material support in the form of protected speech.[22] So not only is the terrorism prosecution's aim preventive, with all the attendant difficulty of knowing when an attack is truly thwarted or a dangerous individual actually deterred, but it also relies principally on the concept of material support, a nebulous notion that has the effect of criminalizing association and political/religious affiliation as terroristic.

These innovations have shifted the terms of the debate on terrorism and political violence quite dramatically. The criminal terrorism prosecution, with its primary focus on the Muslim population and its purported potential to churn out radicalized terrorists, has done away with talk of legitimate or justified political violence. Its investigatory techniques and doctrinal developments do not allow for any type of arguments on the nature of a political struggle. Once a group is branded as terrorist, all associations with it carry that label as well, and courts have been quick to adopt the government's broad view criminalizing such links. Gone are the days when courts would consider the nature of a violent political struggle between a nonstate actor and a nation-state in construing the concept of terrorism.[23] The concept of material support relegates the debate over the contested topic of a universal definition of terrorism and the justice of a particular cause to the sidelines, allowing the government to burrow away, criminalizing more and more tangential links to its increasingly broad concept of terrorism.

Taken in tandem with the preventive mindset of law enforcement and the proactive use of informants and provocateurs, which has seen the government create the threat it subsequently thwarts and prosecutes, the material support ban goes further and allows the government to criminalize charity, solidarity, religious practice, and speech. As opposed to run-of-the-mill criminal cases, terrorism prosecutions are often the product of the government, which initiates the plot, relying on a concept of material support liability that is highly inchoate and clashes directly with protected First Amendment rights. This is not to deny the very real criticisms of the modern American criminal justice system, with its myriad injustices rooted in racial and socioeconomic grounds. However, it is clear that people commit ordinary drug, fraud, and other clearly defined crimes and engage in illegal violence with frequency in the United States; the same cannot be said in the terrorism context. Contrast the tens of thousands of standard crimes prosecuted every year with the around five hundred or so terrorism prosecutions that have occurred since September 11, 2001. One estimate of the data is that only 1 percent of those prosecutions represented an actual security threat, that is, targeted an individual willing to carry out an attack without government involvement.[24] Another more recent study concludes that the real number is 3 percent.[25] Whichever is correct does not affect the analysis here since the point is that the exaggerated nature of the threat has allowed the government to change the very essence of the criminal prosecution under the rubric of terrorist exceptionalism.

In making this argument, this book adopts a linear model that follows the progression of the terrorism prosecution, from the beginning of an investigation through to its final phases when a convicted defendant is sentenced and confined to prison. In this manner, we can examine terrorist exceptionalism at all stages of the prosecution, from the investigation, to the charges brought, the evidence produced at trial, sentencing, and conditions of confinement. While not every single terrorism prosecution occurring in the United States over the past decade and a half is discussed, the book takes up the major themes and trends embodied by the phenomenon. Accordingly, the first chapter focuses on the government's investigations of terrorism, concentrating on the FBI's and NYPD's extensive operations involving the use of informants and spying within Muslim communities. After an explication of the problematic "radicalization" theory of terrorism, the chapter then reviews several prosecutions that demonstrate the ineffectiveness of the entrapment defense in informant-driven prosecutions, before examining, as a final matter, the potential for these tactics to seep into law enforcement practice more generally outside the terrorism context.

The second chapter looks at the material support ban in extensive detail, from its 1996 passage in Congress to the legal battles surrounding its usage as a chief statutory tool in terrorism prosecutions since 9/11. All throughout the history of material support-based prosecutions, the government has adhered to a construct of the terrorist organization as so toxic that it taints everything with which it comes in contact. That produces in turn a mindset that has seen the concept of material support go way beyond funding terrorism under the guise of humanitarian activity, the statute's original aim. All along, the courts have acquiesced in approving the government's expanding theories of material support to include speech and unquestioned humanitarian activity.

The third chapter moves on to consider the evidence used to prove terrorism charges, with an initial look at evidence-gathering techniques, whether via eavesdropping under the Foreign Intelligence Surveillance Act (FISA), or through custodial interrogation. Again, the terrorism prosecution allows for exceptions to well-established and constitutionally mandated rules that govern normal criminal procedures. The chapter then analyzes trends in the introduction of evidence in the courtroom. The government's wide construction of terrorism and association comes squarely into view as courts in the main have allowed highly prejudicial and arguably irrelevant images, videos, and testimony that seek to link a defendant with terrorism—and, wherever possible, al-Qaeda—without an adequate assessment of the evidence's probative value. Finally, the chapter concludes with a discussion of the individuals the government has employed as expert witnesses and finds a startlingly pronounced lack of qualifications and jumbled methodologies that courts have ignored in allowing their admission as experts.

The fourth chapter pauses to consider what the terrorism prosecution signifies through a more thorough discussion of several high-profile cases, including that of Jose Padilla, the so-called al-Qaeda "dirty bomber," whose trial and conviction on criminal charges were unconnected to the government's dirty bomb allegations and glossed over his years of incommunicado military detention as an enemy combatant. The cases discussed in this chapter demonstrate that the government's theory of what constitutes terrorism is essentially limitless and can encompass even the most basic expressions of solidarity or concern with oppressed populations. In other instances, the terrorism prosecution provides an escape hatch for the government to extricate itself from situations where its actions normally would have foreclosed criminal prosecution. The chapter also notes that the government construes terrorism through an American lens, a political posture that represents a kind of selectivity in the counterterrorist scheme, as it can leave very real threats of political violence unprosecuted if they do not correspond to American interests.

The final chapter arrives at the end of the line, where convicted defendants can be sentenced under a special sentencing enhancement that allows for dramatically heightened penalties if the offense somehow can be tied to terrorism. The operation of the enhancement raises serious questions of its fidelity to recent Supreme Court precedent in the field of criminal sentencing generally, where higher penalties are authorized only if the relevant conduct has been proven to a jury beyond a reasonable doubt or a defendant has pled guilty. It also questions the recent phenomenon of courts of appeals overturning district court sentences as too lenient in certain high-profile cases, in contravention of Supreme Court precedent and providing further evidence of yet more terrorist exceptionalism in the criminal model. The chapter then briefly considers the fate of terrorism defendants post-conviction, as they can be subjected to highly restrictive prison units where their ability to communicate with the outside world is severely limited. While the classification procedures for such units are highly opaque, the notion that a terrorism inmate is somehow a different kind of threat persists.

In making these arguments, this volume aims to document critically a phenomenon that threatens to radically change our concept of a free society and the right to be politically or religiously engaged, as the erosion of rights under consideration impacts a particular ethno-religious minority. The stress on the normative prescriptions for these ills is deemphasized because those prescriptions are both relatively clear and uncomplicated to state.[26] For example, law enforcement, both state and federal, should cease using suspicionless spying as a tactic and also stop using informants to drive prosecutions when there is no reasonable suspicion that dangerous activity is afoot. The material support statute should not apply to protected speech, and the government should have to show a defendant's specific intent to further a group's illegal goals to obtain a conviction, particularly in cases where the material support is undisputedly humanitarian aid. Courts should subject to much greater scrutiny the government's evidence-gathering methods, as well as the forms of proof it wishes to introduce at trial. And finally, it is not entirely clear that there is a need for a special terrorism sentencing enhancement. Even assuming such a need, the enhancement should only apply if the government can prove its applicability beyond a reasonable doubt, a higher evidentiary showing than currently required.

Whether or not these recommendations are adopted, the hope is that the analysis here falls into the same category of the larger structural critiques of the criminal justice system and its idiosyncrasies, as well as the literature documenting the legal excesses of the war on terror more generally.[27] After all, the criminal terrorism prosecution is where both of those phenomena converge, oftentimes unhappily, as this volume documents. If the military commission/Guantanamo model represents an attempt by the government to create the air of legality for a fundamentally (at least at the outset) unaccountable process, the criminal prosecution goes much farther in providing a veneer of constitutional legitimacy for many of the government's preferences and predilections regarding the concept of terrorism. Where the military model was originally intended to keep the federal courts out of this adjudicatory effort, the criminal model actively brings them in, largely in the role of a partner to the government's efforts. For, as this book documents, in far too many situations where the courts should have served as a check on the government's wide-ranging tactics and theories, they opted instead to grant their blessing. This is a development worthy of our critical attention, as the specter of terrorism continues to change and distort our criminal justice system in unexpected and novel ways.

1

INFORMANTS, SPIES, RADICALIZATION, AND ENTRAPMENT

A KEY QUESTION raised by the preventive mindset adopted by the government and its law enforcement wings is what types of investigatory tactics can be put to use in stopping terrorist plots before they occur. As the post-9/11 experience reveals, and much like in previous wide-scale campaigns such as the War on Drugs, inside informants and undercover surveillance play prominent roles when attempting to answer the question. Both within the Federal Bureau of Investigation (FBI) and the New York Police Department (NYPD)—the largest municipal police force in the country—authorities have resorted to informants and undercover operatives to probe activities deemed suspicious. However, in direct contrast to crimes like drug dealing and weapons possession, which, in theory, tend to be rather straightforward—possessing illegal narcotics with the intent to distribute is illegal, as are the many variations on unregistered firearms ownership—what constitutes a terrorist plot may be highly inchoate and also involve speech and associational activities protected by the First Amendment. In order to both increase its effectiveness and avoid infringing on constitutionally protected activity, we might expect law enforcement to work hard to understand the distinctions between unthreatening speech or gatherings, no matter how far outside the mainstream they may lie, and utterances or meetings that portend something more dangerous. However, in reality the government's belief as to what constitutes the warning signs of terrorism has been consistently expansive, at times going so far as to reflect an overt suspicion to Islam and Muslims, who are seen as inextricably linked to terrorism. And on that basis, we see repeatedly that the activity under scrutiny could very well be innocuous, and the defendant charged with terrorist crimes unwitting and maybe even innocent, leading to very real doubts about whether a threat actually existed in the first place.

This chapter therefore details the work of law enforcement at the first stage of developing a criminal prosecution, primarily through the use of informants* or undercover officers, to investigate what it deems potentially terroristic activity. The discussion here reveals that law enforcement has become wedded to the notion that terrorists—read Muslim terrorists—can be uncovered based on their exhibiting the signs of a theory called "radicalization," most of which are just behaviors indicating growing religiosity. Ideas of sleeper cells in our midst and hardened terrorists biding their time while waiting to strike have ceded most all of their ground to the fear that American Muslims might become radicalized at home and then wish to launch an attack on their own. This mentality has led to a twofold approach: (1) a strategy of bringing successful prosecutions driven by FBI informants proactively seeking out targets, suggesting a plot, and then providing the means with which to carry it out; and (2) intense spying and surveillance by the NYPD with little regard to the feasibility of making a criminal case. In both situations, the effect has been deleterious to the relationship between the authorities and the communities targeted; perhaps another unexpected conclusion to draw is that the prevalence of the lurking terrorist threat has been overstated. What is undisputed so far is that there is no adequate check on the government's overreach and heavy-handedness; the FBI's use of informants to bring terrorism prosecutions continues apace, as defendants arguing they have been entrapped have met entirely with failure, and all the while, a spying program in the nation's largest city has created fear and paranoia in the minds of some.

This chapter proceeds as follows. After an introduction to the radicalization theory and the assumptions behind it comes a critical examination of the respective undercover activities of the FBI and NYPD, concluding with an explanation of why the sole legal defense to these practices—entrapment—has failed to deter law enforcement excesses in this area. What these developments portend is considered at this chapter's conclusion, in which we see counterterrorism tactics creeping into the realm of ordinary criminal law enforcement and domestic political protest.

---

* At the outset, a quick note on a key term discussed here: an "informant" is someone who never intends to help carry out a terrorist plot, as opposed to a "cooperator," who "conspired with terrorists at one point but [was] induced to cooperate with law enforcement." *See* CTR. ON LAW & SEC., N.Y. UNIV. SCH. OF LAW, TERRORIST TRIAL REPORT CARD: SEPTEMBER 11, 2001–SEPTEMBER 11, 2009, at 43 (Jan. 2010), http://www.lawandsecurity.org/Portals/0/documents/02_TTRCFinalJan142.pdf.

THE ESSENTIAL QUESTION: WHO IS A TERRORIST?

Even the most perfunctory inquiry into the government's mindset regarding which groups constitute the terrorist threat provides the obvious answer: people of the Islamic faith writ large, with no distinction made for all of its sects, groupings and subgroupings, or doctrinal divisions. Consider the list of groups designated as Foreign Terrorist Organizations (FTOs) by the government (discussed in greater detail in Chapter 2 on the Material Support statute). Currently designated are fifty-nine groups, forty-six of which could be described as Islamist or Arab/Muslim in their ethno-religious make-up.[1] Furthermore, thirty-three of the thirty-six groups added since September 11, 2001, have those same characteristics, the vast majority of which are Islamist groups.[2] The U.S. government believes that al-Qaeda and its affiliated groups represent the greatest terrorist threat, although the FTO list includes a significant number of non-al-Qaeda-affiliated Arab and Muslim groups of both religious and secular orientations. The terrorist designation is not limited to mere groupings but can also attach to nations, as the State Department maintains a list of "State Sponsors of Terrorism." Of the four countries on the current list, two—Sudan and Syria—have overwhelming Arab and Muslim majorities, and a third is the Islamic Republic of Iran (the fourth is Cuba).[3] Even were the reader to not disagree with these designations on either political and theoretical grounds, the official figures suggest that the archetypal terrorist comes from a certain background, when viewed in combination with the al-Qaeda network's leading role as a primary terrorist actor and threat. The current media furor surrounding the Islamic State in Iraq and the Levant's (ISIL) emergence as a powerful actor in the Middle East does nothing to dispel this perception.

This state of affairs has led scholars to observe how our societal construction of the typical terrorist is Muslim and/or Arab or, even more puzzling, "Muslim-looking."[4] Of course, since the early 1970s, the government has continually associated Arabs and Muslims with terrorism—a linkage that has produced heightened surveillance of those communities in the United States as well as restrictive immigration policies for nationals of certain Arab and Muslim countries—going so far as to consider, in the mid-1980s, detaining Arab and Iranian Americans on military bases much like the Japanese internment during World War II.[5] Even well before September 11, 2001, Arab and Muslim Americans were "racialized" as "terrorists," an identification practice that had long seeped into the output of Hollywood and other mass media.[6] And after 9/11, the government's immigration crackdown on nationals of certain Arab and Muslim countries was only a more overt expansion of politically motivated deportation cases it brought against individuals from the same list of suspect countries in the 1990s based primarily on secret evidence.[7] This practice of racializing Muslims (and Arabs) as terrorists represents a kind of Islamophobia, which persists to this day in events like the campaign against the building of a mosque at Ground Zero, the numerous legislative efforts to outlaw the incorporation of the Islamic Shari'a into state law,* and the dogged belief of a fair number of Americans that President Obama is secretly Muslim, which is regarded as wholly and unquestionably negative.[8] It is in this specific backdrop of official and popular hostility to Islam in one form or another that law enforcement agencies have articulated a series of markers rooted in a theory for evaluating an individual's propensity for terrorism. The theory is called "radicalization," and it comes as no surprise that the warning signs all correlate with Islam in some way.

RADICALIZATION: THE THEORY

The first articulation of the radicalization theory in any detail came in the form of an FBI Intelligence Assessment issued in 2006. The document, prepared by the FBI Counterterrorism Division and entitled "The Radicalization Process: From Conversion to Jihad," makes clear in unambiguous terms that terrorism and Islam are intertwined. While the focus of the assessment seems to be Americans who convert to Islam from another religion, it uses the following definition of conversion: "a noticeable change in one's religious identity, a conscious self-transformation that may take the form of a change from: [o]ne formal faith to another; [a] secular belief to a formal faith; [a] recommitment to an existing faith."[9] This key definitional decision allows the FBI to view all Americans of Muslim origin who head in the direction of radicalizing with the same lens, regardless of how they initially acquired their Islamic faith, by birth or otherwise. The document identifies four stages in the radicalization process: "pre-radicalization," "identification," "indoctrination," and "action." A chart on the fourth page of the report elucidates the steps a believer must take to move to the next stage as well as the proximity of each stage to violent action. "Pre-radicalization" can be signaled by "conversion/reinterpretation" of the faith but indicates that the individual Muslim will take "no action." "Identification" means "acceptance" of the violent cause, portending a "propensity for action," while "indoctrination" requires "conviction," meaning that the individual is "ready for action." Finally, the "action" stage indicates that "terrorism" is imminent, as the target will now "implement action."[10]

The FBI's assessment notes that the reasons for conversion or recommitment to Islam can be manifold, running the gamut from the need to belong, a desire for

---

* Where is the objective proof that America's state laws are in danger of being overhauled into codes rooted in Islamic law?

acceptance within a group, and deprivation on the social, political, religious, and ethnic levels, among others. The first stage in the radicalization continuum can be initiated between an American Muslim and an Islamic extremist at a mosque, a prison, a university, the workplace, or an Internet chat room; in other words, a series of potentially limitless locations. However, the document makes clear that "an individual may not display overt signs of radicalization because conversion does not always lead to radicalization."[11]

The second stage starts when an individual, once exposed to a cause, identifies "with a particular extremist cause and accepts a radicalized ideology that justifies, condones, encourages, or supports violence or other criminal activity against the US Government, its citizens, its allies, or those whose opinions are contrary to his own extremist agenda."[12] Again, much like the government's baseline definition of any nonstate political violence as potentially constituting terrorism (see Chapter 2 on material support), the sheer number of political and social causes encompassed by this concept of "identification" is large indeed. A key indicator of this stage can come when the individual travels abroad to a Muslim country, and the document does not entertain explicitly the possibility that such travel could be purely innocent. Other indicators are even more controversial, since they simply indicate increased religiosity or political activism, and touch on constitutionally protected activity. Those indicators include "[i]ncreased isolation from former life," "[a]ssociation with new social identity," "[w]earing traditional Muslim attire," "[g]rowing facial hair," and "[f]requent attendance at a mosque or a prayer group."[13]

With respect to the "indoctrination" stage, the document has little to say, featuring borderline nonsensical sentences such as "[p]art of this stage involves becoming an active participant in a group, but could also be initiated within the recruit's self-created jihadist environment" and "[m]oreover, the activities are essential to know at which level the convert can ultimately participate and how much he can prove himself worthy to the cause."[14] Indicators include "[i]ncreased activity in a pro-Muslim social group or political cause," "[a]ttendance at a training camp or participation in paramilitary training," "[c]onducting surveillance activities," and "[p]roselytizing."[15] This list perfectly encapsulates the flaws inherent within the assessment, namely, the propensity to conflate perfectly innocuous activity with preparation to carry out a violent attack. Surely, the line between the two must be more finely drawn, as these examples encompass a wide range of legal behavior that, when performed, would only be chilled by active federal law enforcement's monitoring of one particular religious group. With the FBI's preventive focus on terrorism and these indicators as a guide, it is not surprising that law enforcement officers have sometimes surveilled and investigated religiously or politically active Muslim Americans on the thinnest of pretexts.

The final stage discusses with greater detail than previous sections the forms that "action" by a target can take. Action can be violent or nonviolent and come in support of preparing, planning, or executing an attack. Individuals working toward jihadist violence can also play the role of a facilitator by "providing financial assistance, safe houses, false documents, materials, attack plans, surveillance, or travel assistance." The assessment also notes that "[f]emales may play a role in this step as well."[16] Recruiting individuals is part of the process of taking action, as is providing funding to carry out an attack, although the assessment, perhaps wary of transgressing the constitutional limits of the material support laws, includes this warning: "It is important to differentiate between providing funding for a terrorist attack, either through individuals or nongovernmental organizations, fully knowing that the contribution will go to facilitate an attack, and donating to an NGO without knowing the final destination of the contribution."[17] Key indicators of imminent violent action include "[t]ravel without obvious source of funds," "[s]uspicious purchases of bomb making paraphernalia or weapons," "[l]arge transfer of funds, from or to overseas," and "[f]ormation of operational cells."[18] Again, the document mixes more incriminating activities along with potentially innocent behavior, underscoring the deep suspicion with which the FBI views (apparently overwhelmingly male) individuals of Muslim background when they manifest their political/religious beliefs more outwardly.

Importantly, the 2006 Intelligence Assessment is still in official use as a guide for FBI counterterrorism agents and analysts.[19] Inevitably, the adoption of a radicalization thesis has produced the requisite government counter-radicalization efforts, which seem to be multiplying at an accelerated rate, underscoring the belief that one's association with the practice of Islam must be officially sanctioned to be free from suspicion.[20] Ostensibly motivated by the fear that "American extremists" are traveling abroad to join groups like ISIL, the latest such "pilot" program was announced by Attorney General Holder in September 2014 and aims to "bring together community representatives, public safety officials, religious leaders, and United States Attorneys to improve local engagement; to counter violent extremism; and—ultimately—to build a broad network of community partnerships to keep our nation safe."[21] The program also aims to "identify threats before they emerge," thereby reemphasizing the threat that American Muslims might find themselves profiled on the basis of completely legitimate political and social activity.[22]

While the FBI has denied that it views religious belief as a proxy for terrorism, it is hard to reconcile its continued use of the assessment with those denials.[23] In September 2011, on the eve of the tenth anniversary of 9/11, the FBI was revealed to have been using materials in its counterterrorism training program to instruct its agents that the more devout a Muslim, the more likely he is to be violent, portray the

Prophet Muhammad as a "cult leader," and argue that " '[t]here may not be a 'radical' threat as much as it is simply a normal assertion of the orthodox ideology.' "[24] In other words, FBI agents were instructed to view the Islamic faith, without any qualifiers, as a threat in and of itself. While the FBI began a purge of these materials several months later, it is not clear to what extent their effect has been dissipated and how long that process might take.[25] After all, the latest round of revelations, from July 2014, showed that training materials used by intelligence personnel to request FISA surveillance used the fake name "Mohammed Raghead" as a stand-in for the actual name of the target.[26]

This is not an idle concern that implicates simply one aspect of the FBI's counterterrorism regime, because there have long been hints of a problematic portrayal of Islam at the heart of the government's terrorism prosecutions. Details have trickled into the public domain over the past decade about attitudes within the FBI regarding the American Muslim community. In late 2009, a *N.Y. Times* report on FBI spying quoted a former Bureau counterterrorism official to the effect that there is a split within the FBI between those who believe in the value of working with Muslim community organizations and those who view those groups with hostility and suspicion.[27] The assessment's language and standards, imprecise as they are, certainly reflect the latter type of thinking. And practically, there are legal barriers to such cooperation. In 2007, during the prosecution of the officers and directors of the Holy Land Foundation on material support charges (see Chapter 2 on material support and Chapter 3 on evidence), the government released a list of unindicted co-conspirators that included the Council on American-Islamic Relations (CAIR), the nation's largest Muslim advocacy group.[28] Essentially, the effect of such a listing is to prohibit the FBI from in any way coordinating or working with CAIR in an official capacity, as well as discouraging dealings with the group more generally.[29] Despite the more recent attempts at reconciliation between the FBI and the Muslim community, the relationship remains strained.[30] When considered in light of the still valid FBI Intelligence Assessment, the above factors indicate that the Bureau itself has at best a deeply ambivalent view toward Muslims in the United States, individually and collectively, a situation in which the problematic theory of "radicalization" can thrive.

The theory's development is not limited to the FBI's Assessment; in fact, a more well-developed and detailed document discussing radicalization was issued by the NYPD in 2007. Entitled "Radicalization in the West: the Homegrown Threat," at ninety pages the report is much longer than the FBI document, and it also explicitly identifies its two authors, Senior NYPD Intelligence Analysts, Mitchell D. Silber and Arvin Bhatt.[31] The report defines its focus on "Islamic-based terrorism" of a "Jihadist or jihadi-Salafi ideology."[32] Before analyzing the radicalization thesis in this report, a quick note on the authors and their expertise. While a standard Internet search uncovered little about Bhatt and his professional background outside the NYPD, the report's lead author, Silber, has moved into the private sector, where he works for a corporate risk analysis firm and maintains a publicly available web profile. Prior to joining the NYPD, where he rose to the position of Director of Intelligence Analysis in the Intelligence Division, Silber spent nine years as an investment banker before earning a master's degree from Columbia University's School of International and Public Affairs.[33] There is nothing in Silber's profile that suggests any training or proficiency in the languages and cultures of the Muslim world, let alone study of the Islamic faith or its history and major doctrinal developments. It is therefore curious that one individual with no apparent expertise in the subject matter at hand and another about whom we might only speculate as to his qualifications were commissioned to write such a report. New York is among the world's most culturally diverse cities, and the NYPD certainly understood how to employ that diversity by hiring and training undercover officers with the relevant language and cultural skills from the very communities it spied on.[34] It is a mystery then, why it did not engage individuals with the requisite expertise and background to write such a report.*

Returning to the contents of the document, the authors followed the familiar four-stage construct of radicalization, only with slightly different nomenclature from that of the FBI's assessment. The four phases are "pre-radicalization," "indoctrination," "self-identification," and "jihadization"[35] However, before turning to the terms in greater detail, the report provides this conceptualized warning in its Executive Summary, one worth quoting at length:

> It is useful to think of the radicalization process in terms of a funnel. Entering the process does not mean one will progress through all four stages and become a terrorist. However, it also does not mean that if one doesn't become a terrorist, he or she is no longer a threat. Individuals who have been radicalized but are not jihadists may serve as mentors and agents of influence to those who might become the terrorists of tomorrow.
>
> The subtle and non-criminal nature of the behaviors involved in the process of radicalization makes it difficult to identify or even monitor from a law enforcement standpoint. Taken in isolation, individual behaviors can be seen as innocuous; however, when seen as part of the continuum of the radicalization

---

* This fact bears a resemblance to the lack of linguistic and cultural expertise of the expert witnesses the government has relied on in terrorism prosecutions to date (as discussed in Chapter 3 on evidence).

process, their significance becomes more important. Considering the sequencing of these behaviors and the need to identify those entering this process at the earliest possible stage makes intelligence the critical tool in helping to thwart an attack or even prevent the planning of future plots.[36]

In other words, once an individual has begun the radicalization process, he represents a threat, even when he does not actually threaten anyone, since he could be actively supporting and recruiting other terrorists. The basis for this position is not spelled out, although it engenders another extrapolation—namely, that innocent behavior from someone undergoing radicalization can actually represent the first step on the way to terrorist violence. Therefore, law enforcement must be proactive and construe threats as broadly as possible in order to protect society. Innocent behavior, once the police recognize it as part of the radicalization continuum (that works like a "funnel"), can suddenly morph into dangerous behavior. The key common denominator that allows for a finding of radicalization in progress seems to be that the target in question is Muslim.

This conclusion is borne out by the report's own definitions and markers attendant to each stage. While there is no one-size-fits-all profile for someone in the first, "pre-radicalization" phase, the individuals most susceptible to falling prey to radicalization's grasp are 15- to 35-year-old males living within Muslim communities in "the West." There seems to be a slightly elevated risk for individuals from middle-class backgrounds and students, but the report also highlights that "[a] range of socioeconomic and psychological factors have been associated with those who have chosen to radicalize to include the bored and/or frustrated, successful college students, the unemployed, the second and third generation, new immigrants, petty criminals, and prison parolees."[37] Outside of the slightly more delineated group of young males, the thesis seems to begin with a not-fully-articulated but still somewhat clear profile of Muslims.

In the second, "self-identification," phase, the individual starts to identify more with jihadi-Salafi Islam, a process that can be triggered by a number of factors, all of which correspond to some sort of personal adversity. These factors arise, for example, when someone loses a job or is blocked in career advancement, experiences any type of discrimination—"real or perceived," expresses a sense of outrage at the political situation of Muslims anywhere in the world, or suffers through a personal tragedy like a death in the family.[38] Boiled down to their essence, the events that can push a Muslim down the path to radicalization represent nearly all types of challenges a human being can face in life. According to the report, the police need to be on the lookout for key outward markers such as getting a new set of friends with so-called Salafi inclinations, affiliating with them in a group, and becoming more active within the local Muslim community on social issues. Additionally, other behaviors of concern include "[g]iving up cigarettes, drinking, gambling and urban hip-hop gangster clothes" as well as "[w]earing traditional Islamic clothing, growing a beard," and even more troubling, regular attendance at a Salafi mosque.[39] At this point, the report evinces a general view of Muslims as inherently suspicious, and particularly young Muslim males, taking any signs of greater devotion to their faith as evidence that they are on the path to committing a terrorist act. The focus on aspects of an individual's identification with one theological strain is also of concern, given the authors' lack of any obvious training in the ramifications of such a religious choice.

The third stage, "indoctrination," according to Bhatt and Silber, occurs when an individual accepts "a religious-political worldview that justifies, legitimizes, encourages, or supports violence against anything *kufr*, or un-Islamic, including the West, its citizens, its allies, or other Muslims whose opinions are contrary to the extremist agenda."[40] As opposed to the previous, "self-identification" phase, this stage sees the individual withdraw from attendance at the mosque because it no longer supports his radical agenda and due to his fear or "perce[ption]" that it represents a locus of undercover surveillance by the police. Interestingly, as subsequent sections of this chapter demonstrate, a key aspect of law enforcement's counterterrorist investigatory regime is spying on mosques. This section of the report therefore accomplishes a most amazing feat in a few sentences; it demonstrates disdain for the individual's belief that his mosque is being spied upon, even though such spying is commonplace and almost assuredly occurring, while noting that his withdrawal because of such spying is a sign of greater radicalization. While that may be one conclusion, it certainly is not the only one, as we might expect many people to stop attending a house of worship if it was widely understood to be under government surveillance. The other marker of the "indoctrination" phase is ideological; the individual views the world as us-and-them and regards all conflicts involving Muslims as an attack on Islam. In response, the individual increases the number and secrecy of meetings with like-minded fellow travelers, thereby moving down the road to an attack. The Internet serves as an enabling force, allowing the indoctrinated to support each other in word and deed, both by connecting them to like-minded individuals and passing on operationally valuable data, like information on carrying out an attack.[41]

The report segues to the final phase, "jihadization," which represents the stage at which the individual participates in an attack, either individually or collectively, indirectly or directly. The type of contribution one can make to a violent plot reproduces the FBI's construct of acts in furtherance of terrorism as involving planning, preparing, or carrying out an attack. Targets and methods of attack can vary greatly from one radicalized individual/grouping to another, but the goal is always the same—"to punish the West, overthrow the democratic order, re-establish the Caliphate, and institute sharia."[42] Unlike the other stages of the radicalization continuum, which take place over a two- to three-year period, the "jihadization" stage can come together quickly, in a matter of weeks, the report warns. Here the markers of the phase are more detailed and pointed than in other stages of radicalization, although they are not exhaustive. The individual makes a decision to commit "jihad," which is often expressed by travel abroad, usually to receive training at a military camp and become a "mujahedeen."* Training can also take the form of "Outward Bound" activities, which can include "camping, white-water rafting, paintball games, target shooting, and even outdoor simulations of military-like maneuvers."[43] An attacker or participant needs also to engage in "mental reinforcement," which includes getting emotional support for the decision to carry out violence, as well as activities like watching jihadist videos to help "psych" the individual, and also the drafting of a last will and testament, as suicide bombers have been known to do. Finally, a would-be attacker reveals himself by engaging in planning activities like Internet research, surveillance of a target, and acquiring and/or constructing an explosive device.[44]

The radicalization process outlined in the NYPD report resembles the FBI's model to a large degree, only with a greater level of detail, as it takes the extra step of applying its model to several case studies drawn from actual attacks or plots. They are divided evenly between five from abroad and five from the United States. Silber and Bhatt attempt to show throughout the report how these case studies conform to their radicalization thesis with its four-pronged progression. The five foreign incidents cited in the report are the March 2004 bombing of the central Madrid train station, the arrest and trial of the members of Amsterdam's Hofstad group, the July 2005 bombing of the London Underground, the arrest and prosecution of the suspects in Australia's Pendennis Operation in November 2005, and the arrest and prosecution of the Toronto 18 in June 2006.[45] The five domestic incidents are the arrest and successful prosecution of the Lackawanna Six, the Portland Seven, the Northern Virginia Paintball defendants, the Herald Square Subway defendant, and the al-Muhajiroun Two, the latter two being plots from New York City, with all five taking place in the five-year period after 9/11.[46]

With respect to the foreign incidents cited in the report, it is hard to know what conclusions to draw about such a geographically and culturally disparate set

---

* "Mujahedeen" is one way to transliterate the plural form of the Arabic word "mujahid," so an individual could not become a "mujahedeen," but rather a "mujahid," the report's wording notwithstanding.

of circumstances that each case represents. While two of the case studies, Madrid and London, resulted in violent and deadly mass attacks, the other three were plots thwarted by the authorities in Holland, Australia, and Canada, respectively, with only the Dutch example involving any violence. The plots in Australia and Canada, which occurred most recently in time out of all those listed, were halted before they could take place, so perhaps the Australian and Canadian authorities have developed successful surveillance and investigatory tactics that relied on actual threat levels, as opposed to thinly veiled religious profiles wrapped in pseudo-academic titles like "radicalization." Bhatt and Silber recite details they regard as pertinent to their thesis, which involves an insistent view that the threat posed by "jihad-Salafi" Islam to "the West" can be reduced to a formula. Other than the common denominator of a Muslim community in each country, it is not easy to follow how the logic of the radicalization thesis corresponds to each example. After all, as they admit, "[h]istory, geography, politics, demography, and culture are all factors which affect the ease, speed, and degree of how radicalization occurs."[47] Identifying radical Islam as the sole culprit for law enforcement in "the West" to analyze through one lens that they conveniently provide flies in the face of the examples they give, with the incredibly vast set of factors that draw from each country's particularized "[h]istory, geography, politics, demography, and culture."

Domestically, the authors effectively undercut the relevance of the foreign incidents they cite to the American experience, since the United States has appeared to be somewhat "immune" to the phenomenon of the "homegrown" attack.[48] But the potential that a homegrown threat might emerge is sufficient to adopt the radicalization thesis in their view. The problem is that the report references details from each of the five American examples it cites without sufficiently explaining how those details correlate to the crimes with which the defendants were charged.[49] The five cases do not involve violent acts, and charges in four out of the five do not allege any intention to commit a violent crime.[50] The fifth example, the Herald Square Subway case, involved a sting run by an undercover NYPD officer and an informant who suggested, directed, and provided the means with which to carry out the plot.[51] As one legal scholar observed, "the NYPD participated in what it purported to study," helping create the existence of a dangerous terrorist plot to justify its provocative tactics and the radicalization thesis at their heart.[52] To paper over these obvious cracks in its shaky edifice, the report resorts to the by-now classic post-9/11 obfuscation: referencing 9/11. It concludes its last major study with a look at how the 9/11 plot conforms to its radicalization theory, devoting five pages to showing how the attackers passed through all its identifiable stages, culminating in deadly mass violence.[53]

Before examining the effect of these radicalization-inspired reports, a critical question to consider is the appropriate level of law enforcement investigation when dealing with extremist terrorism proactively. It is undeniably true that the United States, like numerous other nations, has experienced mass attacks resulting in substantial loss of life. The chief actor in the most notorious and deadly attack was al-Qaeda, a grouping based overseas that is made up in large part of non-Americans. Conversely, the radicalization thesis assumes that a key component of the threat of terrorism is domestic, lying within America's Muslim communities. It argues that all we have to do is wait and watch for the signs to emerge. The small number of actual violent plots that did not emanate from a government source gives lie to this claim, as noted below. This is not a mere academic exercise, as the NYPD report corresponds to an entire regime of spying on the Muslim community, even going beyond New York City's borders in its approach. It serves as the intellectual bulwark for a program that seems only to have stigmatized a vulnerable minority while bringing back heavy-handed police tactics long ago discarded in the wake of earlier scandals. The question that radicalization-inspired law enforcement tactics raises is whether those tactics have been proportional and appropriate to the size and nature of the terrorist threat to the United States domestically. The following examination reveals that the answer is "no."

RADICALIZATION: THE NYPD EXPERIENCE IN PRACTICE

To begin with the NYPD, it has become clear that *Radicalization in the West* served as an operational guide for law enforcement to keep tabs on the city's Muslim population. However, changes in the department's makeup set the stage for the report's implementation before it was ever written. In early 2002, the NYPD hired a former deputy director of the CIA to run its Intelligence Division at the rank of deputy commissioner in the wake of the 9/11 attacks. The impetus for the hire was the NYPD's determination to understand the nature of any future terrorist threats to the city so as to actively interdict them before they could materialize.[54] And from there, the NYPD arranged for a high-ranking CIA analyst to direct the operations of the Intelligence Division, while still officially employed by the CIA.[55] The first order of business was revoking the guidelines that governed politically motivated surveillance by the NYPD. In the 1960s and 1970s, the NYPD, like the FBI, engaged in widespread spying on numerous political and civil rights groups without any of the legally mandated level of suspicion that would govern a criminal investigation. This produced units of the Intelligence Division such as "the black desk," which spied on African American groups, with the Division itself earning a reputation as the "Red Squad."[56] In 1971, numerous targets of the spying program filed a federal lawsuit alleging multiple constitutional violations, which was finally settled in 1985 when the NYPD agreed to limit heavily its use of undercover officers and investigate speech and associational activities only when it could meet the legal requirements that criminal activity was afoot. An oversight committee made up of two police personnel and one civilian official was empowered to review and approve by a majority vote any request by the NYPD to investigate political activity.[57]

In 2003, after the NYPD argued that the settlement's terms interfered with its new mandate to fight terrorism in the wake of 9/11, the district court approved a new set of guidelines to govern political spying drafted by the Intelligence Division. Gone were the oversight committee's preapproval requirements and the limits on investigations and undercover activity; all that was needed was the approval of the deputy commissioner for the Intelligence Division to launch investigations of polit- ical activity. The three-member committee was no longer authorized to approve or disapprove actions before they took place, having been limited to reviewing allega- tions of misconduct after the fact. The new standards were "intended to provide the NYPD with the necessary flexibility to act well in advance of the commission of planned terrorist acts or other unlawful activity."[58] Writing in a time of "unprec- edented terrorist threats," the court justified its decision by noting that "the nature of the public peril [had] change[d] with dramatic speed" after 9/11, and that "differ- ent times" demanded different standards.[59]

When read carefully, the new investigatory standards governing police monitor- ing of political activity were practically limitless. The NYPD now had the ability to "act well in advance of the commission of planned terrorist acts *or other unlawful activity*," meaning it could engage in politically driven spying if it could envision that the group or individuals under surveillance would commit any illegal act.[60] Given the remarkably broad nexus of activity covered by the phrase, "other unlawful activity," the potential for far-reaching and intrusive spying on the Muslim community was clear. Based on the new court-authorized standards, the NYPD adopted a strategy it called "zone defense," which saw officers engage in wide-scale preemptive spying of neighborhoods and communities. No longer was the goal simply to stop an attack before it occurred, but to identify terrorists "before they picked targets, before they bought weapons, and, ideally, before a toxic ideology took root," so that the NYPD could "know whether you were going to be a terrorist before you knew yourself."[61]

Using officers drawn from the community under surveillance and identified as "rakers"—in that they were raking the coals of an extinguished fire pit in the hopes of finding a hidden burning ember, that is, a terrorist—the NYPD spied on "hot spots" like restaurants, markets, and cafes to take the pulse of the city's Muslim population and kept diligent reports of its activities.[62] This type of work led to the "mapping" of New York City's neighborhoods by the targeted ethnic groups, such as Moroccans, Pakistanis, and other groups to allow the police to understand the socio-religious geographic layout of New York City. In total, the NYPD identified twenty-eight "ancestries of interest" to map, almost all of which were from immigrant communities, with the exception of "American Black Muslim."[63] Raking even took place outside the city's borders, with Newark, New Jersey, serving as the subject of its own report by the Intelligence Division.[64]

Students were also a great area of concern, and the police monitored Muslim student groups at colleges and universities to determine if radicalization was afoot. However, the NYPD again did not restrain itself solely to New York City but went beyond, spying on student organizations as far away as Buffalo, New York, and New Haven, Connecticut.[65] However, the most controversial aspect of "zone defense" consisted of spying on New York City's mosques and other Muslim religious activity, using individuals it referred to as "mosque crawlers."[66] Despite telling the court that had authorized the new guidelines that officers would not spy on constitutionally protected religious activity, the NYPD engaged in regular surveillance and reporting on what was going in mosques and other religious gatherings.[67] A former senior police official laid out the rationale behind large-scale spying on mosques without any legally cognizable level of suspicion that criminal activity was afoot by stating:

> A mosque is different than a church or temple. It plays a bigger role in society and its day-to-day activities. They pray five times a day. They're there all the time. If something bad is going to happen, they're going to hear about it in the mosques. It's not as sinister as it sounds. We're just going into the mosques. We just want to hear what they are saying.[68]

To engage in such spying, the NYPD's revised surveillance guidelines authorized wide-ranging investigations into what were dubbed "terrorism enterprises," a concept derived from the Racketeering Influenced and Corrupt Organizations (RICO) Act, the chief federal statute used for fighting larger criminal organizations like the Mafia.[69] Before moving on, a quick word on the origin of the term might be useful. Central to the statute's operation is the concept of a "RICO enterprise," which allows law enforcement to investigate all of the activities and members of an entire group in the belief that no matter how innocuous or innocent the activity appears to be, it is part and parcel of a criminal organization whose goals and practices are entirely illegal. For example, when dealing with a gang that extorts local businesses and has carried out numerous killings, RICO authorizes the investigation and prosecution of all members of the gang—or "enterprise"—even the members whose relation to violence and extortion is remote, such as, for example, the group's accountant. The idea is that all members and associates are part of an illegal scheme with no socially redeeming characteristics working toward a common goal of self-enrichment through illicit activities. Rather than be limited through traditional principles of criminal liability to a single transaction, such as a murder or theft carried out by one or several individuals, association with a RICO enterprise allows law enforcement to investigate all members of a criminal organization to attribute to them all of the crimes it carries out.[70] In a small number of terrorism prosecutions post-9/11, the government has brought RICO conspiracy charges against defendants accused of being part of an FTO on the theory that the FTO is a RICO enterprise and has no legitimate goals, but those prosecutions failed to produce a single conviction on those counts.[71]

Based on this RICO-inspired logic, the terrorism enterprise designation developed from a series of guidelines issued in May 2002 by then-Attorney General John Ashcroft to govern the FBI in its criminal investigatory duties.[72] Relying on this designation, a supervisory officer from the Intelligence Division can authorize a terrorism enterprise investigation for "[t]he immediate purpose … obtain[ing] information concerning the nature and structure of the enterprise as specifically delineated …, with a view to the longer range objectives of detection, prevention, and prosecution of the unlawful activities of the enterprise."[73] Terrorism enterprise investigations have no fixed time period, do not have to end, and are not bound by the requirement that there be a completed criminal offense. As long as there is a "reasonable indication" that two or more individuals are operating an enterprise whose goals are engaging in terrorism as defined by law, a series of enumerated crimes, or "furthering political or social goals wholly or in part through activities that involve force, violence or other unlawful acts," then the police can open an investigation.[74] So there is no requirement that illegal acts take place, just that the individuals identified by the NYPD as part of a terrorism enterprise share goals that could include support for terrorism or the catch-all "other unlawful acts." Such an investigation is authorized for a year, but can be renewed by the Intelligence Division supervisor reviewing the application. In fact, as long as a supervisory officer approves, a terrorism enterprise investigation can continue even if the targeted group is "temporarily inactive in the sense that it has not engaged in recent acts of violence or other unlawful activities …, nor is there any immediate threat of harm—yet the composition, goals and prior history of the group suggest the need for continuing law enforcement interest."[75] There is no provision for judicial review. The NYPD has the authorization, therefore, to undertake intrusive and open-ended surveillance of protected religious activity in houses of worship without ever proving that a crime has taken place, let alone terrorist violence, as long as it is convinced that the operations and demographic makeup of a mosque are suspicious.

The concept of construing a group whose goals are essentially political as akin to a criminal enterprise, and transferring the logic of RICO to the terrorism sphere, is certainly questionable. As far back as 1983, United States Circuit Judge Henry Friendly wrote the following in an opinion considering the appeal of Croatian militants convicted under RICO:

> In the ordinary use of language no one would choose "corrupt" as an appropriate adjective to describe members of an organization striving for the independence of their native land even by the most abhorrent means but without any desire for personal gain. Dangerous, vicious, misguided, blinded with anger, even savage and crazed, yes, but corrupt, no. So too with "racketeer influenced" . . . . It would be stretching such words beyond permissible bounds to apply them to the terrorist activities of misguided patriots which, although likewise subject to condemnation, are worlds removed from that of such venal organizations as gambling, narcotics, or prostitution rings.[76]

Even when a group's conduct properly places it within the ambit of a terrorist organization, to assume that it operates like a RICO enterprise is a stretch. As its name indicates, RICO deals with racketeering influenced and corrupt organizations and, echoing Judge Friendly's words, targets "venal" groups concerned with their own enrichment on an almost sociopathic basis. Politics do not enter into the equation. To use the enterprise structure in a charged political context does not necessarily transfer seamlessly. In the case cited above, making the transition a bit less problematic was the fact that the Croatian group on trial was unquestionably violent, having carried out several murders and bombings in North America in support of their political goals. However, the NYPD guidelines provide for terrorism enterprises that have no relation to violence whatsoever, based solely on protected speech or religious activities the police view as having the potential for danger, or "the possibility of unlawful activity." Nothing that went on in the mosques under surveillance ever approached the level of a violent attack, and the illegality of the activities under observation was debatable at best. However, when the authorities view Islam writ large as a suspicious faith that is synonymous with a terrorist threat, spying on mosques and religious activity follows quite naturally. Taking the evidence in its entirety, it is certainly not without basis that some have noted the NYPD has a problem with Islam as a religion.[77] Equating a mosque, which operates openly as a house of worship, with an organized crime organization that, with its multifaceted parts, seeks to avoid criminal liability and law enforcement surveillance, supports this position.

A series of Pulitzer Prize winning articles by then Associated Press reporters Matt Apuzzo and Adam Goldman revealed the existence of all aspects of the

NYPD's spying program discussed above and confirmed that *Radicalization in the West* had served as a kind of field manual to guide the Intelligence Division's putting into practice its recommendations.[78] The NYPD's actions post-9/11 bear out that position. For example, if increased religiosity is a proxy for radicalization and a greater terrorist threat, then spying on mosques logically follows. After all, mosques are different than churches or temples, if the NYPD leadership is to be believed. If students susceptible to radicalization are more likely to propel each other on that path, then increased surveillance of student groups seems like a sound policy choice, under the same logic. And *Radicalization in the West* offers even more extreme examples of police investigatory tactics that have almost no hope of successfully uncovering illegal activity. The report notes a case study where a Muslim convert named Mike requested that his friends start calling him Maher, thereby taking a step further down the path to radicalization in the eyes of the authors. Whether by coincidence or design, the NYPD began monitoring all Muslims who changed their name in New York City, whether from an Arabic to a more anglicized name, or the reverse.[79] A potential terrorist might undergo a name change to blend in, thereby making himself more dangerous, while an individual adopting an Arabic name could be signaling a greater susceptibility to radicalization, according to the report's conclusions. In the NYPD's view, any attempt by Muslims to change their names is evidence of radicalization, one way or the other.

There is more to highlight and criticize about the NYPD program, such as its inability to distinguish between Sunni and Shia Muslims, as well as its propensity to act like an intelligence agency by, for example, spying on the Iranian Mission to the United Nations, but the critically important point is that it did not work.[80] After the existence of the program was revealed, the head of the Intelligence Division admitted in a sworn deposition in 2012 the following: "I could tell you that I never made a [criminal] lead from the rhetoric that came from [the spying program] and I'm here since 2006."[81] The elaborate, expensive, and extensive pattern of surveillance predicated on the idea of a city under threat failed to uncover any threats because there were almost no plots being hatched. Although numerous individuals affiliated with the program in one form or another, from then New York City Mayor Michael Bloomberg to Mitchell Silber, tried to argue that the spying program foiled some fourteen violent plots, those claims were proven false.[82] That did not stop former NYPD Commissioner Raymond Kelly from defending the program as entirely legal throughout his tenure, and he made sure to indicate repeatedly that any criticisms could undermine public safety.[83] It seems that the program was geared to effectuate a kind of paradigm shift in what law enforcement should be entitled to do in a post-9/11 world. As former Mayor Bloomberg argued: "We live in a complex world where you're going to have to have a level of security greater than you did back in the olden days, if you will. And our laws and our interpretation of the Constitution, I think, have to change."[84] Perhaps this is the critical point; the police believe the program to be legal, and it is not clear that a court would hold otherwise. Individuals subject to spying have filed two lawsuits against the NYPD. In one, a New Jersey federal court has already ruled that the program was legal and dismissed the challenge; in the other, the lawsuit is still pending.[85]

Despite the unlikelihood of a successful legal challenge, with a new mayor and police commissioner in New York City, the NYPD has responded to the diverse criticism in the media and community organizations by disbanding the main unit that spied on the Muslim population.[86] Initially called the Demographics Unit, and later renamed the Zone Assessment Unit, the move appears to be an attempt to improve the NYPD's damaged relationship with the city's Muslim community. Additionally, two years earlier, in 2012 the NYPD confirmed that a CIA officer was no longer working alongside the department in its spying program.[87] As welcome as these actions have been for that monitored population, there are three points of concern with which to evaluate this issue in the future. First, because there has been no judicial ruling or legislation indicating that the NYPD's tactics were illegal, a new political crisis or attack that—however plausibly or implausibly—can be attributed to Muslims, could herald the return of the spying program. Now that these tactics have survived at least one legal challenge, that is a solid indication that they can be revived if a political crisis permits. It looks very much like a stigma of collective guilt has been attached to the Muslim community in the NYPD's eyes, and even though it may be dormant for the time being, that stigma can be reaffirmed in the case of new crisis. Second, there is the concern that the activities of the unit could simply be moved to other units of the Intelligence Division, like the Terrorist Interdiction Unit, which is responsible for deciding if a mosque can be deemed a terrorist enterprise.[88] Because most of the inner workings of the NYPD and its investigational priorities and tactics are not made public, the public will be hard-pressed to monitor if the department really changes its tactics or simply decides to shift them to a bureaucratically more obscure location. Finally, the NYPD seems to be moving toward a surveillance model like that of the FBI; while spying on First Amendment activities such as religious worship is impermissible, law enforcement can rely on publicly available census and government data to "map" communities.[89] And presumably, mapping will allow the NYPD to continue to identify and make liberal use of informants within the Muslim community. In fact, shortly after the announcement that the NYPD was shutting down the Demographics/Zone Assessment Unit, the *New York Times* reported that the police continued to recruit actively within the city's Muslim community for informants.[90]

However, as discussed in the next section, the experience in federal criminal prosecutions reveals that relying on informants has proven to be a problematic and much-criticized method utilized by the FBI. The next section thus examines the FBI's record in terrorism investigations and prosecutions and evaluates the danger that the informant phenomenon constitutes on multiple levels.

THE FBI EXPERIENCE: INFORMANTS AND THE DEATH OF THE ENTRAPMENT DEFENSE

The Attorney General's Guidelines for Domestic FBI Operations, the latest version of which was issued in 2008 by then-Attorney General Michael Mukasey, govern the FBI's investigatory practices. Of particular relevance is the FBI's ability to open an "assessment," a type of initial investigation that has subsequently played a significant role in national security probes. Assessments, which "require an authorized purpose but not any particular factual predication," should be initiated "proactively" by the FBI "with an eye towards early intervention and prevention of acts of terrorism before they occur."[91] The Guidelines urge the FBI to use assessments actively and to consider them a tool to eliminate terrorist threats before they can materialize and to not be content waiting for criminal leads to come in before taking action. In conducting an assessment on a target or lead, an agent can access or request information from any government entity—federal, state, or local—as well as search the Internet for information, engage in overt surveillance not requiring a warrant, interview the target or other relevant sources, and gather information through informants.[92] The decision to open an assessment is at an agent's discretion upon a supervisor's approval; it is not subject to outside or independent judicial review.

The use of assessments as an investigatory and information-gathering tool is widespread. Documents disclosed by the FBI pursuant to a Freedom of Information Act (FOIA) request by the *New York Times* revealed that in the two-year period between 2009 and 2011, the FBI opened 82,325 assessments, a majority of which (42,888) were focused on national security threats.[93] The Bureau closed most of these assessments without taking additional action but retains the information in its files. However, assessments do not exist solely on an individual basis, but also can be used to "map" a particular ethnic or religious community viewed as susceptible to terrorist penetration. The FBI's Domestic Investigations and Operations Guide, which serves as a field manual for its agents, provides examples of the appropriateness of the practice:

A related category of information that can be collected is behavioral and cultural information about ethnic or racial communities that is reasonably likely to be exploited by criminal or terrorist groups who hide within those communities in order to engage in illicit activities undetected. For example, the existence of a cultural tradition of collecting funds from members within the community to fund charitable causes in their homeland at a certain time of the year (and how that is accomplished) would be relevant if intelligence reporting revealed that, unknown to many donors, the charitable causes were fronts for terrorist organizations or that terrorist supporters within the community intended to exploit the unwitting donors for their own purposes.[94]

Although the Guide refers in numerous places to the inappropriate practice of using race or religion as a proxy for criminality or terrorism, the theoretically plausible situation of terrorists exploiting the community—which can have multiple permutations and exist in numerous situations—justifies collective spying or intelligence gathering on the basis of race or religion. So even as Attorney General Eric Holder seems poised to issue new guidelines that ban racial profiling on the basis of race, religion, national origin, and sexual orientation as well as do away with a national security exception to the use of such profiling, those new guidelines will leave the FBI's assessment powers untouched.[95] Specifically, as long as federal agents can imagine a situation in which assessments can be used strategically to combat terrorism, they can proceed to collect information on whole communities if those communities are perceived to be at risk of terrorist infiltration or exploitation. And once a community is mapped, a process that depends on informant activities, law enforcement can use that data to select more individuals it wishes to employ as informants, thereby bolstering the practice on both ends.

While the FBI and NYPD both engage in informant-intensive mapping of communities, where they differ is in the FBI's use of those informants to bring actual criminal prosecutions. The NYPD has admitted that its systematic spying on New York's Muslim community did not lead to one successful prosecution, in contrast to the FBI's longer and more fruitful history in garnering federal criminal convictions in the post-9/11 period. As an initial matter, the Department of Justice has its own guidelines for how the FBI should handle informants—"confidential human sources" in the official parlance—although those guidelines concern the relationship between the agent and source only, not the target of the investigation.[96] There are also operative standards for undercover operations and the use of informants, but those guidelines do not provide any judicially enforceable remedies for individuals negatively impacted by undercover work.[97] Much like the NYPD's spying program, the decision to use informants and how to treat them is within the discretion of the FBI and federal authorities and not subject to any type of outside review.

The period after September 11, 2001, and the adoption of the preventive mind-set have seen the numbers of informants officially employed by the FBI rise significantly. While law enforcement agencies are generally loath to release statistical information on the number of informants on the books, information can make its way into the public record. An official FBI budget request submitted to Congress in 2008 put the number at 15,000, a significant rise from past practices.[98] Unofficially, the figures could be three times as high, given that agents are known to rely on informal arrangements with unregistered informants for informational purposes or tips. But having an informant does not guarantee information sufficient to support criminal charges. In the first ten years post-9/11, around five hundred defendants were charged with terrorism-related crimes in the United States, with just under half ensnared in cases driven by an informant.[99] Of critical importance, however, is the fact that criminal charges generally result in some information making its way into the public record about informants and the tactics they employ against a target, which are often provocative, to say the least.

The use of informants in ordinary criminal cases, such as drugs and weapons prosecutions, is structurally problematic because, as a practical matter, informants generally have an incentive to fabricate charges against others since they are paid or—more often—rewarded in the form of reduced criminal penalties.[100] Informant use has also had a deleterious effect on the communities it targets, as significant numbers of African American and Latino youth have been swept up in its wake, leaving behind significant social devastation.[101] The theory behind informant use is that with many criminal organizations or transactions, law enforcement would not be able to successfully learn about and prosecute the individuals behind them without a source working for the police on the inside. That the informants are often criminals themselves is seen as a necessary condition for infiltrating larger criminal organizations and transactions.[102] This logic remains consistent in the terrorism context, at least in theory. Law enforcement cannot be expected to learn about secretive terrorist plots unless an insider can be persuaded to divulge information. But, as discussed below, the terrorism context raises a new concern. The examples that follow demonstrate how law enforcement, mainly the FBI, has constructed terrorism plots via an informant, who uses a wide range of tactics and remarkable persistence to get the target to go along. The entrapment defense, often the sole legal defense to informant-driven charges, provides no relief.

A look at the contours of the defense shows why. The Supreme Court first recognized entrapment as a defense in 1928, but it was not until 1973 that the Court articulated the legal test now in place in the federal courts and the majority of state courts. Dubbed the "subjective test" for entrapment, the Court explained that "the principal element in the defense of entrapment [is] the defendant's predisposition to commit the crime."[103] This is in contrast to the "objective test," which examines the conduct of the government agent/informant to judge if entrapment has occurred; this test is in force in the minority of states and is generally favored by academic commentators.[104] In 1992, the Supreme Court issued its most recent decision concerning entrapment in the case of *Jacobson v. United States*, upholding the defense of "a 56-year-old veteran-turned-farmer who supported his elderly father in Nebraska" convicted of ordering child pornography after a twenty-six-month-long government investigation involving a series of inquiries and solicitations by fictitious government entities regarding his sexual proclivities that framed their approach to him as anti-censorship.[105] The case was considered to have revived the entrapment defense and its focus on predisposition, which the Court ruled has to be evaluated before the defendant was approached by the government.[106]

Defining what "predisposition" means in the entrapment context is an extremely difficult exercise in that it attempts to predict what a given defendant would have done had law enforcement agents not intervened.[107] As the Supreme Court has never articulated a legal test for proving predisposition, it has come under widespread criticism, and there remains a great deal of confusion regarding how predisposition may be proven or disproven in any given case.[108] Perhaps the most straightforward application would be in an ordinary criminal case involving, for example, drug distribution charges, where a defendant would have a difficult time arguing he was entrapped if he has already been convicted of drug distribution charges in the past. Although the current charges may have nothing to do with the past convictions, and may even have been fabricated or trumped-up, the fact that a defendant has been convicted of similar charges in the past militates in favor of finding predisposition. The terrorism prosecution presents a further wrinkle in that it can allow a defendant's statements to be used to prove predisposition, given the political nature of terrorism charges. If a defendant has no criminal or other record indicating past involvement in terrorism but tries to assert an entrapment defense, the government can introduce statements and practices indicating support for terrorism. Demonstrating predisposition can transform a criminal prosecution into a referendum on a defendant's political or religious views when the inquiry turns to the matter of how sympathetic the defendant is to terrorist objectives. An analysis of predisposition to commit a given crime therefore focuses on an individual's general character and beliefs, something the law normally rejects outside the entrapment context.[109] Instead, in the case of an entrapment defense, the more an individual can be shown to be predisposed to commit crime—"through proof of prior crimes, prior bad acts, bad reputation, or other evidence of bad character"—the more extreme the government can be in its inducements to commit the crime.[110]

The examples of pre-9/11 terrorism prosecutions featuring an informant are not plentiful. In a series of related prosecutions in the early 1980s of individuals accused of smuggling weapons for the Provisional Irish Republican Army (IRA) to use in Northern Ireland, one group of defendants successfully argued entrapment to the jury, which acquitted them in spite of at least one defendant's admission that he had smuggled the weapons. Crucial to the defense's success was the fact that the government informants had represented that they worked for the Central Intelligence Agency and were authorized under law to purchase and deliver the weapons. Although the second group to stand trial was convicted of the charges, they were ultimately sentenced to prison terms of between two and seven years, penalties that seem incredibly light for activities directly connected to violence, especially when compared to the typical penalties imposed in connection with terrorist crimes, as discussed later on in Chapter 5.[111]

Perhaps the most prominent pre-9/11 example is that of Emad Salem, a former Egyptian army officer who worked as an informant for the FBI during the investigation of the individuals behind both the first World Trade Center bombing in 1993 and a subsequent plot to blow up several landmarks in the New York City area. The latter conspiracy involved numerous defendants working under the aegis of the leader of the Egyptian Islamic Group (al-Gama'a al-Islamiyya), "the Blind Sheikh" Omar Abdel Rahman, for whom Salem worked as a bodyguard. Salem was a difficult informant who had a strained relationship with the government, even secretly taping his conversations with the FBI and insinuating that the Bureau failed to stop the World Trade Center bombing after he provided information on the bomb plot. As a witness, he admitted on the stand to lying repeatedly, yet his testimony helped successfully convict the defendants in the landmarks prosecution, despite their attempts to argue he had entrapped them.[112] Given the plot's potential for a series of exceedingly destructive attacks, what role the defendants' racial, ideological, and religious beliefs played in crediting his testimony, which was ostensibly undermined by his fabrications and questionable behavior, is anyone's guess.

Outside the rare anomalous case,[113] the pre-9/11 period does not offer many examples of informants involved in terrorism prosecutions. With a turn to the preventive mindset post-9/11, it has become clear that the FBI is motivated to find informants with inside information about terrorist plots so as to stop any attacks from coming to fruition. In ordinary criminal cases, law enforcement is often successful in getting individuals to act as informants as any potential informants are usually looking for relief from their own criminal charges and/or are seeking to be paid. In these situations, law enforcement has the necessary leverage to offer reduced criminal penalties and/or money as inducements to inform. In the terrorism context, however, such leverage often does not exist as law enforcement tends to approach individuals from a particular religious background, who do not have a criminal record or charges pending and are not in need of any relief an agent can provide.[114]

Because of this dynamic, the FBI has resorted to desperate and heavy-handed tactics. For the many Muslims in the United States without citizenship or whose legal status is in flux, FBI efforts to recruit them as informants are often accompanied by the threat, implicit or explicit, to have them deported if they refuse to cooperate. Foad Farahi, an imam at a mosque in Florida, declined the FBI's offers to work as a secret informant and offered instead to work with the Bureau openly, only to have his case for political asylum in the United States thwarted. The government tried to have Tarek Saleh, a Brooklyn-based religious leader, deported after he did not accept to inform on his cousin, a high-ranking al-Qaeda member. Even after the cousin was killed in a 2010 drone attack in Pakistan, the government continued to press to have Saleh deported.[115] Adding to the problematic nature of these tactics are two factors. One is the imbalance in the relationship between the FBI and its noncitizen informant, who is even more legally vulnerable than the average American informant in that the right to remain in the United States hinges on the information provided, an open-ended arrangement that can be terminated solely at the FBI's unreviewable discretion. When an informant is in such a position of dependence, the incentive to lie is heightened, even over and above the normal informant-law enforcement dynamic. Second, and relatedly, the FBI is not required to look for informants with any prior links to terrorism, thereby increasing the risk that the information they provide cannot be verified or trusted.[116]

In dealing with United States citizens without immigration concerns, the FBI also has other options for creating informants. If the target refuses to work as an informant, the Bureau can threaten to charge him with terrorist crimes. That is precisely what happened in the case of Tarek Mehanna, who was charged with and then convicted of numerous terrorism-related crimes stemming from (1) his 2004 trip to Yemen and (2) his online activity translating and distributing Islamist materials after refusing the Bureau's requests to work as an informant.[117] That option may not be feasible in each case, as it is both costly and time-consuming to levy criminal charges, so the FBI has also made use of the no-fly list as a measure to compel cooperation. When Muslim Americans have refused the FBI's offers to work as informants, the FBI has placed them on the no-fly list, resulting in severe restrictions on their ability to travel, work, and so forth. Currently, there are two lawsuits challenging the constitutionality of this practice, which sheds light on the normally secretive process of informant recruitment and the tools at the FBI's disposal.[118] And when Muslim American residents abroad have refused to work as informants for the FBI, they have been arrested, detained without charge, and harshly interrogated by local authorities allegedly at the behest of the United States government in Kuwait, the United Arab Emirates, Kenya, and Yemen, among other countries.[119] Pressure abroad can also be brought to bear in other ways. In the case of Naji Mansour, his refusal to work with the FBI resulted in his forced departure from Kenya, his country of residence, separation from his wife and children, and then detention and interrogation in South Sudan.[120] Additionally, Mansour taped some of his conversations with FBI agents, who threatened not only him but also his family with negative consequences if he continued to refuse to work as an informant.[121] Four days after Mansour declined to work with the FBI, his mother lost her job with a government contractor.[122]

EXAMPLES OF INFORMANT-DRIVEN PROSECUTIONS

When the government employs an informant with an eye toward bringing criminal charges, the central question, both from a practical and philosophical standpoint, has concerned whether the defendants would have committed the crime but for the informant's actions. Consider the following examples. In December 2008, five young Muslim residents of southern New Jersey were convicted of conspiring to attack the United States Army base at Fort Dix. Four of the defendants were given life sentences, and the fifth was sentenced to thirty-three years in prison, with both the convictions and sentences affirmed almost in their entirety by the United States Court of Appeals for the Third Circuit.[123] The government's investigation began when a clerk at Circuit City reported that one of the defendants asked him to digitally transfer a videotape of the men firing guns in the woods and shouting in Arabic. The FBI sent two informants to make contact with the men, and those subsequent conversations made up the bulk of the evidence adduced at trial, comprising seventeen of the twenty-three days of total testimony. Much of what the men talked about was their outrage at American actions in the Middle East, as well as their plot to attack the army base. They were arrested well before they were actually in position to carry out an attack.

Both of the informants had suspect backgrounds. One, an Egyptian national named Mahmoud Omar, entered the United States illegally, was later convicted of bank fraud and then sentenced to prison. When he was suspected of involvement in another fraud case, the FBI asked him to work as an informant, which prompted an attempted escape to Canada. After being caught, he agreed to work for the FBI, resulting in his being paid over $240,000—not including rent and assorted expenses—and receiving relief from his legal troubles. The government's other informant, an Albanian citizen named Besnik Bakalli, agreed to work for the government in exchange for not being deported from the United States. Bakalli had a criminal record in Albania, stemming from his conviction on a weapons charge after shooting a man who had threatened his sister.

Omar in particular was quite aggressive in his interactions with the defendants, many of which he taped. He admitted on the stand to urging the defendants to go ahead with the plan to attack Fort Dix. When Omar asked one of the defendants for a map of the base, the latter actually went to the police to warn them of Omar's intentions, but in the end produced the map. A different defendant stalled Omar, stating that jihad would have to wait, because he had to go get a haircut. Another said that they were "good the way we are. We are not going to kill anyone." These episodes prompted Omar to lash out at the defendants, telling one, "You talk but you don't do nothing."[124]

When the defendants tried to argue that they were entrapped, the government proved their predisposition by playing both the recordings of the conversations with the informants as well as videotapes seized from the defendants that purported to show beheadings carried out by al-Qaeda.[125] Because the Federal Rules of Evidence ordinarily prohibit exhibits that tend to show that a defendant has a bad character and that are overly prejudicial (see Chapter 3), it should have been difficult for the government to introduce such evidence. However, in the absence of any other proof that the defendants were a threat—they had never been suspected of terrorism, let alone charged with a crime in the United States—political discussions and inflammatory videotapes from terrorist groups served the purpose of establishing predisposition. So raising the entrapment defense comes with the real risk that it can open the door to introduce evidence that may well have been excluded had the defense not been asserted. The Fort Dix case thus illustrates one important criticism of the use of informants, namely, whether the defendants would have really done anything in the absence of the informants' actions. It also reveals the limits of the entrapment defense when a jury is presented with evidence of anti-American views expressed from an Islamist perspective.

In addition to the problematic dynamic of the government's agents suggesting violent plots that can later be thwarted in the name of fighting terrorism, informants can also exploit all sorts of misunderstandings—cultural, linguistic, or otherwise—in pushing forward a plot.

Shahed Hussain, code-named "Malik," a Pakistani citizen and informant for the U.S. government in several prosecutions serves as an embodiment of this trend.[126] Facing criminal charges for his role in taking written tests at the Albany, NY, office of the Department of Motor Vehicles in exchange for money on behalf of immigrants who could not understand English, Malik agreed to become an informant for the FBI. This arrangement promised financial respite from his recently declared bankruptcy as well as relief from deportation on fraud-related grounds.

In his capacity as an informant, Malik served first as the principal witness against Yassin Aref and Mohammed Hossain in the 2006 prosecution and conviction of the duo on multiple terrorism charges stemming from a plot to launder $50,000 as part of a fictitious scheme to attack a Pakistani diplomat in New York.[127] Malik later testified in the successful prosecution of the four men charged in the 2009 plot to bomb two synagogues and a National Guard base in New York.[128] Each is discussed in turn.

Malik initially approached Hossain at the latter's Albany-area pizzeria, bringing gifts for the owner's children, and then divulged the details of the money-laundering plot through several meetings. Hossain was neither suspected nor linked to any terrorism-related activities. Malik offered to help Hossain, a Bangladeshi national who was experiencing financial difficulties, renovate his pizzeria with a $50,000 loan. He later told Hossain that he had received the money for his efforts in procuring a surface-to-air missile for a terrorist group as part of its plan to shoot down the plane of a Pakistani diplomat. Malik frequently spoke in Urdu, a language in which Hossain, a native Bengali speaker, was not entirely comfortable. According to their arrangement, Hossain could pay back the loan in small increments, effectively laundering the proceeds of the sale for Malik and the terrorist group. Aref, an imam of Iraqi Kurdish extraction, had come to the attention of law enforcement because his name was found among papers recovered in an American military raid in Iraq, which led to his misidentification as a member of a Kurdish Islamic terrorist group. He was brought into the plot only when Malik schemed to have Hossain ask him to be a witness to the financial transaction, per Islamic custom.

In addition to the dynamic that the defendants would not have even contemplated the crime but for the informant, there was a more troubling aspect to the case. Specifically, throughout the investigation, Malik misrepresented the nature and content of his conversations with the defendants, which became clear when the FBI's reports of those conversations were compared to the actual transcripts. For instance, one FBI report from Malik stated that Hossain supported the plan to bring the missile to the United States and that, were it not for his family, Hossain would be taking up arms in the fight. The transcript actually recorded Hossain as saying: "I don't believe in your method—that's why I don't take that path." Malik's duplicity was exacerbated by the fact that his conversations with Hossain alternated between Urdu and broken English and were vague to the point of raising the issue of whether Hossain understood what was going on. That certainly looked to be the case with Aref—whose English was poor and who did not speak either Urdu or Bengali—as the record of the financial transaction featured Malik using code words and strange pronunciations of the word "missile," which Aref claimed to never have heard. In any event, both men were convicted and sentenced to a prison term of fifteen years.

Where the Aref/Hossain prosecution involved a convoluted money-laundering scheme connected to a poorly articulated violent plot, the sting operation in the second plot Malik worked was more straightforward in that the targets to be attacked were clearly noted.[129] Sometime in 2008, under the supervision of the FBI, Malik began approaching worshippers at a mosque in Newburgh, New York, offering gifts and jobs to individuals not suspected in any way of being involved in terrorism. He ended up meeting James Cromitie and introduced himself as a representative of a Pakistani terrorist organization with ties to al-Qaeda. Malik directed Cromitie to recruit three other men to engage in the plot, which ultimately included plans to bomb two synagogues and attack a National Guard base with missiles.[130] Although Malik recorded several conversations in which Cromitie expressed a desire to attack American targets as well as a synagogue, his "inducements [to commit the attacks] included offers of $250,000, a barber shop at a cost of $70,000, a BMW, and an all-expense-paid, two-week vacation to Puerto Rico for Cromitie and his family."[131] The four men were ultimately arrested by the FBI in May 2009 when they took delivery of the fake bombs and moved into position to carry out the first attack on the Riverdale Jewish Center.

Far from being careful and thorough planners, the defendants were small-time crooks with lengthy criminal records; one of the defendants "was arrested in a crack house surrounded by bottles of his own urine; his lawyer describe[d] him as 'mildly retarded.'"[132] The district court noted that "[i]t is beyond question that the government created the crime here."[133] Specifically with respect to Cromitie, the court remarked that he was "'incapable of committing an act of terrorism on his own,'" and concluded that "'if the Government had simply kept an eye on Cromitie, and moved on to other investigations, nothing like the events of May 20, 2009 would ever have occurred.'"[134] However, none of these observations prevented the defendants from being convicted; they failed to convince the jury that they were entrapped. Their convictions and sentences were upheld on appeal over their arguments that they had been entrapped as a matter of law and also subjected to outrageous government conduct.[135] Both the initial arrests and subsequent trial received wide coverage in the press, allowing many details to come out about Malik's role in concocting and promoting the plot. His actions confirmed that the FBI does not merely allow a paid informant to troll houses of worship looking for recruits to engage in violent terrorism by promising them money, but overtly encourages such activity.

So untroubled did the FBI seem to be by Malik's conduct that it continued to use him, as his failed approach to an American-born Muslim convert named Khalifah al-Akili demonstrates. Having been approached numerous times by Malik, who was operating under a false identity, al-Akili grew suspicious and learned the truth from various Internet searches. In March 2012, he sent out a mass e-mail to journalists, activists, and lawyers asking for help in preventing his being set up or framed by the informant. Shortly thereafter, al-Akili was arrested by the FBI on somewhat shaky charges of being a felon in possession of a weapon, thereby limiting the potential embarrassment to the FBI and further exposure of Malik's provocative methods.[136]

Reports in the popular press continued to note the government's increasing reliance on the sting operation, which centered on a direct plot to carry out a violent act. But such a focus has not eliminated the problems with informant-led stings. The previous examples discussed involved individuals on the margins of American life—either struggling to integrate to a new culture or just trying to survive economically. These men are hardly terrorist masterminds who pose a clear threat to national security. And the FBI is not above exploiting a target's social and emotional problems to win a terrorism conviction. For example, in September 2009, Hosam Smadi, a 19-year-old Jordanian national, was arrested after driving a vehicle loaded with inert explosives provided by the FBI to a skyscraper in Dallas and charged with crimes related to an informant-driven plot to blow up the building. When he came to the FBI's attention by making posts on the Internet in praise of Osama Bin Laden and declaring himself ready for "the jihadi life," he was working at a roadside barbecue restaurant in a town an hour outside of Dallas. He was living by himself and was described by his father as psychologically scarred by the death of his mother two years earlier. His lawyers argued that as a result of her death, Smadi suffered from depression and schizophrenia, leaving him impaired to the point where he was unsure whether the plot was real or not. The undercover operatives exploited his emotional state, bonding with him so deeply that he considered one of them his brother. Facing a potential life sentence, he pled guilty to one count of attempted use of a weapon of mass destruction and was sentenced to twenty-four years in prison. His later attempts to withdraw his guilty plea by arguing that his lawyer provided ineffective assistance in, inter alia, not making an entrapment defense were rejected by the court.[137]

Similarly, Sami Samir Hassoun, a 22-year-old Lebanese national, was arrested in September 2010 when he placed a backpack containing a fake bomb provided by the FBI inside a trash can on a street corner in Chicago. An informant had suggested the plot to Hassoun, whose lawyer tried to point out both his client's incompetence and desire to impress the informant by making absurd claims about his technical abilities. Hassoun was an alcoholic who had witnessed gruesome violence firsthand as a child growing up in the Ivory Coast during that country's civil war, and his psychological frailty made him an easy mark for the informant. Hassoun ultimately pled guilty to two explosives charges and was sentenced to twenty-three years in prison.

The problems with the use of informant-driven prosecutions in the terrorism context go beyond targeting the vulnerable and mirror larger problems inherent to informants generally. In the first instance, there is the matter of their involvement in criminal activity. In more than one case, the FBI has turned a blind eye to an informant's crimes while employed by the Bureau. Documented cases include informants using and dealing drugs without legal repercussions while working a sting, despite the knowledge of the supervisory FBI agent. Also, on one known occasion, an informant engaged in financial fraud during the pendency of the investigation.[138] Additionally, the FBI has exhibited a willingness to work with individuals whose past crimes were particularly reprehensible. In one case, the FBI relied on a convicted rapist and child molester, who was classified as a high-risk sex offender by the state of Washington, to ensnare two mentally ill men in a plot to attack a military base near Seattle.[139]

A further wrinkle relates to the actual investigatory techniques informants employ. Perhaps the most powerful method for obtaining a conviction is for the informant to record conversations with the defendant in which he exhibits a willingness or intention to engage in an act of terrorism in the United States. The defendant's own words thus constitute the ultimate proof that the government was justified in targeting someone willing to engage in violence. Technological advances make such a task relatively easy. However, in many high-profile terrorism prosecutions, key conversations between an informant and target have gone unrecorded, often due to a purported technical malfunction. These tend to come at the most critical times, such as the initial meeting between the informant and target, or when the target expresses a desire not to go through with the plot.[140]

A prominent example of this phenomenon is the case of Mohamed Osman Mohamud, the Somali American college student charged with and ultimately convicted of attempting to blow up the November 2010 Christmas tree lighting ceremony in Portland, Oregon.[141] While the plot was encouraged by the informant, who also supplied the inert bomb to be used by Mohamud, the important first encounter between the two was not recorded due to a technical glitch. The court thus had no opportunity to hear how the informant first broached the idea of an attack and what type of language and methods of persuasion he used. When Antonio Martinez, a 22-year-old Muslim convert from Baltimore, heard the news of the Mohamud arrest the next day in the national media, he asked to speak with the informant orchestrating a similar bomb attack with him because he did not want to be the victim of a sting. Again, the meeting was not recorded due to "a recorder malfunction."[142] Thus, the discussion in which the informant managed to convince Martinez to go through with the plot was not recorded. Martinez ultimately pled guilty to one count of attempting to use a weapon of mass destruction and received a sentence of twenty-five years in prison.[143]

The only time the FBI might be called to account for these types of mistakes or errors, assuming they are not intentional, is in a trial where an informant might have to testify about what precisely happened during the encounter not recorded. However, the likelihood that such a reckoning might occur is remote, in that informant-driven prosecutions are almost always successful. The sole possible defense—entrapment—has proven ineffectual; there has not been one successful instance of an entrapment defense for defendants charged with terrorist crimes in the decade-plus since September 11, 2001.[144] From the perspective of a jury weighing the guilt or innocence of Muslim defendants, it is not hard to recognize the dynamics at play. As an initial point, to the extent that the average American juror understands anything about Islam, that understanding is most likely informed by the official and media representations of Muslims as terrorists.[145] Second, the nature of the plot, coupled with the evidence of predisposition allowed to disprove entrapment, combine to foist upon the jury a picture of a defendant with reprehensible political and/or religious views that are deemed pertinent to the case by virtue of their being produced at trial. The idea that a defendant could hold these views yet not constitute a threat does not seem to enter into the equation. To expect juries to acquit in situations where there is evidence that the defendant before them was willing to carry out a violent plot and possesses radical political views, given what these juries are likely to know about Islam, is perhaps unrealistic.

We might expect courts reviewing claims of entrapment as a matter of law to be more discerning than juries, but in the relatively few instances in which they have adjudicated such claims, they rejected them. A recent example of this trend comes from the 2013 opinion in *United States v. Cromitie*, the plot to bomb synagogues in New York discussed above. The United States Court of Appeals for the Second Circuit affirmed the convictions of all defendants, emphasizing that the evidence to prove predisposition can emanate solely from a defendant's own statements. It is of no consequence that without the government's involvement in the plot via an informant, there would have been no crime, something the court freely admitted. If an individual is predisposed, and even if the evidence of predisposition is only derived from mere words, that is enough to defeat an entrapment defense in the view of the Second Circuit.[146] This point of view reflects something about the nature of terrorism—particularly terrorism of an Islamist bent—as understood by the courts. Courts seem to be articulating their position on terrorism through their rejection of the entrapment defense. The *Cromitie* opinion denied entrapment as a matter of law despite the court's recognition that the informant suggested the plot, provided the means to carry it out, and offered significant monetary inducements to mentally challenged and impoverished men. Therefore, the court seems to be stating that defendants in such a position cannot be saved from the informant's predations since the nature of the crime they are being induced to commit is so heinous.

Compare this ruling with the Supreme Court's opinion in its last major entrapment opinion from 1992. In *Jacobson v. United States*, the Court overturned the defendant's conviction and upheld his entrapment defense as a matter of law precisely because of the government's aggressive tactics in creating the conditions for him to order child pornography, a particularly heinous crime. The majority opinion made sure to note the defendant's status as "a 56-year-old veteran-turned-farmer who supported his elderly father in Nebraska."[147] In a terrorist entrapment case, it is rare to see a defendant's sympathetic attributes highlighted in such a manner. As will be discussed in subsequent chapters, inherent in the expressive function of terrorism prosecutions is a belief in the irredeemable nature of a terrorist, whose crimes are no ordinary crimes. Without belaboring the point too much, courts reviewing entrapment claims are certainly susceptible to such thinking, given the construct of Muslims being racialized as terrorists. Even though the plots noted in this chapter never had any chance of coming to fruition, as they were all the product of an informant's machinations, and the targeted defendants were anything but terrorist masterminds, perhaps the message is that the mere thought of people taking tangible steps toward carrying out an attack is too much for the law to countenance.

There have been some reversals for the government in terrorism stings, but they are few and far between. In the case of a Yemeni sheikh and his assistant drawn into a plot to provide material support to terrorist groups by a Yemeni American informant, the Second Circuit ultimately overturned their convictions and long prison sentences in 2008 due to cumulative errors committed by the trial judge.[148] By the time of trial, the government considered the informant such a liability that it opted not to call him as a witness. Among other red flags, he set himself on fire in front of the White House prior to trial to protest what he considered the FBI's insufficient remuneration for his efforts; he had received $100,000 from the government by that point in time.[149] In any event, the reversal in the case, *United States v. al-Moayad*, was not the result of an entrapment defense. More recently, in April 2014, the government worked out a guilty plea to non-terrorism crimes with a Tunisian man named Ahmed Abassi who had been targeted by an informant. After initially being charged with setting up deadly terrorist plots, the government relented when, according to Abassi's lawyer, he was recorded repeatedly expressing to the informant that he had no intention of engaging in violent activity.[150] However, the about-face by the government was made purely at its discretion, not as a result of a jury verdict or court ruling on an entrapment defense, and therefore does not represent any type of binding precedent.

The government's terrorism prosecution machinery built on informant labor continues to operate. One of the most recent cases involved Nicholas Teausant, a 20-year-old convert to Islam from the Sacramento, California area, who was arrested trying to enter Canada on his way to allegedly join a terrorist group fighting in the Syrian civil war. Teausant, a community college student and National Guard dropout, embarked on the trip after many discussions over several months with an informant. According to his lawyer, once the informant promised to financially "take care of" Teausant's family while he was away at the front, he decided to make the trip. One of the lawyer's allegations was that the informant preyed on Teausant's mental illness, as he was diagnosed as suffering from bipolar disorder after he was jailed for the terrorism charge.[151]

Taking advantage of mental illness is not an isolated theme, as evidenced by the case of Mohammad Hassan Hamdan, a 22-year-old Lebanese legal permanent resident of the United States arrested by the FBI at Detroit Metropolitan Airport in March 2014 on suspicion of traveling to Lebanon to fight with the FTO Hizballah in the Syrian civil war. Hamdan was charged with one count of providing material support to an FTO in the form of personnel—that is, himself.[152] His mother reacted to his arrest and the charge by pointing out that he was physically incapable of fighting as he suffers from a dysfunctional lung. She instead blamed the whole thing on the informant, whom she believed to be exploiting his ties with Hamdan's ex-girlfriend, with whom he was friendly.[153] Whatever the case, after several months in custody, the court ordered Hamdan to be referred for psychiatric evaluation, finding that "there is reasonable cause to believe the Defendant may presently be suffering from a mental disease or defect rendering him mentally incompetent to stand trial."[154]

The above litany of eyebrow-raising details and questionable tactics has resulted in what investigative journalist Trevor Aaronson describes as the FBI "hunt[ing] an enemy that is largely of its own creation."[155] Because around $3.3 billion of the FBI's $8.1 billion annual budget allocation is earmarked for national security purposes, as opposed to the just over $2.6 billion designated for criminal investigations,[156] Aaronson argues that the FBI creates terrorist plots that it then thwarts to justify this budgetary breakdown. Aaronson also warns that the FBI's actions in this area prevent better and more efficient law enforcement practices, thus allowing significant non-terrorist crimes to go uninvestigated. Outside of these practical concerns, the Muslim community in the United States has complained about what it believes is the government equating Islam with terrorism.[157] There has been critical commentary on the use of informants in terrorism prosecutions, particularly the seemingly absurd construct of the government creating fictitious plots that it then stops.[158] That these plots extend from techniques like sending informants into mosques without any suspicion of wrongdoing only exacerbates the problematic nature of an informant's work. As former FBI agent and whistleblower Coleen Rowley put it, "it's much more difficult to catch real terrorists than it is to catch mosque-goers."[159] Additionally, informant use can produce ancillary effects, such as an increased risk of hate crimes for Muslim Americans and communities like Sikhs, who "look Muslim."[160]

However, government officials defend the practice consistently and with vehemence, arguing that it is a vital counterterrorism tool the FBI must hold on to in order to effectively combat political violence. When news broke of the FBI sending an informant to spy on Los Angeles-area mosques and tape his conversations with congregants in 2006 and 2007—an effort that produced no arrests or prosecutions—then-FBI Director Robert Mueller spoke out in defense of the FBI's tactics, downplaying the infringement on religious freedom they represented.[161] In late 2010, Attorney General Eric Holder, speaking to a Muslim advocacy group in the wake of the announcement of the Mohamud and Martinez sting arrests, deemed informant use "'an essential law enforcement tool in uncovering and preventing terror attacks.'"[162] In the same speech, he also called for more and better cooperation with the Muslim community to fight terrorism. Finally, in a 2013 review of Trevor Aaronson's book, former FBI Special Agent Ali Soufan, who spent much of his eight-year tenure with the Bureau working on al-Qaeda-related cases, took issue with what he viewed as Aaronson's overly critical approach. Soufan argued that just because the men ensnared in FBI stings were incompetent, deluded, or both, that did not mean they were not a threat. He noted that terrorism represented a real threat, as evidenced by the 2001 arrest of "shoe bomber" Richard Reid, the 2002 arrest of "dirty bomber" Jose Padilla, and the failed plot to detonate a car bomb in Times Square in 2010 by Faisal Shahzad.[163] None of those plots were foiled by the use of an informant, however. Yet the very real question remains of what the FBI should be doing in light of the threat of terrorism. Soufan, buffeted and inspired by the preventive approach, typifies the government's focus on stopping plots before they can come to fruition, even if those plots have to be midwifed by the FBI's heavy guiding hand.

CONCLUSION—WHAT SPYING AND INFORMANTS HAVE WROUGHT

It is precisely this preventive mindset that is the most difficult to argue with. At the most basic level, the citizenry of almost any political entity is going to want its authorities to stop a threat to public safety before it manifests in the form of actual violence. But the tactics of spying and using informants do not really result in preventing attacks in the manner described by the government. As noted, the examples Soufan gave in his article did not correspond to terrorist attacks thwarted by the FBI's use of informants, but plots that were broken up by chance and/or alert actions by police and observant bystanders. When news of the NYPD's spying on the city's Muslim community came to light, then New York City Mayor Michael Bloomberg rose to the defense of the police, arguing that the department had prevented some fourteen terrorist plots since 9/11. An examination of that claim revealed it to be incorrect, with the spying program responsible for stopping at best only a few plots that its informants had initiated.[164] Despite this, both the NYPD and FBI remain steadfast in their insistence that a preventive mindset, which reacts proactively to a new series of threats, justifies the more intrusive tactics guided by theories of radicalization discussed in this chapter. Law enforcement in general has yet to be weaned off its reliance on the radicalization theory, despite its poor capacity for predicting terrorist activity, in that it focuses too much on religious speech and practice as a proxy for terrorism.[165] Still, the response of the FBI, the NYPD, and their defenders to any criticisms of their counterterrorism actions, however well-intentioned, reveals a refusal to countenance any outside scrutiny of their tactics and methods. After all, their mandate is to prevent attacks from the terrorist enemy, and they cannot afford to leave any stone unturned in service of that goal. If someone can be convinced to commit an attack after interaction with an informant, should the authorities really be forced to consider whether that individual had the capacity to carry out an attack without the informant's help? Isn't that individual a threat that society is better off removing from its midst via a criminal prosecution?

The problem with trying to answer these questions is that they tend to obscure the phenomenon that terrorism investigations and prosecutions demonstrate in their relentless focus on the existential threat of terrorism and the desire to avoid the next attack. What we are witnessing is the transfer of these tactics into the domestic sphere, outside the narrow realm of Islamist terrorism, to the point where law enforcement transforms into a domestic intelligence agency, without a popular mandate or congressional authorization for such a transformation. In a general sense, this book aims to demonstrate the terrorism prosecution's outsize influence and effect on criminal law and procedure, despite the relatively small number of such prosecutions. The Center on Law and Security documented 578 national security prosecutions in the decade after 9/11, 431 of which had been resolved in that time period.[166] By contrast, in 2013 alone, there were over eighty thousand federal criminal cases in which a sentence was issued.[167] The numbers of terrorism prosecutions therefore are not significant statistically in the grand scheme of federal criminal prosecution. But the specter of terrorism allows for a creeping implementation of preventive tactics that perceive as criminal highly inchoate activity that may never result in illegality, as well as construe political activism as suspicious and potentially subversive.

By way of example, Matt Apuzzo and Adam Goldman, the former Associated Press reporters who broke the NYPD spying case, illustrate how terrorism investigations could take an improper political turn. They describe how the investigation of a suspect in the March 2008 bombing in Times Square led to the Intelligence Division sending an undercover officer to New Orleans to collect information on future demonstrations in support of labor and prisoners' rights. Within a few weeks, the investigation had "metastasized to include broad intelligence gathering on liberal groups with no connection to [the suspect] or the Times Square Bombing."[168] In the case of the FBI, outside of the investigations and prosecutions discussed in this chapter are the tens of thousands of national security assessments that result in no further action but generate a great deal of information that the Bureau can access going forward. What those files hold remains available only to the FBI and its agents, with no external review of their contents contemplated.

Slowly but surely, details of cases from beyond the realm of Islamist terrorism have emerged that demonstrate the FBI's willingness to use informant and spying tactics more broadly in politically tinged cases.[169] The 2011 documentary film, *Better This World*, details the story of two young men from Texas who go to protest at the 2008 Republican National Convention in Minneapolis and find themselves facing federal terrorism charges as a result of the constant prodding and provocations of a government informant, who was a well-known radical political activist.[170] Also in 2008, Eric McDavid, a member of the Earth Liberation Front, was found guilty of plotting to bomb several targets, including federal government facilities and cell phone towers, and received a sentence of around twenty years in prison. An informant known to McDavid as "Anna" was paid $65,000 by the FBI for her services leading to his arrest, and she was also given money by the Bureau to buy gas, food, and supplies to facilitate the purported bombing plot. There was also the indication that Anna used the prospect of a romantic relationship with McDavid as an incentive to carry out the planned bombings.[171] Notwithstanding McDavid's argument that he was entrapped by Anna, his conviction and sentence were upheld on appeal; he was later released when the government was found not to have turned over legally required materials to his defense team.

Recently released FBI documents show that the Bureau conducted surveillance on and monitored the nationwide Occupy protests that began in 2011. Despite the FBI classifying the Occupy Movement as peaceful, it carried out its investigation of the organization under counterterrorist rubric, and played a role in coordinating the eventual dispersal of the protests by law enforcement across cities.[172] In a case strongly resembling the terrorism prosecutions discussed above, four young men active in Occupy Cleveland were charged and ultimately convicted of plotting to blow up an Ohio highway bridge. The FBI sent an informant to the protest based on an initial report of illegality being committed by anarchists there. The informant, Shaquille Azir, had a long criminal record involving numerous convictions on fraud charges, as well as spending nearly three years in prison for robbery. The defendants, several of whom were destitute and/or suffering from mental health problems, were led into the plot by Azir, who helped suggest targets and arranged and financed the sale of the explosives to be used. He also provided the men with drugs, alcohol, food, and housing. After the FBI broke up the sting its informant had created, the four were convicted in 2012 for their roles in the plot and sentenced to prison.[173] Also in 2012, seven members of Occupy Austin were charged for their roles in obstructing a road in Houston by tying themselves together during a protest. It was later discovered that undercover officers with the Austin Police Department had encouraged the use of a device called a "lockbox," which triggers enhanced criminal penalties, as the device makes it much harder for the police to separate the protestors tied together. After the officers suggested employing the device, one of them purchased the components required to make it and then provided the protestors with the finished lockboxes to use.[174]

The undercover phenomenon continues to grow, reaching more areas where the government operates. In November 2014, the *New York Times* reported that entities such as the Department of Agriculture, the Internal Revenue Service, and the Small Business Administration had "significantly expanded undercover operations" over the last few years.[175] The impetus for the push seems to have been a fortuitous confluence of interests between stopping terrorist attacks and adopting a more preventive mindset to law enforcement in general. While much of the activity focused on problems or crimes unrelated to national security and terrorism, such as fraud and misuse of federal funds, the potential adverse effect on First Amendment protected activities was evident. Perhaps the most disturbing aspect of the report in this regard was its revelation that the Supreme Court Police engage in the practice of sending undercover officers dressed as students to monitor demonstrations and protests by groups supporting one or the other side in cases outside the Supreme Court building.[176]

What the post-9/11 phenomenon of informant use and domestic spying represents, therefore, is the overturning of a carefully struck legal and societal balance that emerged in the United States out of the political upheaval of the 1960s, both domestically and internationally. Under the framework of safeguarding national security, law enforcement has focused on a despised and misunderstood minority to exploit legal gaps and ambiguities that have in turn regularized a new, lowered tolerance for spying and provocateurs in our midst. The national trauma of 9/11 and foreignness of the perpetrators of the attack have contributed most obviously to the tolerance for this wrong-headed approach to law enforcement in a free society. The relatively low proportion of Muslims in the population and the small number of terrorism prosecutions also allows for these tactics to pass without too much fuss. With other public debates occupying the national security agenda—such as the NSA spying program and the controversy over the use of drones to kill American citizens abroad extrajudicially—informant activity and spying on Muslim communities seem relatively inconsequential. There does not seem to be a Watergate-level tipping point that might spur the public and Congress into action to curtail law enforcement's powers to act as a new type of domestic intelligence service. As opposed to the congressional Church and Pike Committees investigating the actions of the CIA and FBI at home and abroad in the 1970s, American Muslims have actually themselves been investigated by Congress, whose Homeland Security Committee, in a move reminiscent of the McCarthy era, examined the supposed links between them and Islamist terrorism in 2011.[177]

American Muslims have not succeeded in bringing political weight to bear to meaningfully stop the correlation between them and terrorism in the public and official mind. This is in contrast to non-Muslim constituencies potentially described as terrorists. When a 2009 Department of Homeland Security report identified right-wing extremism as a potentially violent threat—highlighting individuals concerned about illegal immigration, abortion, and gun-control—and specifically mentioned returning military veterans as particularly susceptible to committing violent acts, Republicans in Congress criticized the report so heavily that the government ordered it be rewritten.[178] This episode in no way diminished the threat of domestic extremists, as a 2013 report from the Combating Terrorism Center of the United States Military Academy at West Point makes clear.[179] American Muslims have little to no political clout to lobby the government on its national security policies that place them under suspicion and have not been successful in preventing the spread of spying and informants in their communities. For its part, the FBI remains committed to a focus that favors national security investigations, essentially demonstrating its transformation into a domestic intelligence agency, a process begun under former Director Robert Mueller that continues under his successor James Comey.[180] This trend persists despite statistics showing that the terrorism threat from American Muslims, historically low, keeps decreasing, even when accounting for 2013's Boston Marathon bombing.[181] Additionally, almost all large urban police forces have developed cooperative relationships with their local Muslim communities, with some two-thirds of these partnerships generating real intelligence for the police to work with, demonstrating that such arrangements actually enhance national security.[182] Yet for the largest municipal police force, the NYPD, and the premier federal law enforcement agency, the FBI, spying and informants remain part and parcel of their counterterrorism-based strategy.[183] Viewing Muslim communities through the prism of radicalization, hardly a coherent or effective theory, is the practice most often utilized. It is certainly debatable if this approach is the best for protecting national security. What has not been really debated is the benefit to society of these organizations' shift toward internal security and domestic intelligence at the expense of a vulnerable minority population.

2

THE CONTINUAL EVOLUTION OF THE MATERIAL

SUPPORT BAN

SECTION 2339B OF Title 18 of the United States Code (§ 2339B), the federal criminal ban on providing material support to a foreign terrorist organization (FTO), is, by the government's reckoning, the most important statute employed in terrorism prosecutions.[1] Its central place as the premier statutory tool used to tackle the phenomenon of terrorism in American courtrooms is well established, even if its contours are not necessarily well understood. David Cole has called it "the centerpiece of the Justice Department's criminal war on terrorism."[2] Norman Abrams has described it as a "catch-all . . . that can be invoked in widely varying situations where individuals engage in conduct that may contribute in some way to the commission of terrorist offenses."[3] Although passed in 1996, the near-ubiquity of the statute in terrorism prosecutions post-9/11 correlates with the government's focus on preventive law enforcement, that is, stopping plots before they reach fruition. This is in contrast to the pre-9/11 "punishment" model of prosecution in which the government would generally prosecute individuals who had already committed some sort of politically motivated violence.

But before beginning a detailed examination of the history and use of the statute, a few points are worth mentioning. First, the original animating force behind the passage of the law was simple—Congress was concerned that terrorist groups were raising money in the United States under the cover of charitable activity. The facts in the *Rahmani/Afshari* prosecution speak neatly to this scenario.[4] In that case, seven Iranian nationals were indicted and ultimately pled guilty to violating § 2339B because, among other activities, they solicited donations from travelers at Los Angeles International Airport to a charity called the Committee for Human

Rights. The government investigated the group and found that the money had not been sent to an actual charity, but rather went to a Turkey-based bank account of the Mujahedin-e-Khalq (MEK, also known as the People's Mojahedin of Iran, or PMOI), an Iranian opposition group then listed as an FTO. From there, large sums of the money were used to buy rocket-propelled grenades and other weapons for fighting the Iranian government.[5] This prosecution corresponds perfectly with Congress's intent to stop money flowing to terrorist groups under the cover of humanitarian activity. However, as this chapter details, § 2339B prosecutions have come to target more than just money and surreptitious funding of terrorist groups.

Second, the statute is written to operate regardless of one's view on the justice of a particular cause. For example, in 1998, Fawzi Mustapha Assi, a naturalized U.S. citizen of Lebanese origin, was stopped by customs officers when he tried to board an international flight out of Detroit Metropolitan Airport. The officers searched his luggage and found two global positioning modules, night vision goggles, and a thermal imaging camera. In subsequent interviews with federal agents, he allegedly told them that he had been contacted by a member of Hizballah, a Lebanese FTO, who asked him to purchase the equipment, and that he "was willing to help Hizballah in its struggle to expel the Israelis from southern Lebanon."[6] After being indicted on charges, including providing material support to the FTO, he moved to dismiss on the basis that § 2339B violated his First Amendment rights and due process, among other contentions. While not casting doubt on the sincerity of Assi's beliefs, the district court rejected his arguments, stating that to accept them "would invalidate any attempt to outlaw contributions of military hardware or weaponry to any organization, no matter how heinous its actions or abhorrent its mission, so long as the donor could identify some political aim he sought to advance through his donation. The First Amendment does not sweep so broadly in restricting the Government's efforts to fight terrorism."[7] In this case, even though Assi believed that his providing material support was for what he believed to be a good and just cause, the court ruled that it is illegal if the support goes to an FTO, regardless of the motivation or conflict.

The above examples adhere to what could be called the contours of "traditional" material support. If they represented the full scope of material support prosecutions, that would be one thing. However, § 2339B has come to encompass far more kinds of activity, including things like speech and the tricky concept of material support as providing legitimacy to an FTO. What follows, then, begins with a two-part discussion of the history of the statute and its language. After that brief introduction comes an examination of the legal debates § 2339B engendered in the wake of its passage, starting from the issue of the process of designating FTOs on through to the legal challenges to the statute's constitutionality. In the ensuing analysis, we will see how the statute has come to impinge on notions like pure speech as well as push the boundaries of what types of conduct fall under its strictures, thereby going beyond the confines of what Congress envisioned when it passed the law.

THE STATUTE—18 U.S.C. § 2339B

Enacted by Congress in 1996, § 2339B was regarded as an attempt to close the loophole left open by previous terrorism-support statutes; namely, it was designed as a tool to combat the purportedly pressing problem of terrorist groups raising money for violence under the cover of charity.[8]

Passed in the wake of various acts of violence in the Middle East and the 1995 Oklahoma City bombing (a decidedly domestic act of terrorism), the statute prohibits the provision of material support to a designated FTO. The penalty for violating the statute is fifteen years in prison, rising to a life sentence if the material support results in the death of a person. The technical term "material support" involves not just money but also "any property, tangible or intangible, or service, including currency or monetary instruments or financial securities, financial services, lodging, training, expert advice or assistance, safehouses, false documentation or identification, communications equipment, facilities, weapons, lethal substances, explosives, personnel (1 or more individuals who may be or include oneself), and transportation, except medicine or religious materials."[9] Critical to the statute's promulgation was the following key congressional finding that justified the need for such a sweeping ban: "foreign organizations that engage in terrorist activity are so tainted by their criminal conduct that any contribution to such an organization facilitates that conduct."[10]

The wisdom of this congressional finding on the nature of terrorist organizations and their irreducible irredeemability is highly debatable; how Congress created such a metric and the limits of its logic are left unaddressed.[11] Additionally, the position that the designated terrorist groups were engaged in any significant fundraising in the United States was almost assuredly exaggerated prior to and after the passage of the ban. To be sure, the legislative record contains ample evidence of opponents of the ban articulating their concerns that passage of the statute would greatly inhibit protected First Amendment activities. Although these are all worthy points to press and debate, they do not form the focus of the remainder of this chapter. Accordingly, the legal discussion of § 2339B's ramifications is concentrated in a few areas. At the outset is an overview of the process by which FTOs are designated, which leads into a discussion of the law's constitutionality, and then the chapter concludes with an examination of how the concept of material support has gone far beyond money or weapons.

THE DESIGNATION PROCESS

The U.S. Secretary of State has the power to designate a group as an FTO if, after consulting the Attorney General and the Secretary of the Treasury, he or she makes the following findings: (1) the group is foreign; (2) it has engaged in "terrorism" or "terrorist activity"; and (3) it "threatens the security of United States nationals or the national security of the United States."[12] While the "security of United States nationals" is clear enough, by statute "national security" is defined as the far more nebulous "national defense, foreign relations, or economic interests of the United States."[13] This third finding is essentially insulated from challenge in the courts and therefore unreviewable.[14] The designation process takes place in secret; the group being considered receives no notice that it is under review and has no access to the administrative record, which may contain classified information. A designation remains in place until the Secretary, in his or her discretion, decides to revoke it or a court judicially overturns it.

A designated FTO can challenge its status, but only before the D.C. Circuit in a process in which its ability to present any countervailing evidence and receive access to the administrative record compiled by the Secretary are highly circumscribed. By contrast, the Secretary has the right to present new evidence in support of the designation, which may be classified and denied to the FTO.[15] The court will overturn a designation only if the Secretary has acted contrary to the law, in an arbitrary and capricious manner, or the administrative record does not support a designation. It should be noted that because the D.C. Circuit is the sole forum for challenging a designation, a criminal defendant charged with violating § 2339B cannot argue in a terrorism prosecution that the FTO in question was improperly designated.[16]

To date, not one FTO has been successful in having its designation revoked by the D.C. Circuit. The only group to obtain any partial relief at the D.C. Circuit was the MEK/PMOI, which mounted several legal challenges to its designation. On two occasions spanning a decade—first in 2001 and then again in 2010—the court found that the MEK/PMOI had been denied due process by the Secretary's decision to designate it, thereby rendering the designation itself unconstitutional.[17] The court also ordered that the nonclassified portions of the administrative record be turned over to the group so that it could properly challenge its designation, along with the ability to put on evidence in support of its position.[18] While its first challenge centered on the fact that the group maintained a presence in the United States, thereby entitling it to due process in the designation decision, its second challenge in 2010 was rooted in actions it had taken to renounce violent activity and cooperate with the United States in Iraq, where the group maintained a training camp.[19] Neither decision represented a total victory since all the while, the D.C. Circuit left the FTO designation legally in effect. Two years after the second decision, in response to the government's failure to afford the group a hearing on its status, the D.C. Circuit granted the group a writ of mandamus, compelling the government to either make a decision on its petition or drop the group from the list of FTOs.[20] Throughout the duration of the legal challenges, the group lined up an array of high-profile American supporters, including two former CIA directors, a former FBI director, a former Attorney General, and a former national security adviser.[21] At one point, supporters of the MEK/PMOI organized a holiday party in Congress, which was attended by several members of the House of Representatives, including the Republican Chair of the House Foreign Affairs Committee, Ileana Ros-Lehtinen.[22] Finally, a few months later, in September 2012, Secretary of State Hillary Clinton dropped the group from the FTO list, ending a long-running legal saga involving a small and somewhat obscure Iranian opposition group that managed to attract many prominent American names to its cause, perhaps because of its positions that are consistently critical of the current Iranian government, but also oftentimes through large sums of money.[23]

The group and its members and sympathizers also generated the only serious challenge to the designation process outside the D.C. Circuit. In the *Rahmani/Afshari* prosecution referenced above, the district court ruled in favor of the defendants by rejecting the notion that the D.C. Circuit was the sole arbiter of a designation challenge and held that the statute providing for designation itself was unconstitutional.[24] The Ninth Circuit disagreed, finding that it was not empowered to interfere with the D.C. Circuit or Secretary of State's decisions on the group's designation.[25] Even though the D.C. Circuit had held the MEK/PMOI's designation unconstitutional in the years 1997–2001, precisely the time frame the defendants were accused of providing material support, the court of appeals held that the government retained the power to prosecute them.[26] In support of this point, the court cited Supreme Court precedent allowing felon-in-possession charges where the underlying felony had been overturned on appeal, noting that in the FTO's case, the designation had not been set aside, and the group had admitted its commission of numerous violent acts.[27] It also likened § 2339B to a violation of the Export Administration Act, where the issue is not whether the restriction on the commodity in question was valid, but rather whether the defendant knew of the existence of the restriction.[28]

The Ninth Circuit also took the unusual step of addressing the defendants' First Amendment claims—the First Amendment argument is addressed below in greater detail—even though the district court had not ruled on them. The court of appeals remarked that "[g]uns and bombs are not speech," and that "[t]here is no First Amendment right 'to facilitate terrorism by giving terrorists the weapons and explosives with which to carry out their grisly missions.'"[29] It rejected the defendants' attempt to make an "enemy of my enemy is my friend" argument, stating that those types of political decisions are for the executive branch alone to make. When the en banc Ninth Circuit denied review of the panel's decision, Judge Alex Kozinski dissented, joined by four other judges. He took the position that there could be no prosecution where the designation at issue was invalid during the years the material support was allegedly provided. While also casting doubt on the legality of not allowing a § 2339B defendant to challenge the validity of an underlying designation, he rejected what the prosecution had transformed into: a "uniquely unconstitutional (and oxymoronic) practice: an *ex post facto prior restraint*."[30]

The issue of national security and constitutional limits loomed large in the litigation, as evidenced by the numerous written opinions. But Judge Kozinski cut to the heart of the matter in making his views known:

> I can understand the panel's reticence to interfere with matters of national security, but the entire purpose of the terrorist designation process is to determine *whether* an organization poses a threat to national security. Under the Constitution, the State Department does not have carte blanche to label any organization it chooses a foreign terrorist organization and make a criminal out of anyone who donates money to it. Far too much political activity could be suppressed under such a regime.[31]

The record of designation-related litigation contradicts the above statement. As much as Judge Kozinski's position on the State Department's powers sounds in both common sense and constitutional safeguards, nothing in recent designation practice indicates that the Department is in any way bound when banning foreign groups as FTOs. The unreviewable nature of the Secretary of State's determination that a group impacts U.S national security, which can be made legally from an incredibly broad factual basis, indicates a kind of carte blanche. As the MEK/PMOI saga shows, after a fifteen-year struggle, the group finally managed to get removed from the list. Although the organization had suffered through several constitutional improprieties in the designation process, that was not enough to have its name removed. Coincidentally, it carried out a wide-ranging publicity campaign, which involved payments to many high-profile American political, military, and journalistic figures. Then, and only then, was its name removed. It is certainly debatable how much impact this campaign actually had on the Secretary's decision to de-list, but both the timing and circumstances of the decision do not inspire confidence in the likelihood and effectiveness of any relief to be had via litigation at the D.C. Circuit.

The designation decision, in its unreviewability, also makes plain a type of double selectivity. The FTO list currently contains fifty-nine groups, forty-seven of which are Islamic in ideology or Arab/Muslim in ethno-religious composition.[32] Thirty-three of the thirty-six groups added since September 11, 2001, meet those criteria, with the vast majority being Islamist groups.[33] With its smattering of leftist and nationalist groups, the FTO list clues us into the current concept of who the United States considers the enemy, with a few outliers from the Cold War-era and the odd fringe group thrown in for good measure. As the MEK/PMOI saga shows, arguments that the United States and the FTO share a common enemy are unlikely to enjoy traction in any legal challenge to a designation, but a publicity campaign and political lobbying can bear fruit in the right circumstances. Some of the groups on the list represent a more immediate direct threat to the United States than others, so the practical effect of designation is greater where the FTO tries to be more active, although the legal consequences of designation are the same regardless of whether the group is actively planning violent acts or effectively moribund or defunct. In other words, providing material support to al-Qaeda is just as illegal as providing material support to the Revolution Organization November 17, a small Greek faction that was effectively disbanded in 2002 when its members were arrested, convicted, and later imprisoned for a series of violent politically motivated attacks in Greece spanning two and a half decades.[34]

However, it must be noted that those designated are not the sole groups to meet the American definition of a terrorist organization—just those that the government has decided it needs to designate, which has the effect of ceasing all activity by the group in the United States and prohibiting the provision to it of material support. This state of affairs presents numerous issues with which to grapple. Let us leave to one side temporarily the fact that definitions of terrorist activity and terrorist groups for material support purposes can be quite expansive. The selectivity inherent in deciding which groups make the FTO list certainly requires some comment. But even when focusing on the list itself, it becomes clear that the unfettered discretion prosecutors enjoy to bring or withhold charges has allowed for a sort of secondary type of selectivity.

A prime example of this phenomenon involves the Israeli FTO Kahane Chai, also known as Kach, an anti-Arab party founded by the late Meir Kahane.[35] Though the group has been designated as an FTO since the first incarnation of the terrorist list in 1997, to date, the government has not indicted anyone on charges of materially supporting it. Although several groups on the list probably fall into a similar category, Kahane Chai is known to operate in the United States, and its activities have not escaped the attention of the press. In late 2000, the *New York Times* reported that a charitable organization had organized a fundraising dinner at which two leaders of the group were going to speak.[36] A month later, in January 2001, the FBI raided a community center in Brooklyn run by followers of Meir Kahane, and the government revoked the visa of one of the leaders.[37] But whatever investigation the FBI conducted over a decade ago did not result in any material support charges against any individuals. As recently as 2010, the *New York Times* again reported that a former high-ranking Kahane Chai leader solicited donations in the United States for his own charity in support of Israeli settlement activity. When consulted, U.S. Treasury Department officials merely noted that "a group's presence on the terror list does not necessarily extend to its former leaders."[38]

To be fair, it may very well be that for a host of complicated reasons, material support charges against anyone affiliated with the group were infeasible due to lack of evidence, logistical challenges, and so on. It is curious that for the first several years after the statute was passed, members of the group felt secure enough to hold large fundraising dinners, and the government apparently approved visas for its leaders. Even though at least one of those visas was revoked, it is hard to imagine the government approving a visa for another FTO leader from any number of groups all across the ideological spectrum, from the Kurdistan Workers' Party (PKK) to Hamas and beyond. Many years after the FBI raided the group's offices, figures associated with the movement continued to solicit donations in the United States for causes that it espoused. While this may seem relatively insignificant, in one of the largest terrorism funding prosecutions—the action against the directors and officers of the Holy Land Foundation for Relief and Development (HLF) for materially supporting Hamas (discussed in detail below), the government's theory of the case stemmed from just this type of associative activity—namely, raising funds for an FTO via ostensibly nonaffiliated charities. The point here is that while each case is different, a statute with an overtly political aspect, like § 2339B, lends itself to suspicions that it is being selectively enforced. Although that standard is nearly impossible to satisfy in a legal proceeding,[39] that does not mean the signs of prosecutorial selectivity are not evident.

The issue of selectivity is also of critical importance when we consider that the definition of what constitutes "terrorism" or "terrorist activity" is potentially very broad for § 2339B purposes. While there is a long-standing and entrenched debate about the meaning of terrorism under international law,[40] the basic contours of any legal definition involve politically motivated violence against civilians with the intent of coercing or intimidating a government into a course of action, a position tracked by domestic U.S. law.[41] Under the American definition, a terrorist is generally a nonstate actor, which has the effect of excluding state terrorism in all but the most extreme examples, such as when the government has taken specific legal measures to single out a particular state.[42] There is a worthy debate on the topic of the suitability and fairness of distinguishing between state and nonstate terrorism, but that discussion is outside the scope of this book.[43] But even with this narrowed focus, what constitutes terrorism for purposes of material support is quite broad.

Since all of the groups on the FTO list have engaged in violent activity that easily meets the definition of terrorist activity, a turn outside the realm of criminal prosecutions reveals how far the term can be stretched. The definition of "terrorist activity" that a group must engage in to be designated also governs in immigration law, as they both spring from the same statute.[44] In the immigration context, noncitizens are barred from obtaining asylum in the United States if they provide material support to a group engaged in "terrorist activity" in its full expansive definition.[45] But the definition is so broad as to govern conduct that normally would not be considered terrorism, which, according to Gerald Neuman, encompasses "the unlawful shooting of an abusive husband by a battered spouse, and perhaps more importantly, . . . include[s] any locally unlawful use of a firearm for political purposes, including self-defense or use in insurgency consistent with the laws of war."[46]

The definition certainly has the potential to produce counterintuitive results, with *In re S-K-*, a 2006 decision of the Board of Immigration Appeals (BIA) serving as an example indicative of this dynamic.[47] S-K-, a Burmese applicant for asylum in the United States, had donated money—and tried to donate other items like a camera and binoculars—to an organization called the Chin National Front (CNF), which is dedicated to the "goal of securing freedom for ethnic Chin people" within Burma.[48] The BIA took up the question of "whether the use of justifiable force against an illegitimate regime and the right of people to self-determination" falls within the definition of "terrorist activity" under immigration law.[49] Because S-K- had provided material support to the CNF, which "us[ed] firearms and/or explosives to engage in combat with the Burmese military," the BIA denied the application for asylum and withholding of removal.[50] Even though the CNF was fighting a notoriously repressive and insular regime, the BIA relied on the fact that "Congress intentionally drafted the terrorist bars to relief very broadly, to include even those people described as 'freedom fighters,' and it did not intend to give us discretion to create exceptions for members of organizations to which our Government might be sympathetic."[51] Agreeing with Professor Neuman's analysis, the BIA vice chairman pointed out in a concurring opinion that "[a]ny group that has used a weapon for any purpose other than for personal monetary gain can, under this statute, be labeled a terrorist organization," including, for example, the Northern Alliance during its battles with the Taliban regime in the 1990s.[52]

S-K- ultimately obtained relief when Congress authorized the Secretary of State and Secretary of Homeland Security to make exceptions to the terrorist bar on asylum in their discretion.[53] The Secretary of Homeland Security then granted a special waiver, which resulted in S-K- receiving asylum. Concurrently, the government issued a list of groups that included the CNF, which would not be considered terrorist organizations for immigration law purposes on the basis of any conduct carried out previously.[54] Despite all of this, the expansive definition of terrorist activity remained intact, as the subsequent BIA opinion in S-K-'s case made clear.

The government's preferred construct, encapsulated by S-K-'s case, is to rely on the expansive definition of terrorist activity, which encompasses virtually any armed action by any nonstate actor. If the result seems at all incongruous with American foreign policy, the government retains the right to issue a waiver, but the definition does not change. However, within such a construct, any arguments about the justice of a particular cause are de jure irrelevant and may only make a difference if they harmonize with the predilections and policy stances of the government. Without any standards for making this determination, it therefore becomes impossible for any politically active organization to know if it has acquired the right, under American law, to break out from the restrictive confines of "terrorist activity." This scenario transcends immigration law and can directly implicate American foreign policy. As an example, up until 2008, all members of the African National Congress (ANC), including former South African President Nelson Mandela, were considered members of a terrorist organization by the State Department and needed a special waiver to enter the United States.[55] This status dated back to the 1980s, when the State Department determined that the activities of the ANC's armed wing rendered the entirety of the group's anti-apartheid activities as subsumed within the terrorism rubric, in large part due to Cold War sensibilities, with the apartheid government seen as anti-communist and the ANC perceived as riddled with communists.[56] When this scenario was brought to light, Congress, at the administration's urging, quickly passed legislation changing the ANC's status and that of its members, thus ending a saga then Secretary of State Condoleeza Rice deemed "embarrassing."[57]

Congress's decision perhaps seems obvious, given the near-universal celebration of the ANC and Mandela's hard-won victory over apartheid in South Africa. But without any preexisting standards or metric to work out when a group can be considered terrorist in nature, we cannot know precisely why the ANC was removed. Was it because of the group's legitimization and participation in governing South Africa? Other groups on the FTO list with the same legal status have served in the government of their fully sovereign home country, so that cannot be the reason. Is there something different about the type of violence carried out by the group, or when the violence took place? We cannot really know based on how the FTO list functions and the fact that the government's determination cannot really be challenged in court. In the MEK/PMOI case, the Secretary of State provided some information about why she delisted the group, citing the group's "public renunciation of violence, the absence of confirmed acts of terrorism by the MEK for more than a decade, and their cooperation in the peaceful closure of Camp Ashraf, their historic paramilitary base."[58] But the group enjoyed support and benefited from the lobbying efforts of many prominent Americans on its behalf. Would other groups on the FTO list be removed if they publicly renounced violence and did not engage in an attack for over a decade? It is clear, however, that fighting in coordination with the United States against a common enemy, such as the PKK's clash with the militants of the ISIL in Syria, has done nothing toward getting the PKK removed from the FTO list.[59] Essentially, the government did not state a standard or series of benchmarks that a group must meet to be delisted, but rather provided a rationale for one action in the case of one organization.

It is advantageous for the government to hold on to an expansive model of what it considers terrorist activity—namely, all nonstate political violence, regardless of target or motivation—and then choose to offer exceptions as it sees fit, based on an unarticulated political calculus. This model has the capacity to disregard complex factual situations involving political conflicts with a significant humanitarian dynamic and also pertains in the criminal context. Pointedly, there are scenarios in which a humanitarian crisis demands immediate relief, but the problem is that § 2339B views any aid distribution efforts as presumptively illegal if they occur in areas where an FTO is in control and involved. Such a scenario arose in connection with a recent famine in Somalia, which led international aid organizations and individual donors to complain of being chilled in their efforts to distribute relief in the stricken region, due to the fact that the designated FTO al-Shabaab was in control of the afflicted areas.[60] Their concern was that they would not be able to undertake relief efforts because of the possibility that they might be prosecuted for violating § 2339B, since any aid might go directly into the hands of al-Shabaab.

In 2011, the State Department responded to these concerns by conducting a press briefing during which officials articulated a general guideline that allowed for U.S. aid organizations to operate in Somalia without fear of prosecution under § 2339B, provided they had a good faith belief that they were engaged in legitimate humanitarian activity on behalf of actual famine victims.[61] Note that there was no policy change or statement of immunity for aid workers in Somalia—just a declaration of some type of relaxed prosecutorial discretion for those whose conduct could fall afoul of the material support ban. This action sparked criticism of the sparse and ad hoc nature of the State Department's remarks on aid to Somali famine victims, and commentators have urged a more comprehensive set of reforms that allow humanitarian organizations operating in good faith to carry out their work even in areas dominated by a designated FTO.[62] Underpinning this position is the argument that the statute functions to chill the protected speech of the American Muslim community, whose cooperation is critical for success in the government's counterterrorism efforts. If the community's religiously driven charitable efforts can be criminalized, then the community itself ends up alienated to such a degree that it ceases cooperating with law enforcement. Further, there is the concern that if the aid flow stops, the affected areas of the world would suffer from even greater deprivation, which only entrenches the power of the FTO. Such a scenario seems counterproductive to the government's national security objectives both domestically and internationally.[63]

But these arguments, however well considered and reasonable, clash with the basic rationale of § 2339B as articulated on its passage and cited affirmatively by courts on numerous occasions: "foreign organizations that engage in terrorist activity are so tainted by their criminal conduct that any contribution to such an organization facilitates that conduct." The original impetus for the statutory innovation of a law criminalizing support in and of itself and not an act of terrorism stemmed from the debatable notion that there was supposedly a crisis of terrorist groups raising money for violence under the cover of humanitarian activity. Therefore, § 2339B was crafted with the express purpose of cutting back humanitarian activity, however legitimate, provided there existed a nexus between the activity and a terrorist group, under the basic principle that money is fungible. The congressional record documents instances of lawmakers and groups unsuccessfully arguing against the law's passage by noting that without a requirement that the government prove a defendant has a specific intent to further the illegal goals of an FTO, § 2339B is unconstitutional.[64]

That position proved unavailing in the mid-1990s, and there does not appear to be a wellspring of support for reviving that same logic in service of basic § 2339B reform, humanitarian crisis or not. By way of example, in November 2013, Representative Christopher Smith of New Jersey introduced a bill in the House of Representatives to allow for the good faith provision of humanitarian aid in times of genuine emergency, such as the famine in Somalia, thereby immunizing donors from prosecution under § 2339B.[65] So far, the proposed legislation has only attracted three co-sponsors, leading the government transparency website, govtrack.us, to conclude that it currently has only a 4 percent chance of being enacted.[66] The message the government is sending in response to a catastrophe like the famine in Somalia seems to be that one-off exceptions, not fundamental legal or policy change, are the answer to a crisis. Much like the decision in *In re S-K-*, rather than tinkering with the broad notion of what constitutes material support to terrorism, the Somalia famine example highlights how the government maintains maximum flexibility to tailor its response to a given situation, however desperate, without in any way letting go of its core belief in the inveterately evil nature of an FTO. Arguments about the potential for humanitarian aid to improve people's lives in hard-hit areas and thereby decrease the likelihood of terrorism taking root fell on deaf ears then and appear to suffer the same fate now. Further, the humanitarian argument has even failed to sway the government in cases of American citizens being abducted and held for ransom by an FTO. After the journalist James Foley was killed by ISIL in August 2014, reports emerged that the government had dissuaded his family from paying any ransom to the group by informing them that such payments would likely violate § 2339B.[67] Whether this was a smart decision on the part of the government—it is unlikely a family member would be found guilty in such circumstances—is beside the point; the government interprets the law in a broad manner and is strongly resistant to humanitarian arguments.

CONSTITUTIONAL CHALLENGES TO § 2339B

While the money-is-fungible theory resonated greatly with Congress and the Executive in their efforts to prevent humanitarian aid from reaching FTO-controlled areas, § 2339B still faced opposition in the courts. From its passage in 1996 through the 2010 Supreme Court's decision in *Holder v. Humanitarian Law Project* (discussed in detail below), the statute successfully withstood essentially all legal challenges to its constitutionality. Initially, much like the opposition to the passage of § 2339B in the congressional record, litigants initially attempted to argue that the statute violated the First Amendment because it did not require the government to prove that an individual charged under the law had a specific intent to further the illegal goals of an FTO. But the response from the courts was indicative of how the "money-is-fungible" mindset had taken hold. The most well-developed passage that sets out the logic behind the rejection of this First Amendment challenge came from the Ninth Circuit in 2000:

> [All] material support given to such organizations aids their unlawful goals. Indeed, as the government points out, terrorist organizations do not maintain open books. Therefore, when someone makes a donation to them, there is no way to tell how the donation is used. Further, as amicus Anti-Defamation League notes, even contributions earmarked for peaceful purposes can be used to give aid to the families of those killed while carrying out terrorist acts, thus making the decision to engage in terrorism more attractive. More

fundamentally, money is fungible; giving support intended to aid an organization's peaceful activities frees up resources that can be used for terrorist acts. We will not indulge in speculation about whether Congress was right to come to the conclusion that it did. We simply note that Congress has the fact-finding resources to properly come to such a conclusion. Thus, we cannot say that [§ 2339B] is not sufficiently tailored.[68]

Phrased a bit differently, courts confronting this type of challenge to § 2339B's constitutionality were unlikely to second-guess Congress's judgment on the matter of how terrorist groups operate financially, even if that judgment was the result of speculation. The mere fact that Congress and the statute's supporters had articulated a plausible basis for its strictures was enough for most courts.

Another attempt to argue for a specific intent requirement came in the context of the Fifth Amendment's guarantee of due process, which closely tracked the First Amendment claim previously rejected.[69] This challenge took its cue primarily from the 1961 Supreme Court decision in *Scales v. United States*, which held that an individual could not be convicted under the membership provisions of the Smith Act without the government demonstrating the defendant's specific intent to bring about a targeted group's—in this case, the Communist Party—illegal goals, that is, the overthrow of the United States government.[70] The key passage from *Scales* reads as follows:

> In our jurisprudence guilt is personal, and when imposition of punishment on a status *or on conduct* can only be justified by reference to the relationship of that status *or conduct* to other concededly criminal activity . . . that relationship must be sufficiently substantial to satisfy the concept of personal guilt in order to withstand attack under the Due Process Clause of the Fifth Amendment.[71]

This claim analogized banning material support without demonstrating a defendant's specific intent to further the illegal goals of an FTO as akin to banning membership, something the *Scales* decision said was unconstitutional. However, almost all courts to encounter this argument dismissed it.[72] Again the Ninth Circuit weighed in to rule that for a conviction to stand under § 2339B, the government had to show that the defendant knew (or should have known) that what was provided was material support and that it went to group designated as an FTO.[73] In light of this ruling, in 2004, Congress amended § 2339B to make explicit that knowledge of an FTO's designation, not specific intent to further a group's illegal goals, was the proper legal standard for conviction under the statute.[74]

The two Ninth Circuit opinions discussed above stem from the same case, *Holder v. Humanitarian Law Project*. The lawsuit was a civil challenge to § 2339B by individuals in the United States who wished to provide financial support and specialized training, and engage in advocacy in service of the political and humanitarian goals of two FTOs: the Liberation Tigers of Tamil Eelam (LTTE), also known as the Tamil Tigers, a Sri Lankan rebel group, and the PKK, a Kurdish separatist group in conflict with Turkey.[75] The plaintiffs brought the lawsuit as a preemptive measure; rather than wait to be prosecuted under § 2339B, they challenged the statute's constitutionality, based on the fact that the advocacy work they wished to pursue would likely expose them to criminal liability under the law's terms. The litigation was a long and protracted affair, already twelve years old when the case reached the Supreme Court, and one that had produced numerous rulings from both the district court and the Ninth Circuit, as discussed partially above.[76] By the time the dispute made its way to the Supreme Court in 2010, the issues had been distilled into a general challenge to the statute's criminalization of material support in the form of speech under the First Amendment, as well as an argument that four types of material support—"training," "expert advice or assistance," "service," and "personnel"—were unconstitutionally void for vagueness under the Fifth Amendment.[77]

In an opinion authored by Chief Justice Roberts, the Court quickly dispensed with the idea that the statute contained a specific intent requirement, finding that Congress had clearly established knowledge of an FTO's activities as the standard. It went on to distinguish *Scales'* holding, which focused on the unconstitutional restriction of mere membership in a group from § 2339B's much more permissible criminalization of conduct.[78] Although there is much to criticize in this part of the Court's holding, its central flaw, however, is that it ignored the congressional record accompanying § 2339B's passage, which featured statements from proponents of the ban to the effect that it was not to be construed as restricting freedom of speech or association.[79] The majority opinion declined to discuss this point, engaging more fully with the First Amendment issues later on in the opinion, but still rather doggedly sticking to the line that material support, even in the form of speech or association, could be criminalized because of its link to an FTO without elaborating further.

With respect to the Fifth Amendment vagueness claim, the plaintiffs had expressed a desire to help the PKK use international law to resolve disputes peacefully, advocate on behalf of Kurds in Turkey, and petition representative bodies like the United Nations and Congress for relief. As for the LTTE, since, by 2010, the Sri

Lankan military had defeated the group, the plaintiffs limited their proffer to support in the most basic terms. The Court took the view that the plaintiffs' proposed advocacy on behalf of the PKK and LTTE—which would expose them to criminal liability under § 2339B—was far too speculative.[80] On that basis, the Court rejected the challenges to the four terms at issue. Specifically with regard to the terms "personnel" and "service," the Court made sure to note that independent advocacy of an FTO was permissible under the statute, just not working under the direction of an FTO, in coordination with a group, or running its affairs. In other words, it is illegal under the statute for someone to work for an FTO or provide a service by acting as, for instance, a spokesperson for the group, but doing the same thing independently is allowed.

There were several problems with the Court's logic in this regard. First, even assuming that the proposed material support was too general, it is not hard to imagine what advocacy on behalf of an FTO might look like based on the description above. Second, there was at least one concrete example the plaintiffs gave—distributing publications in support of the PKK and Kurdish liberation—that the Court glossed over in its characterization of the plaintiffs' proffer. Finally, and most importantly, the material support encompassed by the vagueness challenges was geared to having an FTO move away from violence and toward peaceful means of resolving conflict. As a policy matter, it is problematic that the Court's ruling discourages advocacy with the goal of steering a group away from violence, the *sine qua non* of any terrorist label. As a legal matter, however, this point reflects the fundamental problem with criminalizing material support in an expansive sense. If we are to believe that FTOs are "so tainted by their criminal conduct that any contribution to such an organization facilitates that conduct," there is a legitimate question as to why it should make any difference whether the contribution—in this case, advocacy—came independent of the group, so long as the contribution provides a tangible benefit.[81] The Court declined the opportunity to pursue this matter further.

The majority opinion then proceeded to the key First Amendment issues presented by the lawsuit—namely, whether material support in the form of actual speech could be criminalized. Normally, for speech to be banned without offending the First Amendment, it must serve as a precursor to imminent lawless activity under the Supreme Court's opinion in *Brandenburg v. Ohio*, issued in 1969.[82] At this point, it was clear that the money is fungible logic had only served to propel § 2339B toward greater and broader constructions of what might be outlawed, up to the quintessential American concept of freedom of speech. All the support that the plaintiffs were attempting to provide could be construed as protected speech under the First Amendment, and that support went to the legitimate, as opposed to illegal, goals of an FTO. But the Court rejected the distinction by focusing on the congressional language that "any contribution" to an FTO furthers its illegal activities, thereby eliminating whatever daylight the plaintiffs tried to exploit between a group's illegal and legal goals. To that end, in holding that material support in the form of speech could be criminalized, the Court relied on the idea of material support that provides "legitimacy" to an FTO where it operates. Specifically, that type of material support that generates "legitimacy . . . makes it easier for those groups to persist, to recruit members, and to raise funds—all of which facilitate more terrorist attacks."[83]

To draw this conclusion regarding legitimacy, the Court relied on a 1998 affidavit from a State Department official, an amicus brief from the Anti-Defamation League, and a book about the FTO Hamas by Matthew Levitt, a former Treasury Department official and FBI analyst [see Chapter 3 for discussion of Levitt as an expert witness for the government in terrorism prosecutions].[84] These sources were employed to describe how FTOs operate—by raising money for violence under cover of charity and other seemingly benign activities—and the manifold ways material support supposedly aids them. But the use of an affidavit from 1998 raises the question of why, after more than a decade of a war on terror and concomitant generous budget allocations, the government did not produce a more up-to-date document in support of its position. The Anti-Defamation League brief and Levitt's book both posited the solitary example of Hamas as the FTO that somehow represents and personifies all terrorist organizations. Further, the example of Hamas allowed the Court to bring up the notion of Islamist terrorism, since both the PKK and LTTE are secular organizations that almost assuredly do not occupy much space in the popular imagination.

In dissent, Justice Breyer noted that the Court's theory on material support as speech providing legitimacy offered "no natural stopping place" and suffered from a lack of empirical evidence.[85] In response, the Court's majority opinion made sure to point out the distinction between lawful independent advocacy and illegal material support in coordination with an FTO.[86] And at the heart of the disagreement was a divergence of views as to the nature of a threat posed by an FTO to the nebulous and disputed concept of national security, since both the PKK and LTTE did not target the United States. Where national security concerns might trump the First Amendment in situations directly involving attacks on the United States or its nationals, suppressing material support as speech to an FTO not in any active conflict with the United States is much harder to justify. If no American citizen is targeted or threatened, then the rationale behind banning material support in the form of speech to a group not targeting the United States is unpersuasive.

One scholar has remarked that the goal of the government, as endorsed by the Supreme Court in its majority decision, was to achieve "minimum-compliance with constitutional rights."[87] But taken to its logical conclusion, the implication of the *Humanitarian Law Project* decision is that terrorism is now an existential threat to the United States wherever it occurs, and—as long as the government has designated an organization as an FTO—that existential threat must be thwarted, even to the detriment of the First Amendment.

MATERIAL SUPPORT PROVIDING LEGITIMACY—THE HOLY LAND FOUNDATION PROSECUTION

The problem with relying on material support as enhancing an FTO's legitimacy is that it has the potential to stretch the rationale behind § 2339B beyond the constitutional breaking point. This was true even before the Supreme Court's decision in *Holder v. Humanitarian Law Project*, as evidenced by the prosecution of the officers and directors of the Holy Land Foundation for Relief and Development (HLF), which stands as one of the government's most high-profile terrorism prosecutions to date. In 2008, after a re-trial, the defendants were convicted of violating § 2339B by providing material support to the FTO Hamas via the then largest Muslim charity in the United States, the HLF.[88] The government's theory of the case was that the HLF funded Hamas through a series of charities in the West Bank and Gaza Strip known as zakat committees, which collected the religiously mandated donations of observant Muslims for distribution to the less fortunate.[89] Although initially the government indicated that the committees laundered or channeled money into Hamas' coffers,[90] at trial it backed off that theory, arguing instead that through their undisputed humanitarian activity, the zakat committees served to enhance the reputation of Hamas in the community. The government's case hinged on linking Hamas to the zakat committees through expert testimony, which was problematic in its own right and is discussed further in Chapter 3. Stated another way, instead of the money-is-fungible logic that helped § 2339B overcome numerous challenges to its constitutionality, the theory underpinning the HLF prosecution did not connect the money sent to the Middle East to Hamas so as to indirectly buy weapons. Rather, it alleged that the defendants, in donating to the zakat committees, enhanced Hamas's reputation and legitimacy in the eyes of the community through their funding of the committees' charitable endeavors.[91]

Let us consider the full implications of the HLF case, based on this understanding of the theory of prosecution. First, the language of the indictment seemed to target all zakat committees in the West Bank and Gaza Strip in their entirety as acting on behalf of Hamas's charitable network, as there was no qualifying language on this point.[92] This position effectively rendered all Muslim charitable giving in the West Bank and Gaza Strip as inherently terroristic, a sweeping accusation with severe consequences for religiously observant Muslims wishing to alleviate clear humanitarian suffering in a war-torn region. Second, this position also implicates the question of what standards are used to adjudge when a charitable institution can be considered part of an FTO. The legislative record in support of § 2339B's passage speaks of an integrated terrorist movement, sporting a violent wing and a charitable wing of inextricably linked finances. The indictment in the HLF prosecution speaks of "Hamas members, operatives, and terrorists" making up the membership of the zakat committees.[93] What is the magic number of "members, operatives, and terrorists" that renders a zakat committee a part of a designated FTO? There is also the inverse: does this mean that a zakat committee could have no Hamas members on its board or staff yet still provide banned material support? Are there situations where a zakat committee has a large number of Hamas members involved with it but does not violate the ban? All of these questions remain unanswered.

Finally, with respect to the zakat committees at issue, the U.S. government has yet to designate them as terrorist organizations, which it has done in similar cases involving an FTO and organizations the government regards as its front groups.[94] Even with the HLF case effectively finished, a designation would signal that the government views the committees as part and parcel of Hamas, thereby underscoring the seriousness of the verdict. That it has not done so at least leaves open the possibility that the zakat committees do not constitute an urgent target of United States counterterrorism efforts and are not properly linked to terrorism. In addition to the legal and security questions raised by the case is the chilling effect the prosecution had on American Muslims and their ability to engage in charitable donations according to their religious belief, a fact highlighted by the ACLU in a 2009 report on the topic.[95] In the final analysis, the HLF prosecution resembled an argument on American foreign policy in a federal courtroom more than it did a criminal case. The money-is-fungible logic of a material support ban expanded into the strange new realm of material support as legitimacy. The HLF prosecution allowed the government to widen the range of criminalized material support based on political calculations, with the issue of dangerousness and violence shunted off to the side. And so the door to a terrorism prosecution based on political—as opposed to security—considerations was opened. While that is a handy development for the government, the effect on individual constitutional rights is far more worrisome.

CONTINUAL EXPANSION—*UNITED STATES V. MEHANNA*

The saga of § 2339B's evolution is not over. The case of Tarek Mehanna, a young Egyptian American charged with violating § 2339B—and several other laws—by providing material support to al-Qaeda in the form of translating material and posting it on the Internet, serves as the prime post-*Humanitarian Law Project* example.[96] The charges against Mehanna stemmed from two separate series of activities. The first was a 2004 trip to Yemen he undertook with two friends in search of a terrorist training camp (according to the government) or to pursue Islamic studies (according to Mehanna); the second was related to his work translating Arabic-language materials into English and posting them on a website called "at-Tibyan," which, in the government's view was "for those sympathetic to al-Qaida and Salafi–Jihadi perspectives."[97] The government alleged that some of the material translated by Mehanna "constituted al-Qaida-generated media and materials supportive of al-Qaida and/or jihad."[98] After a thirty-five-day jury trial, Mehanna was convicted of all the charges against him and sentenced to seventeen and a half years in prison.

The critical issue that arose at trial concerned the idea of material support as speech. The *Humanitarian Law Project* decision made clear that § 2339B only criminalized material support in the form of speech if it was done at the behest of or in coordination with an FTO. The key piece of evidence was a text by a Saudi religious scholar Mehanna had translated and posted online entitled "39 Ways to Serve and Participate in Jihad," which the government characterized as "a training manual for terrorism," a position challenged strongly by the defense.[99] However, although much evidence was adduced about his political views in favor of jihad against the United States, the government's case included no evidence that Mehanna met or corresponded with anyone representing al-Qaeda, or that the "39 Ways" text was ever seen by al-Qaeda, which, in any event, was not alleged to have written it.[100] Even so, the jury convicted him on the material support charge, leading to extended discussion about the First Amendment implications of the case from an academic and policy standpoint.[101]

However, when Mehanna appealed his conviction, the First Circuit opted not to confront the issue of coordination with al-Qaeda or the lack thereof in the context of the terrorism charges. Its opinion began with an alarmist tone that reflected the government's mindset post-*Humanitarian Law Project*: "Terrorism is the modern-day equivalent of the bubonic plague: it is an existential threat."[102] The government had offered two theories of material support, one stemming from the 2004 Yemen trip and the other from Mehanna's translations. The court of appeals reasoned that the jury was entitled to base its guilty verdict on either of the factual scenarios. So, the First Circuit remarked that "[e]ven if the government's translation-as-material-support theory were factually insufficient, we would not reverse: the defendant's convictions on the affected counts are independently supported by the mass of evidence surrounding the Yemen trip."[103] In other words, even if Mehanna's translations and online activity were the type of constitutionally protected independent advocacy exempted from § 2339B's strictures—as noted by the *Humanitarian Law Project* decision—evidence of Mehanna's trip to Yemen in search of a terrorist training camp was sufficient to sustain his convictions.[104] Of course, Mehanna vigorously disputed the government's contention that he went in search of a terrorism training camp, and it even admitted that there was no such type of camp in Yemen in 2004.[105] His argument that the prosecution was in part retaliation for his refusal to become an informant for the FBI was rejected by the jury, even though it was hardly far-fetched.[106]

So the *Mehanna* prosecution and consequent conviction, which essentially pushed a theory of material support in the form of speech without properly setting forth a link between the speech and an FTO, was allowed to stand based on an alternative factual predicate for material support. But this ruling looked like a sort of ad hoc type of solution to what may have been a reversal on a terrorism conviction, something that courts post-9/11 have only rarely entertained, let alone granted. The dividing line between independent advocacy and material support as speech in coordination with an FTO remains unelaborated, although the toxic example of material support to al-Qaeda is probably close enough to the line that the distinction may very well be immaterial, if the First Circuit's *Mehanna* opinion is any indication.

FURTHER PERMUTATIONS OF MATERIAL SUPPORT

The construction of what constitutes material support continues to evolve, pushing the concept into novel areas and uses. Section 2339B is innovative in that the support itself is the crime, but the recent prosecution of Craig Baxam, a former U.S. Army serviceman and convert to Islam, demonstrates how even the provision of support can be highly inchoate. Baxam was arrested in Kenya on suspicion of wanting to join the Somali FTO al-Shabaab as he headed toward Kenya's border with Somalia.[107] He was arrested and returned to the United States, where he was charged with violating § 2339B by attempting to provide material support to al-Shabaab. Although his lawyers argued that as a pious Muslim, Baxam was simply looking to live in a state governed by Islamic law, he eventually pled guilty to lesser charges, again saving § 2339B from a searching inquiry as to the extent of its contours.[108] But the charges had served the purpose of wringing a conviction out of an individual whose actions did not definitively represent a threat to the United States, and may not have resulted in material support of any kind.

Material support as a crime has proven so useful to the government that it has codified it as a war crime and sought, albeit unsuccessfully, to apply it retroactively to individuals charged in military commissions and held at the detention center in Guantanamo Bay, Cuba.[109] The need to stop the provision of material support has also served the government in its efforts to gain acceptance for the National Security Agency's (NSA) bulk electronic eavesdropping program. The government highlighted the case of Basaaly Moalin, a Somali American cab driver from San Diego, who was convicted of providing $8,500 to al-Shabaab, as a successful example of the NSA's bulk data collection leading to an actual conviction.[110]

Overall, the success the government has garnered in charging individuals with violating the material support statute is no doubt impressive. And the Moalin example reinforces the centrality of the money-is-fungible logic. But concerns about the selective and nebulous nature of what groups get designated and what material support gets criminalized have yet to adequately subside.[111] And in the interim, new concepts like legitimacy and material support as speech have gained traction. The resulting admixture is one that is no doubt agreeable to the government but raises serious questions about the limits of constitutionally protected expressions of support and solidarity with various political causes, not to mention religious freedom. Where § 2339B goes next is no doubt open for speculation, but if the government continues to expand its parameters and uses, we can expect the courts to continue to approve them, constitutional limits notwithstanding.

3

EVIDENCE AND THE CRIMINAL TERRORIST PROSECUTION

AS DISCUSSED IN the preceding chapters, the widespread use of informants is the government's primary driver of terrorist prosecutions, and the ban on providing material support to foreign terrorist organizations represents the chief statutory tool for bringing those prosecutions. Working in tandem, they represent the embodiment of the Department of Justice's preventive focus on terrorism. Prior to September 11, 2001, the government's approach regarding terrorism was to punish individuals for crimes—primarily acts of violence—previously committed. After the attacks, the focus shifted toward the prevention of terrorism before it occurred. But an examination of the use of informants reveals the controversial and provocative nature of this tactic, which in many cases involves identifying vulnerable or naive targets, winning their trust, suggesting a violent plot, and then providing the means to carry it out. From the government's perspective, however, the use of informants has been a great success, as the main legal tool available to a defendant ensnared by an informant—the entrapment defense—has failed in every instance it has been raised.

Likewise, the definition of what constitutes "material support" has gone beyond mere funding or provision of weaponry to terrorist organizations to preclude the provision of support in the form of speech, as the Supreme Court's 2010 decision in *Holder v. Humanitarian Law Project*[1] makes clear. Further, the manifold other legal challenges to the material support ban have also been unsuccessful in the main. Given that the statute does not require any nexus with an act of violence, the government has been able to widen the net of what it believes constitutes support for terrorism to target humanitarian activity and what would otherwise be protected speech.

From this backdrop, we can begin to evaluate the methods by which the government gathers evidence and then seeks to have it admitted in terrorism prosecutions. These methods, which are discussed in detail throughout this chapter, include electronic surveillance, interrogation, and the use of expert witnesses. The net result is that from the perspective of the outside observer, once the government decides to indict someone on terrorism charges, the evidentiary floodgates open, no matter how dubious the origin of any given piece of evidence. Rather than look simply into the applicability of the Federal Rules of Evidence in terrorism prosecutions, the goal here is to evaluate all types of evidence—how it is generated and how the government intends to use it—across a varied stream of legal doctrines and practices. In this way, we can imagine a linear sequence that roughly comprises law enforcement's investigatory tactics at the outset and then moves on to contemplate the admission of evidence in the courtroom. This chapter considers first the issue of evidence derived from eavesdropping, then continues on to discuss the fruits of interrogation, classified evidence, the relevancy versus prejudice conundrum, and concludes with an examination of the use of expert testimony.

FISA

The investigation begins with a look at the surveillance powers of the government, specifically, the communications that federal authorities can lawfully monitor under the Foreign Intelligence Surveillance Act (FISA). Signed into law by President Carter in 1978, FISA was the result of congressional efforts to monitor the warrantless wiretapping and electronic surveillance of individuals by the executive branch, particularly in light of the information unearthed by the discovery of the Watergate break-ins.[2] With the revelations that former FBI Director J. Edgar Hoover had authorized a wide-ranging surveillance program of anyone—Communist dissidents, student radicals, congressmen, federal officials, Supreme Court Justices, foreign ambassadors, etc.—who engaged in "suspicious" activity, Congress recognized the need to institute a regulatory structure limiting the government's powers to protecting against actual foreign threats to national security. This was in contradistinction to the FBI's long-standing practice of opening "files" and secretly listening in on those American citizens and residents it perceived as a threat, often on nothing more than disapproval of the target's political views or statements.[3]

FISA was intended as a compromise; it explicitly recognizes the government's power to listen in on communications that implicate national security, while seeking to safeguard the rights of U.S. citizens and residents to be free of invasive eavesdropping. Specifically, the original bill permitted a government agent to request the Attorney General's approval to carry out electronic surveillance of a target in the United States, based on a showing the target was a "foreign power" or an "agent of a foreign power" engaged in foreign intelligence activities while in the country.[4] The term "foreign power" encompasses both countries and organizations, including nonstate organizations like a terrorist group. Once the Attorney General's approval was secured, the agent could then approach one of the judges of the Foreign Intelligence Surveillance Court (FISC), originally a seven-member body of federal judges appointed by the Chief Justice of the United States Supreme Court, to apply for a warrant to conduct the surveillance.[5] If the judge found that there was probable cause to believe a target was a foreign power or agent of a foreign power, FISA would authorize the electronic surveillance. In contrast, when the government wishes to establish a wiretap for ordinary criminal law enforcement purposes, it must show that there is probable cause that the crime being investigated is afoot.[6]

This is not an insignificant distinction. The lower standards for a FISA wiretap reflect congressional deference to the executive's powers to safeguard national security. But those standards also underscore the fact that information from a FISA-derived surveillance scheme ordinarily will not make its way into a criminal prosecution in open court. The Patriot Act, passed by Congress in the wake of the 9/11 attacks, amended the statute in several ways that were designed to make the FISA regime more amenable to the government in its reinvigorated counterterrorist function. First, no longer would a high government official have to certify to a FISC judge that the sole purpose of FISA surveillance was foreign intelligence-related. Congress changed the operative language to require only "a significant purpose" of the surveillance to be foreign intelligence gathering.[7] Second, the Patriot Act also broke down what had come to be referred to as "the wall" between the foreign intelligence and law enforcement divisions of the FBI. While not mandated by FISA as it was originally written, Department of Justice regulations that were in effect up through the passage of the Patriot Act imposed restrictions on sharing information between FBI agents investigating foreign intelligence activity in the United States under FISA and those involved in criminal probes, with the idea being that FISA should not serve as an end run around the normal rules of criminal procedure governing electronic surveillance. After 9/11, the wall was blamed for several failures by federal agencies to share information on the attackers and affiliates prior to the attacks.[8] Additionally, to handle the expected increased workload, the Patriot Act increased the number of judges on the FISC from seven to eleven.[9]

These first two changes had the effect of making it easier to use evidence derived from FISA surveillance in criminal cases. But there was a real question as to whether the government needed these amendments, based on the fact that all of the examples cited as proof of the wall's negative effect turned out to not have been actually affected by its presence. And in the government's signature prosecution highlighting how the elimination of the wall had supposedly permitted more effective counterterrorism investigations—a case on which I served as co-counsel—the parties learned that the foreign intelligence wing of the FBI had in fact been sharing information with its law enforcement counterpart from before 9/11.[10] But after the 9/11 attacks and the passage of the Patriot Act, closing the gap between foreign intelligence surveillance and law enforcement investigations was not a high priority.

In 2002, the FISC took the extraordinary step of publicly issuing an opinion for the first time in its history to document its disapproval of certain DOJ regulations that blurred the lines between the intelligence and law enforcement functions of the FBI too drastically. Specifically, the court worried that, under the proposed reforms, "criminal prosecutors will tell the FBI when to use FISA (perhaps when they lack probable cause for a Title III electronic surveillance), what techniques to use, what information to look for, what information to keep as evidence and when use of FISA can cease because there is enough evidence to arrest and prosecute."[11] Those concerns were not enough to thwart the government; the Foreign Intelligence Surveillance Court of Review overruled the FISC's decision, finding that the FISC explicitly had overstepped its bounds in subjecting the new regulations to what was, in its view, unwarranted scrutiny.[12] The net effect was to make it easier for the FBI to bring a criminal case against individuals whose activities can be lawfully monitored under FISA.

Despite the government's success in garnering legislative and judicial support for greater surveillance powers under FISA, it has continued to press for even more expansive surveillance powers. In late 2005, the *New York Times* revealed that the government was bypassing FISA entirely to eavesdrop on the calls and e-mails of individuals in the United States when one party to the communication was linked to al-Qaeda or, what the government termed, "an affiliated organization."[13] Where subsequent reporting on the issue turned up riveting tales of high-level government officials clashing over the legality and utility of the spying program, ultimately Congress acted to codify much of the warrantless surveillance program as practiced by the government and bring it under FISA's aegis.

With the FISA Amendments Act (FAA) of 2008, Congress allowed the government to monitor communications where one party was in the United States, provided that the foreign participant was the target. The new regulations presume that a party located abroad is foreign and do not adequately require the government to confirm that fact. As opposed to FISA as originally passed, there is no requirement that the government establish probable cause that the target is an agent of a foreign power, only that a government official have a "reasonable belief" that the foreign target is outside the United States.[14] And once a foreign target has been identified, the government is permitted to track not only the target's communications but also communications referencing the target. Coupled with standards that authorize the government to retain in large part the contents of captured communications, the FAA essentially created a scheme that resembles the government's original warrantless wiretapping program, revealed by the *New York Times* in 2005. The key distinction was that so long as the government did not explicitly admit it was targeting Americans, it could continue to monitor communications involving Americans under FISA while subject to less stringent oversight than ever before.

Moreover, the government has continued to push for even fewer constraints on the use of FISA-derived evidence. In February 2013, the Supreme Court denied a challenge brought by human rights organizations to the FAA on standing grounds, reasoning that any injury to them is purely speculative.[15] During oral argument, the government stressed that it was not rejecting all challenges to evidence introduced from the wider, programmatic type of surveillance authorized by the FAA; it argued, however, that only someone against whom it intended to use the evidence, like a criminal defendant, could mount such a challenge.[16]

The impact of the FAA did not receive full airing in the press until the emergence of former NSA contractor Edward Snowden in June 2013, who revealed that the government was recording pertinent information (but not the contents of the call itself) about the calls of all subscribers on a major wireless network, also known as metadata.[17] While the Snowden revelations resulted in the government revealing to criminal defendants when it intends to rely on evidence derived under the authority of the FAA, the limited record to date indicates that courts find no fault with the use of such evidence.[18]

Further, under the express authorization of the FISC, the government has been collecting vast amounts of data from the servers of the world's largest internet companies, such as Google, Yahoo, and Apple, among others.[19] Subsequent revelations included disclosures that the government also had recorded the Internet and e-mail metadata of Americans in bulk for nearly a decade after 9/11. While the bulk surveillance initially was part of the government's warrantless wiretapping program, in 2004, the government sought and received approval from the FISC to continue to gather the data, thereby bringing it squarely within FISA's ambit.[20] Subsequent disclosures about the government's spying program were that an internal audit from within the National Security Agency (NSA), which directs and conducts the government's mass electronic surveillance programs, found that the agency violated the even more permissive privacy rules of the FAA "thousands of times a year" in the period after 2008.[21] Legal challenges to the NSA's bulk metadata collection program have met with mixed results.

One federal court found it to likely constitute an unreasonable search under the Fourth Amendment, but immediately stayed the effect of its decision, pending appeal.[22] Another found no constitutional violation.[23]

The revelations about the government's expansive construction of FISA and the FISC's granting its imprimatur to much of the government's agenda have dominated the headlines about privacy and surveillance in contemporary society. As a result, discussion of how FISA-derived evidence makes its way into a criminal prosecution is rendered largely an afterthought. At the outset, the FISC's record in allowing the government to conduct surveillance is clear. Since the passage of FISA, the FISC has approved 35,080 surveillance requests, while rejecting a mere 12 in the period spanning 1979–2013.[24] From 2011 through 2013, the latest three years for which statistics are available, the FISC did not deny any requests "in whole or in part."[25] These numbers paint a stark picture of what looks like ineffectual oversight of the government's electronic surveillance regime. This pattern holds in criminal prosecutions, albeit on a much smaller scale. When the government seeks to introduce evidence from secret surveillance methods, it meets largely with success. To date, not one of the some twenty challenges to FISA's constitutionality in a criminal prosecution has been successful, with courts routinely ruling that FISA does not violate the Fourth Amendment in any way.[26] Legislative and administrative changes, such as requiring that a "significant purpose," as opposed to "the purpose," of the investigation under review be for foreign intelligence surveillance, have also been approved by the courts.[27] As long as the government follows the procedural rules set forth by FISA, any evidence derived from subsequent surveillance will almost certainly be admitted in a criminal prosecution.[28] For defendants charged with national security crimes, the fact that the government had been listening to their calls and monitoring their e-mails pursuant to FISA is no barrier to introducing the evidence of those investigations at trial.

The government's powers of surveillance have expanded to such a degree that much of American Internet and telephone traffic can be included. And when the government wishes to use that information in a criminal prosecution, the federal courts have consistently allowed for the admission of FISA-derived evidence. The theme of admitting evidence is one taken up by the remainder of this chapter.

INTERROGATION

In addition to the government's ability to produce evidence against a defendant as a result of surreptitious surveillance and electronic wiretaps, a defendant's own statements remain an attractive source of evidence in a criminal prosecution. Police interrogation retains a prominent place in the hierarchy of evidence-gathering tools available to the government because of the seemingly irrefutable nature of the defendant's own inculpatory words. Though we now know much more than ever before about the phenomenon of the police eliciting false confessions through questioning,[29] the modern terrorism prosecution presents a novel series of situations that implicates the use of evidence generated by interrogations at home and abroad, by both domestic and foreign law enforcement and intelligence agencies. The analysis below touches on three basic constructs: (1) interrogation of terrorism suspects in the United States by American law enforcement; (2) interrogation of terrorism suspects abroad by American government agents; and (3) interrogation abroad by foreign law enforcement and intelligence agents. An examination of all these examples demonstrates the courts' willingness to find exceptions to generally accepted standards for the admission of confessions in a terrorism case.

The starting point for this discussion begins at home with the constitutionally required warnings that the police must give to individuals suspected of a crime upon arrest, as mandated by the Supreme Court in its 1966 decision in *Miranda v. Arizona*.[30] As anyone who has ever watched an American police serial or movie knows, prior to beginning custodial interrogation, the police must inform a suspect of the right to remain silent, the right to the assistance of an attorney (at state expense if the suspect cannot afford one), and the fact that if he chooses to speak with the police, anything he says may be used against him in future legal proceedings. In a terrorism prosecution, as in any other criminal case, it would seem that the *Miranda* rule applies if and when the police wish to question a suspect. However, given the intense unease terrorism inspires, the government has taken advantage of an exception to *Miranda*'s strict warning regime to come up with an approach that allows its agents to question a suspect without informing him of his rights. Before investigating the history of this exception and its updated application, it is worth pointing out the construct that animates the discussion. Simply put, assume that the government managed to apprehend an individual it believed had planted a bomb set to explode in the heart of a major city—should law enforcement agents be required to administer the warnings before trying to obtain information that could stop the attack? The great fear is that the suspect, duly warned, would refuse to speak further to law enforcement, thus allowing the attack to proceed, with the attendant loss of life and injury. Without more analysis, this scenario—also referred to as the problem of the "ticking bomb"—suggests that both the Fifth Amendment and society would countenance a deviation from *Miranda*'s warnings regime to save lives.

The April 2013 attacks at the Boston Marathon saw this issue debated in the media as the FBI indicated that it would forego Mirandizing the surviving bombing suspect to ensure that no further violent attacks were in the offing. While some of the journalistic coverage of the Boston bombings indicated this was perhaps a novel approach, in truth, the government had already begun the practice of not giving warnings in cases where the threat of terrorist violence loomed.[31] In December 2009, an al-Qaeda operative, using an explosive device hidden in his underwear, failed in his attempt to blow up an international commercial flight bound for Detroit and was arrested upon landing in the United States. The attacker, a Nigerian citizen, was initially cooperative with the FBI agents interrogating him, but later stopped answering their questions, only to then begin speaking again.[32] In the wake of this incident, which prompted fears that a dangerous terrorist might refuse to give up information of a violent attack if apprised of his Fifth Amendment rights, the FBI drafted a memorandum governing the standards that give rise to a decision to interrogate a suspect without administering warnings.[33] The document permits the government to conduct questioning in situations where a suspect is an "operational terrorist" who can provide information about potential future attacks.[34]

In issuing the memorandum, the government took the position that it was not breaking new ground, but rather was relying on existing Supreme Court precedent, namely, the 1984 decision in *New York v. Quarles*, which articulated a "public safety" exception to *Miranda*.[35] In *Quarles*, a woman approached the police in Queens, New York, to report that she had been raped and gave a description of the suspect. The police then tracked Quarles to a supermarket and duly arrested him after a brief chase. Upon noticing his empty shoulder holster and before giving Quarles *Miranda* warnings, the police inquired about the location of his gun, and he led them to it. While he tried to challenge his conviction on illegal gun possession charges as improper due to the admission of pre-warning statements, the Supreme Court ruled against him, reasoning that those statements were an exception to the *Miranda* requirements because of the danger to the public that Quarles' gun represented were it to have remained hidden in a public grocery store.

The extension of *Quarles'* logic to the terrorism context does not appear to have broken much new ground, despite the fact that it took around nine years after 9/11 to recognize the public safety exception in such a context. There exists at least one instance of a federal appeals court recognizing a public safety exception in a terrorism prosecution pre-9/11. In 2000, the Second Circuit upheld the admission of pre-warning statements by a suspect that he intended to commit a suicide attack in the New York City area and identified the location of pipe bombs he had stored for the operation.[36] Although the "ticking bomb" hypothetical at the heart of the public safety exception has been severely criticized,[37] the government has invoked the exception in several high-profile prosecutions over the last several years. In 2010, Faisal Shahzad, an American citizen of Afghan heritage, was arrested after being implicated in a plot to set off a car bomb in Times Square, denied *Miranda* warnings, and interrogated about future attacks under the public safety doctrine, which helped lead to his pleading guilty.[38] In 2011, the U.S. military captured Ahmed Warsame, a Somali citizen, in the Red Sea between Yemen and Somali on suspicion of working with the banned FTOs al-Shabaab and al-Qaeda in the Arabian Peninsula. According to the government, he was then interrogated over the course of two months "for intelligence purposes" before finally being read his *Miranda* warnings. At that point, he waived his Fifth Amendment rights and was subjected to further questioning for several more days. He ultimately pled guilty to a variety of material support, conspiracy, and weapons charges.[39] In October 2013, alleged al-Qaeda leader Nazih Abdul-Hamed al-Ruqai, also known as Anas al-Libi, was seized in Tripoli, Libya, and interrogated by American authorities on a U.S. Navy ship in the Mediterranean.[40] Charges against him for allegedly participating in the 1998 attack on the U.S. Embassy in Nairobi, Kenya, were pending until his death in custody in January 2015.[41] Finally, in June 2014, the government seized Ahmed Abu Khattala, a suspect in the September 2012 attack on the U.S. mission Benghazi, Libya and interrogated him on board a U.S. Naval vessel before taking him to the District of Columbia to face charges related to the attack; he is expected to be tried in early 2015.[42]

The FBI memorandum did not address just the public safety exception, however. Drawing from Supreme Court precedent that makes clear a *Miranda* violation occurs only when the government seeks to admit unwarned confessions during a trial, the memorandum allows an FBI agent, in certain circumstances, to interrogate a suspect without warnings even when there is no threat to public safety. Upon approval by FBI supervisors, with no need to seek an order from a court, an agent can continue questioning for intelligence purposes when "the government's interest in obtaining this intelligence outweighs the disadvantages of proceeding with unwarned interrogation."[43] The factors that go into making this determination are left unarticulated and solely within the discretion of the FBI. From this nebulous standard, we can see the basis of a special and novel terrorism exception to *Miranda* take shape. The novelty of this provision stands in contrast to the public safety exception, which considerably predates 9/11 and has been applied almost exclusively in ordinary criminal cases.

Allowing agents to question a suspect for intelligence purposes even when there is no threat to national security is problematic for two reasons. First, there is the inherent unfairness of a so-called "two-part" or "two-step" interrogation. In 2004, the Supreme Court found unconstitutional a Missouri police practice of questioning a suspect before arrest, obtaining a confession, and then administering the warnings while asking that the suspect simply repeat what was said previously, as the cat was already out of the bag.[44] As the *Warsame* case demonstrates, once suspects have been interrogated for two months and then Mirandized, the likelihood that they would recognize the distinction between intelligence and law enforcement-driven questioning and therefore refuse to speak to the FBI is remote, to say the least. This is particularly true in Warsame's situation, where he had no prior contact with the United States, let alone its law enforcement practices. Second, the implication is that interrogation for intelligence purposes is different than for public safety purposes because the former is not tied to a criminal prosecution, unlike the latter. But, as the above examples show, those individuals interrogated for intelligence purposes ended up confessing and pleading guilty to terrorist-related crimes once given *Miranda* warnings.[45] Perhaps this is an intentional narrowing of the two aspects of the FBI's counterterrorism mandate, much like what occurred with FISA and the elimination of "the wall" between its intelligence and law enforcement divisions. If so, the FBI document does not make this explicit, in its one sentence aside about an agent choosing to obtain intelligence via interrogation—a decision not subject to outside scrutiny. As with many aspects of the legal regime governing terrorist prosecutions, what begins as a seemingly narrow and delineated exception can easily morph into something much greater. Where the extension of the public safety exception into the operational terrorist realm has generated public debate, the intelligence exception has been added on and put to evident use with little controversy.

The discussion of *Miranda*'s applicability also extends to the interrogation of suspects abroad by American law enforcement. Although never addressed by the Supreme Court, several lower federal courts have recognized the Fifth Amendment's applicability to interrogations conducted by American agents outside the country. The leading example of this trend involves the prosecution of the defendants charged with blowing up the United States Embassy compounds in Kenya and Tanzania in August 1998. Mohamed al-'Owhali, a Saudi national apprehended in Kenya shortly after the bombing, was questioned by FBI agents in Nairobi regarding his role in the attack and given an "advice of rights" form that discussed Fifth Amendment standards in American police interrogation.[46] When al-'Owhali, who had been in the van loaded with explosives that crashed into the Embassy, was transferred to the Southern District of New York for prosecution, his lawyers challenged the admission of statements he made to the FBI in Kenya. Although the district court initially granted the motion to suppress his statements, the government moved successfully for reconsideration of that decision, and the statements were admitted.[47] Critically, the district court noted that *Miranda* was applicable even to foreign nonresidents when interrogated abroad by American agents in connection with a criminal case.[48] To the extent that *Miranda*'s right to counsel proved impossible or impractical to satisfy, the district court required that the American agents make efforts to learn the law in the foreign jurisdiction governing the right to counsel and even advocate for foreign counsel to be appointed, when requested by the suspect.[49] On appeal, the Second Circuit agreed with the district court that the Fifth Amendment applied, without explicitly finding *Miranda* applicable to foreign questioning, even though it "generally governs the admissibility in our domestic courts of custodial statements obtained by U.S. officials from individuals during their detention under the authority of foreign governments."[50] The court of appeals also disagreed with the district court's requirements of American agents operating abroad with respect to the right to counsel.[51]

Even with the retreat from the original *al-'Owhali* opinion, however, the clear implication is that government agents must administer some sort of warning system rooted in the Fifth Amendment when conducting an interrogation abroad. In the wake of the FBI memorandum on interrogation and the public safety exception, however, it is not difficult to see how the government can get around any requirement to provide warnings in a terrorism prosecution. Again, the *Warsame* prosecution provides the clearest example of this phenomenon. Once someone has been interrogated for intelligence purposes for a period of time—in *Warsame's* case, two months—it seems unlikely that he will invoke his rights to silence or counsel. After all, once there has been a confession or admission of unlawful activity, a suspect will most probably feel that there is no harm in confessing after the administration of warnings, since the authorities already know what happened. Further, if, during plea negotiations, the government bargains for a waiver of the right to appeal, as is standard in many guilty pleas, the likelihood that the FBI's granting itself the right to forego *Miranda* warnings for intelligence purposes will be subject to meaningful judicial review is small, at best. While *Miranda's* applicability in the terrorism prosecution at both home and abroad remains intact, the government's ability to get around its strictures has expanded.

Where there is no American involvement in an interrogation conducted abroad that produces statements federal prosecutors wish to use in an American prosecution, *Miranda* has no applicability, because foreign officers have no obligation to adhere to American criminal procedures. In such cases, the voluntariness test, which requires an inquiry into whether any confession given was "voluntary," governs the admission of statements given to foreign agents.[52] This is a highly fact-specific question that mandates a court decide the issue of voluntariness by looking at the "totality of the circumstances" of the confession under the preponderance of the evidence standard; it also served as the test governing police interrogation in the period preceding the *Miranda* decision.[53] A notoriously tricky proposition, the voluntariness test drew criticism from both legal practitioners and academics prior to the decision in *Miranda*, and the test's imprecision played a large role in the Court's decision to abandon it.[54]

There are two exceptions that apply even if a court finds a confession to be voluntary. First, it cannot be admitted if it is found to "shock the conscience." Second, a confession must be excluded if it is the result of a joint venture between U.S. law enforcement and foreign agents.[55] Turning to the "shocks the conscience" standard, the phrase comes from the U.S. Supreme Court's 1952 decision in *Rochin v. California*, in which the police tactic of pumping a suspect's stomach to uncover drugs he had ingested during a raid was declared a violation of due process.[56] This exception suffers from two distinct problems. First is the very valid issue of how a confession could be voluntary if it came about in circumstances that "shock the conscience," a question posed by at least one federal court.[57] Second is the issue of defining what conduct actually "shocks the conscience," as both *Rochin* and the cases that cite to the standard do not provide a ready metric. The late Professor William Stuntz characterized the test as "thoroughly unlawlike," so it is of questionable utility when a court examines foreign confessions.[58]

The "joint venture" exception allows for the suppression of an otherwise voluntary confession where the government has coordinated with foreign agents to have the latter conduct an interrogation. The rationale behind this exception is that, if it did not exist, the government could strategize with foreign law enforcement and intelligence agencies to get around *Miranda*'s strictures by having the latter interrogate a suspect. The joint venture exception applies to both the Fourth and Fifth Amendment contexts and includes the same analysis in each situation: that of "active" or "substantial" participation by U.S. law enforcement agents. However, like the voluntariness inquiry itself and the "shocks the conscience" exception, this is a highly fact-specific inquiry, and case law has not produced a set of clearly articulated standards. Mere presence by U.S. agents at a foreign interrogation is not enough to trigger the exception, but beyond that, figuring out a metric to gauge the required level of participation has proven elusive.[59]

THE VOLUNTARINESS TEST IN PRACTICE: THE CASE OF AHMED ABU ALI

In a terrorism prosecution, determining the voluntariness of a confession is fraught and contentious. The paradigmatic example of this difficult inquiry is the case of Ahmed Omar Abu Ali, an American citizen who had been studying in Saudi Arabia when the authorities there arrested him in June 2003 on suspicion of being part of an al-Qaeda cell after the group carried out a deadly bombing in the capital city, Riyadh.[60] For nearly a year and a half, Abu Ali was held incommunicado by local authorities, not allowed an attorney, and interrogated extensively—including a stretch of forty-seven straight days, mostly at night. He ultimately confessed to belonging to the cell and plotting attacks within the United States. His father, coincidentally an employee of the Saudi Embassy in Washington, D.C., tried to use his contacts to obtain information on his son's predicament, only to be told that Abu Ali was an "American case," over which the Saudi government was not exerting control. When Abu Ali's parents filed a petition for habeas corpus on behalf of their son in the United States District Court for the District of Columbia, the government refused to say anything about his detention and moved instead to dismiss the petition on the grounds that the court lacked jurisdiction. After the court denied the motion and ordered the government to produce information on Abu Ali and his plight in Saudi Arabia, a grand jury in the Eastern District of Virginia indicted him for various terrorist crimes, including a plot to assassinate President George W. Bush, thereby mooting the basis for the habeas petition. Abu Ali was brought to Virginia from Saudi Arabia and prosecuted.

The key issue in his prosecution centered on the voluntariness of his confession while in the custody of the Saudi Interior Ministry's secret police, the Mabahith. In the hearing on Abu Ali's motion to suppress his confession, the court allowed the Saudi agents who interrogated him to testify via VideoLink from Saudi Arabia under pseudonyms. While this was an unprecedented development in the history of American-Saudi relations—the Saudi government had never before allowed access to its security officers—the structure of the proceedings provided no guarantee against the agents lying. For example, how would a court hold a Saudi officer accountable if it discovered he had testified falsely? Despite one Mabahith officer boasting that he had never failed to secure a confession from a detainee and another admitting that he had once tied a prisoner to a tree during an interrogation, the district court ruled that Abu Ali confessed voluntarily. Neither his own extensive testimony nor that of several medical experts, all of whom spoke at length of his being tortured, was sufficient to convince the court otherwise. The confession, duly admitted, led the jury to convict on all charges. On appeal, the Fourth Circuit affirmed the conviction on all counts and found no fault with the voluntariness of the confession. The court also rejected Abu Ali's challenge on the basis of an alleged joint venture between the FBI and the Mabahith. The Saudi authorities allowed FBI agents to subject Abu Ali to an extensive interrogation during which they threatened, inter alia, to declare him an enemy combatant if he did not cooperate with them. However, because the district court ruled that the FBI had not played a role in obtaining the confessions, the Fourth Circuit majority found that no joint venture existed.[61]

What was striking in Abu Ali's prosecution was the fact that the district court rejected any attempts to raise the issue of the systematic use of torture as an interrogation tactic by the Saudi authorities in national security matters. For example, the district court rejected as irrelevant Abu Ali's proffer of two British former residents of Saudi Arabia prepared to testify to their abusive treatment at the hands of the Mabahith.[62] Even more notably, the jury never heard about the State Department's own human rights reports, which discussed the Mabahith's record of abusive practices, especially in politically motivated cases.[63] Strangely, the district court dismissed all of this evidence as "news reports." The net result was a situation where the agents of a foreign intelligence agency—named by the State Department as one that routinely abuses its detainees—testified that they, in fact, routinely abused prisoners, but somehow managed not to do so in this case, and the court credited their testimony. The court found this to be the case even where the Mabahith prevented American agents from being more involved in Abu Ali's interrogation. These conclusions require, in the face of the evidence, an assumption of extraordinary good faith and restraint on the part of foreign agents accustomed to exercising neither. To assume such good faith on behalf of the police in the United States is one thing, but to extend that presumption to the secret police agents of a monarchical dictatorship is another.[64] As much of this book explores, however, high-profile terrorism cases have a habit of producing rulings and outcomes that seem illogical in any other context.

Ahmed Abu Ali's case stands in marked contrast to that of Sameh Khouzam, an Egyptian Coptic Christian who fled Egypt in 1998 after being charged with murder and made his way to the United States. He asserted an asylum claim on the basis of his belief that he would be tortured if returned to Egypt because he would not convert to Islam.[65] Given that he was charged with an ordinary, nonpolitical crime, the immigration court denied his claims of asylum and withholding of removal to Egypt. However, Khouzam was able to obtain relief under the United Nations Convention against Torture (UNCAT), based on the July 24, 2000, finding by the Board of Immigration Appeals that torture was rampant in Egyptian police investigations—a point stressed by the Second Circuit in its opinion upholding the UNCAT relief.[66] Not content with that outcome, the Department of Homeland Security later detained him and sought diplomatic assurances from Egypt that he would not be tortured if extradited to Egypt. The Third Circuit ultimately blocked the government from doing so, ruling that the diplomatic assurances were insufficient to protect Khouzam's due process rights and therefore stayed his deportation to Egypt.[67]

Because Khouzam's case was an immigration/extradition matter and Abu Ali's a criminal trial, these two examples underscore the fact that allegations of terrorism can shift a court's perception of how an interrogation should be characterized. Abu Ali was charged with terrorist crimes, while Khouzam was accused of committing murder, a serious nonpolitical crime. The Second Circuit and the Third Circuit found Khouzam's fear that he would be tortured upon his return to Egypt to be credible and ruled against his deportation, while another court, the Fourth Circuit, found voluntary a confession given to Saudi intelligence agents notorious for abusing their detainees. Abu Ali was the victim of what appears to be an unstated, but understood, terrorism exception; in this case, the exception applied to what otherwise looked like a relatively easy application of the voluntariness test.

Finally, it is worth considering the effects of the ad hoc nature of the voluntariness test even within the narrow confines of those post-9/11 cases that analyze a foreign confession. Shortly after the decision in *Abu Ali*, a federal district court in Chicago ruled on the voluntariness of the confession of Muhammad Salah, a naturalized American citizen of Palestinian origin charged with terrorist crimes based on his alleged activities on behalf of Hamas, a banned FTO.[68] Over a decade before he was indicted in the United States, Salah had been arrested and interrogated by the Israeli authorities on suspicion of his Hamas links; he was ultimately indicted, convicted, and incarcerated there, spending some four years in prison.[69] The court allowed the introduction of his Israeli confession in the federal prosecution against Salah, ruling that it was voluntarily made in great part.[70] Controversially, the court allowed Salah's Israeli interrogators to testify under pseudonyms in a closed courtroom, where they denied his claim that they mistreated and tortured him.[71] Like the Saudi agents in *Abu Ali*, they did not deny using coercive methods as part of their routine interrogation tactics, but stated that they did not use those methods with Salah because he was an American citizen.[72] What was never contested was the fact that Salah was held incommunicado by the Israeli authorities and interrogated for over a month, all the while being consistently denied the right to counsel. Regardless, the court allowed into evidence almost all the statements Salah made while in Israeli custody.[73]

Abu Ali and *Salah* stand in contrast to the 2006 decision of the federal district court in Washington, D.C., on the voluntariness of the confessions of three Rwandan rebels charged with killing two American tourists in Uganda. The three men were interrogated by Rwandan officials and subsequently confessed, under conditions the court ultimately decided were coercive.[74] The court also made the effort to distinguish Abu Ali's interrogation from that of the Rwandan rebels before it, but the distinction was both unconvincing and underscored the difficulty anyone making allegations of torture faces when trying to argue their point in adverse litigation.[75] More critically, the court took into consideration the State Department's own human rights reports on the abusive conditions in the Rwandan detention facility, as well as allowed testimony from third parties who had suffered through interrogation at the same facility.[76] The *Abu Ali* trial court specifically rejected this type of evidence in its evaluation of his confession's voluntariness. Why? One might think that the actual murder of Americans abroad is at least as serious as mostly inchoate terrorist plots and conspiracies. Without needlessly belaboring the point, Abu Ali (like Salah) was charged with crimes of a terrorist bent, whereas the Rwandan defendants were not, however violent and horrible their alleged crimes were. The extent to which the counterterrorist rubric affects courts making the relevant voluntariness determinations is certainly debatable. However, in its current state and based on recent practice, the voluntariness test has not served as a barrier to the admission of confessions taken abroad in terrorism cases. The government therefore retains the ability to bring prosecutions when foreign agencies carry out the interrogation in a terrorism prosecution.

* * *

The preceding sections detail some of the more prominent methods for generating evidence to be used in a criminal terrorist prosecution as well as the legal challenges those methods can pose. The question of what evidence is admitted in court operates under a different set of rules and precedents but follows a similar pattern of deference to the government's theories of the case and the defendant's perceived dangerousness. There are two particularly pertinent subjects of study. Initially, there is the question of what evidence is relevant and should be admitted, which is subject to a limitation rooted in the potential prejudice a given piece of evidence may engender. Second, there is the more specialized regime covering the use of expert testimony, which differs from that of a lay witness in that, once qualified, an expert may give an opinion on the evidence and rely on hearsay in support of that opinion. The following sections consider the relevant rules and precedent in the context of a terrorism prosecution to uncover the trends at work.

THE FEDERAL RULES OF EVIDENCE—RELEVANCE AND ITS DISCONTENTS

For evidence to be admissible, it must be relevant, under Federal Rule of Evidence 401 (Rule 401).[77] As the federal rules governing the introduction of evidence make clear, irrelevant evidence is inadmissible, leaving only relevant evidence to be admitted in a trial.[78] However, just because evidence is relevant does not mean that it must be admitted. It must also satisfy the strictures of Rule 403, which allows a court to exclude even relevant evidence when "its probative value is substantially outweighed by a danger of one or more of the following: unfair prejudice, confusing the issues, misleading the jury, undue delay, wasting time, or needlessly presenting cumulative evidence."[79] There is also a further legal rationale for denying a Rule 403 motion—the idea that excluding relevant evidence "'is an extraordinary remedy that should only be used sparingly.'"[80] While these principles are not hard to follow

in the abstract, making determinations based on their contours is highly depen-
dent on the specific facts and circumstances of a given case. The Supreme Court has
recognized that there is no set formula for determining relevance and that courts
proceed on an individual case-by-case basis, as no two prosecutions are identical.[81]
Within the framework of these basic rules, we must look at how the question of
relevance arises in terrorism prosecutions. Typically, the inquiry involves an attempt
by the government to introduce items, words, or images that are particularly damning, like an act of violence or praise for terrorist groups or leaders.[82]

Violent plots tend to include evidence that is both relevant and prejudicial, as
the balance can seem clear in context. The prosecution of the men charged with
bombing the World Trade Center in February 1993 featured the introduction of
bomb-making manuals, replete with a defendant's handwritten notes, as well as
a document entitled "Facing the enemies of God terrorism is a religious duty and
force is necessary."[83] The court upheld the admission of the materials over a Rule 403
objection because, although clearly prejudicial, they were of great probative value
and tended to show both the motive and preparations behind what was a deadly
and destructive bombing. Had these materials been introduced to show that the
defendants were terrorists who acted in accordance with their character, they would
have been excluded under Rule 404(b).[84] But since this evidence was geared to the
specific point of demonstrating that the defendants had the intent and had taken
steps to carry out a violent attack, it did not fall afoul of the rule. Likewise, when a
defendant is charged with being part of a violent conspiracy, the First Amendment
does not protect against the admission of documentary evidence tending to show
the conspirators' plans to blow up certain targets. When the first World Trade
Center bombing defendants made such a challenge, the Second Circuit rejected it,
reasoning:

> Neither Ajaj nor Abouhalima was prosecuted for possessing or reading
> terrorist materials. The materials seized from Ajaj were used appropriately
> to prove the existence of the bombing conspiracy and its motive. Moreover,
> any prejudicial effect they might have had was ameliorated by the trial court's
> instruction that mere possession of the literature is not illegal and that the
> defendants' political beliefs were not on trial.[85]

The above excerpt serves as a useful example of the reasoning behind a court making its evidentiary rulings on an individualized basis, as a per se rule might have
the effect of excluding evidence when it crosses the line to prejudicial, despite being
highly relevant. But of course, not all examples will be so clear-cut as the case of those

caught after setting off a bomb under what was a major American landmark. The more inchoate and attenuated the plot, the more significant becomes the evidence that links a defendant to terrorism. Consider the case of Muhammad Hammoud, a Lebanese national charged with running a smuggling ring whose members purchased cartons of cigarettes in North Carolina, where sales tax on a pack was low, and sold them in Michigan, where the taxes were much higher, thereby pocketing the difference.[86] The government suspected him of sending a portion of the profits from the smuggling operation to Hizballah, a banned FTO. Though he was indicted before 9/11, Hammoud was the first individual tried after 9/11 on money laundering, conspiracy, and material support charges. Based on a cooperating witness's testimony, Hammoud was found guilty on one charge of providing material support to Hizballah in the amount of $3,500.

As part of the government's case against him, the district court allowed the prosecution to play for the jury "Hizballah videotapes" found in Hammoud's home; the segments of the tapes played featured footage of crowds of Hizballah supporters shouting, among other things, "Death to America," as well as referring to the United States as the "enemy."[87] Although Hammoud offered to stipulate that the videotapes were produced by Hizballah and found in his home, thereby obviating the need to play them for the jury, the government rejected his offer. In addition to finding that the tapes were relevant and admissible under Rule 403, both the district court and the Fourth Circuit recognized the government's right to put on the case of their choosing. Another critical strain of thought animating this ruling was the notion that the videotapes were admitted to demonstrate Hammoud's knowledge of Hizballah's violent aspect and to counter his arguments that he supported only the humanitarian aspects of its work.[88] In a material support prosecution, the government must show that the defendant has knowledge of the FTO's status and knows that what he is providing is material support, which in this case was money. Rejecting precedent from another circuit in non-terrorism cases, the Fourth Circuit reasoned that the videotape evidence "provided evidence of Hammoud's motive in raising funds for Hizballah" and cited to the World Trade Center bombing decision in support.[89]

The *Hammoud* prosecution was flawed in several respects, which are addressed elsewhere in this book. For purposes of the Rule 403 discussion here, however, a few points are in order. While a trial court is authorized to make relevance/prejudice evidence rulings on a case-by-case basis, the analysis in *Hammoud* seems to hinge on the fact that the Fourth Circuit panel believed that the facts more closely resembled that of the Second Circuit's World Trade Center decision—cited by the government—than the Fourth and Ninth Circuit precedents cited by Hammoud. Perhaps this was a fair conclusion, given all the facts in the case, but perhaps not. The sole conviction on a substantive material support charge was supported only by the testimony of an admitted liar who had been charged as part of the cigarette-smuggling ring and later made a deal with the government in exchange for his testimony. The facts of the solitary $3,500 donation to the FTO were extremely convoluted, and the money may have never actually reached the group, even accepting the cooperator's testimony in its entirety.[90] What emerged looked more like a group of garden-variety fraudsters with unpopular politics, as opposed to the dangerous and violent bombers of the World Trade Center conspirators, a distinction that could have had a real impact on the nature of the evidence admitted against Hammoud.

Even more troubling in the Rule 403 analysis is the matter of whether a defendant should be able to stipulate to certain facts before the jury.[91] Certainly, from the government's perspective, being able to show videos containing footage of members of a group the defendant is charged with supporting chanting things like "Death to America" can be powerful. However, a much-litigated and debated issue that dates from the passage of the material support ban in 1996 is what standard of proof must the government demonstrate to convict someone. The majority of courts considering the issue have settled on a knowledge standard, meaning, as noted earlier, that the government must prove that a defendant knew he was providing material support to a banned FTO. Opponents of the law and defense attorneys advocated at length for a specific intent standard, meaning that, to meet its burden, the government must prove that a defendant supports the illegal—as opposed to humanitarian—goals of the group, but those efforts largely failed. This standard thus raises the issue of what purpose the introduction of highly inflammatory evidence serves. Both the district court and Fourth Circuit rejected Hammoud's argument in favor of a specific intent standard, leaving the issue of his knowledge as the critical one for the jury.[92] Stipulating to his ownership of the videotapes and their contents goes a long way to meeting the government's burden without injecting potential prejudice. The message sent by playing the videotapes to the jury is that Hammoud is a person who supports America's enemies, which is not really the point of a material support charge, but can certainly go a long way to ensuring a conviction.

Consider also how terrorism-related charges have a way of widening the net of relevant evidence for a court, which in turn can allow for underconsideration of the evidence's prejudicial impact. The paradigmatic example is that of Osama Bin Laden/al-Qaeda-related evidence. When the government can introduce this type of evidence against a defendant, the chance of obtaining a conviction increases exponentially. The stakes on the introduction of evidence are therefore heightened in such cases, although it must be said that where an indictment alleges crimes linked directly to the group, the evidence is clearly relevant, and even a Rule 403 challenge is unlikely to be successful. It is those cases where al-Qaeda links are tangential to the government's case that the admission of Bin Laden/al-Qaeda-related evidence is most fraught.

Lynne Stewart, an attorney who defended Omar Abdel Rahman (the Blind Sheik), the former head of the designated Egyptian FTO al-Gama'a al-Islamiyya (IG), was indicted herself on material support charges several years after her client was convicted and sentenced to life in prison for terrorism-related crimes.[93] While in prison, the Blind Sheik was subjected to a series of restrictions—"special administrative measures" (SAMs)—imposed by the Federal Bureau of Prisons that regulated his communication with the outside world. As part of the restrictions, he was forbidden from speaking to the press about IG-related matters. Stewart was indicted on charges that she ignored the SAMs, which she had pledged in writing to respect, and that she had knowingly deceived the prison authorities by helping to solicit the Blind Sheik's opinion on the IG's then recently declared ceasefire with the Egyptian government. Subsequently, the Blind Sheik's opposition to the ceasefire was disseminated to the press.

Although the government did not allege or attempt to show that anyone had been harmed as a result of the public leaking of Abdel Rahman's position on the ceasefire, it indicted Stewart and two others—one was her translator and a graduate student, and the other a follower of the Sheik's living in the New York City area. After a jury trial, Stewart and the other two defendants were convicted of various material support and fraud charges stemming from her violation of the SAMs, with the Blind Sheik's follower also being found guilty on charges of conspiracy and solicitation to commit murder. Among the items the court admitted into evidence against the follower was a videotape of an unindicted co-conspirator and IG leader appearing alongside Osama Bin Laden, discussing planning an attack to secure the release of the Blind Sheik.[94] Even though Stewart and her translator complained that the videotape was both irrelevant and highly prejudicial to them, the district court found that its limiting instructions to the jury to not improperly consider the videotape were sufficient to thwart any prejudicial effect.[95] The Second Circuit agreed, citing the first World Trade Center bombing opinion referenced in *Hammoud* for the established proposition that this type of evidentiary decision is best left to the court overseeing the prosecution.[96]

On the one hand, this decision, while perhaps difficult for the district court, was a relatively straightforward evidentiary matter involving a defendant (the Blind Sheik's follower) who supported the IG, even when the group latched itself onto al-Qaeda and Bin Laden as a kind of affiliated force. On the other hand, admitting any evidence tied to Bin Laden/al-Qaeda in a trial at a courthouse a few minutes' walk from the site of the former World Trade Center is a difficult issue, to be sure. That the court thought it could cure any prejudicial effect with a limiting instruction in such a situation a mere three or so years after the 9/11 attacks seems a bit optimistic, to be charitable about it. Also, there is the more difficult question of whether Stewart and her translator were properly exposed to Bin Laden evidence, notwithstanding the district court's limiting instruction, given that they probably knew nothing about the IG's links to al-Qaeda. It is one thing to prosecute someone for disregarding SAMs in a matter involving the limits of zealous representation, but quite another to bring the specter of 9/11 into the trial of defendants having nothing to do with anything violent outside their representation of a criminal terrorist defendant.

While cases like the Lynne Stewart prosecution push up against the government's theories on what can be considered relevant evidence, terrorism prosecution defendants face another evidentiary conundrum. As discussed in Chapter 1, a primary tool the government employs to drive prosecutions is the use of informants, who play a prominent role in selecting a target and concocting a violent plot, which the government later thwarts. As this scenario unfolds, a defendant seeking to argue that he was entrapped faces the proposition of confronting the government's argument that he was "predisposed" to carry out the plot. In such situations, evidence involving a defendant's political or religious views can become relevant when an entrapment defense is attempted.[97]

The prime example here is that of Shahawar Matin Siraj, a young Pakistani immigrant to the United States who was convicted in 2006 on charges of conspiring to blow up a major subway station in Manhattan.[98] His entrapment defense focused on the role of the NYPD's informant, who, among other things, suggested the plot, recommended obtaining Russian nuclear material from a fictitious entity called "the Brotherhood" to carry it out, and constantly spoke critically about American actions in the Muslim world, in an effort to rile him up.[99] Given that Siraj raised the defense of entrapment, he opened the door to evidence regarding his predilection—his "predisposition"—to engage in terrorism, which was presented by an undercover police officer who had investigated the case.[100] The evidence detailed Siraj's support for the FTOs al-Qaeda and Hamas, along with books and videos extolling violent jihad and violence against Jews.[101] The *Siraj* court explained its decision to allow the testimony this way:

Defendant also argues that allowing the undercover officer's testimony raises "considerable First Amendment concerns" by criminalizing legitimate political discourse. However, even if the undercover officer testified to statements made by defendant that may be described as reflecting defendant's political views, those statements were properly admitted as discussed [previously]. That defendant's statements contain political expression does not insulate defendant from their use at trial where the statements also rebut his testimony and prove predisposition.[102]

What was once highly prejudicial and possibly irrelevant evidence became admissible, even in the form of protected speech.

The net effect of charging someone with terrorist crimes can amount to an indictment of that individual's thoughts, associations, religious views, and political positions. Again, if one is convinced that terrorists are de facto dangerous, whether based on affiliations, plots that government agents cook up, or direct evidence of violent or dangerous activity, the net of relevance is wider. Courts focusing on the narrow confines of relevance within the framework of a given case can understandably allow in evidence of a highly prejudicial nature in a charged atmosphere that portends threats to national security. Viewing the trend as a whole via the cases discussed in this chapter, there is a real danger that the nature of terrorism charges can cause a court to view a defendant's evidentiary objections as unalterably tainted. And from that position, opinions, associations, and beliefs can come into evidence.

A court can go too far in allowing the government to put on its case. There is one post-9/11 example of a court of appeals reversing a conviction on material support charges in part because of the introduction of highly inflammatory testimony. In *United States v. al-Moayad*, two Yemeni nationals were convicted on charges of conspiracy and material support to the FTOs al-Qaeda and Hamas.[103] The named defendant was a prominent religious figure in Yemen who, along with his assistant, had been lured by an informant from his homeland to Europe under the pretext of soliciting support for his charitable foundation. The informant claimed that al-Moayad had long been a significant fundraiser for Bin Laden, hence the al-Qaeda link, and also videotaped a group wedding presided over by al-Moayad in Yemen during which a Hamas leader gave a speech praising the organization's 2002 bus bombing in Tel Aviv. What seemed clear from the prosecution was that what the defendants viewed as legitimate charitable activity, the government considered code for violent terrorism.

During the trial, the district court admitted the testimony of two witnesses that the Second Circuit ruled was improper. In the first situation, the witness—a survivor of a bus bombing carried out by Hamas in Tel Aviv—testified at length about the experience, introducing personal details about the loss of his cousin in the bombing and repeating himself often.[104] The court noted that the defendants were not charged with "planning or carrying out the Tel Aviv bus bombing," and the government failed to introduce any evidence connecting the defendants with a terrorist act.[105] The testimony was supplemented by photos and video, which the court felt "amounted to a blatant appeal to the jury's emotions and prejudices."[106] Even if the testimony had been correctly admitted to show that a bombing had occurred, the court of appeals ruled that allowing the testimony to continue once the bombing was established was improper.[107]

In the second instance, the district court allowed the testimony of an individual convicted of providing material support to al-Qaeda, based on his experiences at an al-Qaeda training camp in Afghanistan.[108] The Second Circuit explained that the district court failed to make a "conscientious assessment of the testimony's prejudicial effect" in part because of the government's "misleading proffer" as to the testimony.[109] The witness was supposed to testify about the business practices of the training camp, but his testimony went far beyond that, resulting in the admission of a video of Osama Bin Laden's visit to the training camp.[110] Because there was no link between the witness and the defendants, and the district court failed to offer a limiting instruction for the testimony, the Second Circuit found the testimony to be in error.[111] The convictions were reversed, with the court of appeals taking the unusual step of remanding the case to a different district court, given the fact that the trial was riddled with evidentiary improprieties.[112]

As noted, *al-Moayad* is, to date, the sole decision in which a court of appeals reversed the convictions of defendants convicted of terrorism charges in the period after 9/11. It is the single instance of a court refusing to accept the government's expansive theories of what constitutes relevant evidence, and the fear that harmful prejudice to a defendant can result if improper evidence is admitted. There can be any number of extraneous explanations for the Second Circuit's position that go beyond mere criticism of the government's conduct during trial—the exaggeration of the main FBI informant, who incidentally set himself on fire prior to trial in front of the White House to protest what he believed was a lack of sufficient remuneration by the FBI; the almost willful blindness to the fact that the defendants were referencing actual charitable endeavors during the sting operation; and the Yemeni government's long battle to secure the sheik's release, and so forth. Although we will ultimately never really know all of the factors that helped shape the *al-Moayad* opinion, it remains the anomalous decision that regulates somewhat the overreach of a terrorism investigation. It has yet to become a harbinger of a more active and skeptical federal judiciary when dealing with terrorism prosecutions. Essentially, the decision, while maybe setting a floor for proper evidentiary standards in a terrorism case, only goes so far in regulating the government's use of the evidence against a defendant. The opinion itself alludes to the district court's failure to offer more detailed rationales for its rulings and limiting instructions to blunt their effect, indicating that the decisions to allow the testimony noted above was not in and of itself unimaginably wrong. For the time being, we should not expect too many decisions like *al-Moayad*.[113]

THE EXPERT WITNESS

In prosecutions with complicated facts, the use of an expert witness allows a party to explain and contextualize its arguments, because an expert may provide an opinion and analysis of the evidence, something a lay witness may not do. A terrorism prosecution may very well be the type of forum that demands expert testimony. However, a review of expert testimony in terrorism prosecutions reveals several troubling trends in how the government and courts evaluate an individual's expertise and scope of testimony.

An expert is allowed to opine on the evidence at issue in a case provided the testimony to be offered is relevant, detailed, helpful to the trier of fact, and the product of a reliable and recognized methodology.[114] According to the Supreme Court, a district court serves as the "gatekeeper" for which expert testimony will be admitted, and both Supreme Court precedent and the Federal Rules of Evidence provide nonexhaustive standards to guide a court in ruling on the admissibility of expert testimony.[115] The Supreme Court has also clarified that the district court's gatekeeping function extends to nonscientific expert testimony.[116] Unsurprisingly, courts have found that the "nature, structure, methods, and means" of terrorist groups are the kinds of subjects for which expert testimony is appropriate.[117]

The nature of expert evidence in the scientific context contemplates that an expert can make reference to studies that support the argument being advanced. While the studies themselves are inadmissible hearsay, one of the special privileges of properly admitted experts is that they can rely on such hearsay to bolster their point.[118] But in the terrorism prosecution, the government's expert can enjoy an informational advantage that the defense is hard pressed to challenge.

Evan Kohlmann is the government's most high-profile,[119] and perhaps most used expert witness.[120] The government generally offers Kohlmann as an expert witness on al-Qaeda and affiliated groups.[121] Courts have qualified him as an expert witness in over two dozen prosecutions in the United States, and he helpfully links to several court rulings reflecting that fact on his website.[122] However, a closer look at his credentials reveals knowledge gaps that cannot be brushed aside easily. Kohlmann does not know Arabic, or any other foreign language in which al-Qaeda purportedly communicates, and must use a translator to sort through the data he collects.[123] As an initial matter, a lack of language ability is a serious impediment not likely to be tolerated in other areas of research—could we imagine that an expert in dissident French movements would not know French?

In addition to the issue of language capabilities, there is also the matter of educational and professional background. Kohlmann has no advanced degrees other than a law degree from the University of Pennsylvania.[124] He has never worked in law enforcement, the military, or in an intelligence service.[125] He has, however, authored a book on al-Qaeda in Europe, which was cited in the 9/11 Commission official report.[126] Does that qualify him as an expert? According to Kohlmann, he tracks al-Qaeda and ideologically related groups, mostly on the Internet, collecting and storing the data he studies.[127] The following is a description of his work and methodology:

> [It] consists of gathering multiple sources of information, including original and secondary sources, cross-checking and juxtaposing new information against existing information and evaluating new information to determine whether his conclusions remain consonant with the most reliable sources. He describes his work as a study of the micro-history of al Qaeda and its involvement in regional conflicts. His methodology is similar to that employed by his peers in his field; indeed, he explained that he works collaboratively with his peers, gathering additional information and seeking out and receiving comments on his own work.[128]

Outside the specific mention of al-Qaeda, the above paragraph is too general and diffuse to evaluate adequately how Kohlmann goes about verifying the information he analyzes. All we know about the peers in his field is that he says he relies on them, but he does not elaborate further. There is also the related question of how Kohlmann can determine accurate information and reliable sources when he cannot read or understand the foreign language source material. Regardless, this description of his work and methods has been enough for courts to permit him to testify as an expert in almost all the published judicial opinions ruling on the matter.[129]

A 2010 academic study of those judicial opinions regarding Kohlmann's expertise and proposed testimony described his approach:

> In his expert reports, Kohlmann deftly links a particular Arabic publication, website, or organization (typically the one the defendant allegedly supported) to terrorist recruitment. He then establishes the link between recruiting terrorists and Osama Bin Laden. And then, obviously, he links Bin Laden to the jihadist objective of killing American nationals. In these cases, Kohlmann repeatedly, vividly, and emphatically highlights these connections throughout his expert reports.[130]

Specifically, the study, by evidence scholar Maxine Goodman, found that "courts routinely backtrack to prior admissibility decisions as a means of assessing Kohlmann's reliability."[131] That is, once he has been accepted as an expert in one case, he will be qualified as such in others going forward, to the point where defendants have given up trying to challenge his suitability as an expert.[132] But the problem, according to Goodman, is "the published . . . opinions illustrate that courts accept his methodology and conclusions 'hook, line, and sinker' without any real scrutiny. . . . [allowing] Kohlmann to rely primarily on Internet sources without ever having to explain to a court how he assesses the authenticity of those sources."[133]

A compelling example of the consequences associated with courts accepting Kohlmann's methodology without the required level of scrutiny occurred in the prosecution of the two men charged with participating in a convoluted plot to buy a missile intended to shoot down the airplane of the Pakistani ambassador to the United Nations discussed previously in Chapter 1.[134] The government named Kohlmann as its intended expert on the Bangladeshi wing of a terrorist group active in Southeast Asia.[135] Despite the fact that Kohlmann had never written about the group or interviewed any of its members, and was not even able to name the group's leader, the court admitted him as an expert based on information he had obtained from the Internet.[136] In that case, as in many others, Kohlmann's testimony tied al-Qaeda to the defendants—a Bangladeshi immigrant who owned a pizza parlor and an imam of Kurdish descent, both of whom lived in the Albany, New York, area—essentially guaranteeing a guilty verdict.[137] Kohlmann's effectiveness as an expert witness is obvious, but his technique is highly controversial and has been strongly criticized by leaders in the field of terrorism studies, leading one to call it "junk science."[138] Perhaps the most telling statement on the use of Kohlmann as an expert witness comes from Kohlmann himself. Referring to the government, he noted that "[i]f they had other options, don't you think they would take them?"[139]

Beyond methodology lies the problematic issue of foreign language fluency. Intentionally downplaying the lack of linguistic capability of the government's expert allows for testimony that exploits the general unfamiliarity a court or jury has with geopolitics in general. Dr. Ronan Gunaratna is the head of a think tank focused on terrorism in Asia and author of several books on terrorism. He served as the government's expert in the prosecution of Jose Padilla—the accused al-Qaeda "dirty bomber"—and two others on material support charges unrelated to the dirty bomb plot. Gunaratna was qualified by the court as an expert and proceeded to testify at length about al-Qaeda, even though the defendants were not accused of materially supporting the group.[140] Part of Gunaratna's testimony was based in part on interviews with individuals abroad—intelligence officers, terrorist detainees, government officials—who were covered by confidentiality agreements, leaving the defense to object on the grounds that it could not establish the reliability of the information in the interviews. The court was unmoved and refused to order Gunaratna to disclose the details and identities of those involved in the interviews.[141] In essence, he was permitted to testify regarding secret information about the world's most reviled terrorist group and its relationship to the defendants without the defense having a substantive informational basis from which to mount a challenge.

Additionally, both Gunaratna and an FBI agent testified at length regarding the defendants' use of code words in the electronic communications intercepted by the government, terms such as "soccer" or "football" as a code for violent jihad, "egg-plant" for a rocket-propelled grenade launcher, and so on.[142] What is astonishing about these facts is that both Gunaratna and the FBI agent did not know Arabic, the language of the communications at issue. As already discussed, expert witnesses testifying on behalf of the government in terrorism trials frequently do not know the language in which the defendants communicate. Courts tend to dismiss this threshold challenge as immaterial, which represents a marked contrast with cases involving expert witnesses interpreting drug codes from Spanish. In such cases, the critical basis for allowing the expert, whether a translator or law enforcement officer, to provide an interpretation of the code is knowledge of Spanish.[143]

Second, even if language competency is not enough to disqualify someone as an expert, it can lead to other types of questionable testimony and evidence. Over relevance and Rule 403 objections, the district court admitted seven minutes of a twenty-four-minute CNN interview conducted with Osama bin Laden in 1997 on the grounds that it could serve as evidence of two defendants' state of mind, but not that of Padilla, who never viewed or discussed the video. Part of the rationale in admitting the presentation of the interview to the jury was that the district court condensed the time span of the video presentation and did not allow the government to question witnesses about the interview. However, another aspect of the justification the court gave was that the two defendants discussing the interview referred to Bin Laden by his "nickname," Abu Abdullah (father of Abdullah), which, according to Gunaratna, "was known only to his supporters and identified him as one of the biggest backers of jihad in Afghanistan."[144] How could Gunaratna possibly make this statement, given his lack of knowledge of the Arabic language and, presumably, culture? The tradition of referring to someone by a kunya ("Abu" + other name or attribute) is a well-known cultural practice in the Arab world, most frequently, but not exclusively, involving the name of the eldest son after "Abu." Recent years have witnessed the widespread use of this practice in the political/revolutionary sphere, with perhaps the most famous example being Yasser Arafat, who was well known in the Arab world by his nom de guerre, Abu 'Ammar, which was used by friends and opponents alike. In referring to Bin Laden by his kunya, the defendants were dis-cussing a 1996 fatwa he had issued, which has been widely interpreted as declaring war on the United States, among other targets. But the idea that the defendants were somehow privy to a secret nickname that was used only by Bin Laden's supporters is questionable at best. The 1996 fatwa they referred to was published in a widely circulated Arabic-language newspaper based in London that same year, so knowledge of its contents and Bin Laden more generally was obviously not a secret. At the time in question, Bin Laden's kunya cannot have been too hard to find out, and certainly should not have served as a basis to bring the former al-Qaeda leader before the jury in a case where the defendants were not charged with materially supporting the group. Allowing the testimony to serve as the basis for introducing video of Osama Bin Laden in a criminal terrorism trial was therefore an example of a court not performing its gatekeeping function with respect to the limits of Gunaratna's testimony.

The extrapolations laid out by Gunaratna are by no means unique. In the prosecution of the former officers of the Holy Land Foundation for Relief and Development (HLF), at one time the largest Muslim charity in the United States, for materially supporting the FTO Hamas (discussed previously in Chapter 2), the government offered Dr. Matthew Levitt as its expert on the movement. Levitt, the Director of the Stein Program on Counterterrorism and Intelligence at the Washington Institute for Near East Policy, is a former Treasury Department official and FBI intelligence analyst with a doctorate in law and diplomacy who testifies frequently as an expert for the government in terrorism prosecutions.[145] His testimony on Hamas in general and the role of its social wing was not challenged.[146] However, once qualified as an expert, some of his most damaging testimony seemed to verge on unsupported guesswork. Specifically, in response to the defense's argument that the presence of telephone numbers of senior Hamas leaders in the defendants' personal phone books was unremarkable and not evidence of a special relationship, Levitt averred that it was "personal and direct evidence of a relationship.... [T]he fact that there are connections with so many Hamas leaders is not coincidental, cannot be coincidental."[147]

It is one thing to be an expert on a group and describe its historical formation and basic makeup, even if a defendant's stipulation that he or she knows about the group and its aims should suffice. But in this situation, the court allowed Levitt, who does not speak Arabic and was not admitted as an expert in Palestinian society, to offer an opinion totally unsupported by his own credentials.[148] He was not admitted as an expert on whether Palestinian political figures, even those of Hamas, provide their phone numbers with regularity or otherwise make themselves available to their constituent public. Based on his qualifications, he could not opine about how social exchange in Palestinian society works, making his statement a startlingly conclusive assertion without much basis behind it. Although affirmed on appeal by the Fifth Circuit, this ruling demonstrates far too much deference to the government's expert on matters that lie beyond his area of expertise.

In those rare instances where the government manages to produce an expert with the requisite language capabilities, the results can be even more dramatic. Hamid Hayat was convicted on material support charges stemming from what the government alleged was his preparation for a violent attack in the United States by attending a terrorist training camp in Pakistan.[149] While much of the government's case was driven by an informant (see Chapter 1), its expert, Khaleel Mohammed, a professor of Islamic studies, provided crucial testimony regarding Hayat's state of mind. Mohammed testified that a supplication found on Hayat was evidence of his violent jihadi proclivities. Specifically, his translation of the supplication was "Oh Allah* we place you at their throats and seek refuge in you from their evils." During the course of his testimony, Mohammed noted that "the 'kind of person' who would carry that supplication would be one 'who perceives him or herself as being engaged in war for God against an enemy' . . . '[someone] completely ready' to commit 'an act of warfare against a perceived enemy.' "[150] He repeatedly stated that in having the supplication, the individual was "a jihadist," "part of the mujahideen," "engaged in jihad," and "in the act of being a warrior," and that "*there [was] no other way it could be used.*"[151] The Ninth Circuit upheld the district court's admission of this testimony as reliable and within Mohammed's area of expertise, even if he did not know Urdu, the national language of Pakistan, as he testified as to the meaning of a Islamic supplication in Arabic, a language he knows.

On the issue of mens rea, Hayat objected to Mohammed's testimony under Federal Rule of Evidence 704(b), which prohibits experts generally from offering an opinion on the issue of whether the defendant had the mental state required by the statute.[152] But the Ninth Circuit rejected that argument as well, noting that although it may have agreed with Hayat's position were it to interpret the rule for the first time, circuit precedent allowed Mohammed's testimony on this matter.[153] The court cited its line of Rule 704(b) cases, all of which upheld a law enforcement agent's testimony as an expert on drug transactions that a defendant caught with a certain amount of drugs and/or a weapon is consistent with intent to distribute the drugs.[154]

As an initial matter, this specific type of testimony in drug cases has been criticized as both unnecessary and in contravention of Rule 704(b)'s plain language.[155]

---

* "Allah" is simply the Arabic word for God, used by Arabic-speaking adherents of all three major Abrahamic faiths to connote the same monotheistic deity. The troubling trend of not translating the word is outside the scope of this book, but is noted here as yet another way terrorism prosecution defendants can be marked as somehow different and apart from mainstream society.

In Hayat's case, the expert testimony prompted a strong dissent from Judge A. Wallace Tashima, who noted that there was something quite different between individuals apprehended with large quantities of illegal narcotics and weapons on them and someone carrying a religious supplication.[156] With respect to the seemingly violent language of the supplication, Judge Tashima pointed out that no court would allow expert testimony to the effect that someone carrying a copy of "Onward, Christian Soldiers" in their pocket is the "kind of person" on the cusp of engaging in war and violent jihad.[157] Quite simply, "the conceivable variations in understanding and motivation are too great."[158] In his words, "[t]here is an absence of clarity in this case simply because the testimony was given in relation to Islam, a religion whose tenets are unfamiliar to the vast majority of Americans."[159]

Judge Tashima's dissent is a clear and courageous example of a principled stand against the double-edged sword of fear-mongering and lowering the standards of proof that terrorism prosecutions have become. As it was a minority position, Hayat's conviction and sentence were affirmed. Where the cases involving experts and their lack of language ability allowed those witnesses to draw inferences their expertise did not support, *Hayat* represents a more alarming development. An expert who knew the language in question was permitted—acontextually[160]—to state that Hayat had the mens rea required for conviction on material support charges, essentially substituting his judgment for that of the jury. The court of appeals upheld this result because of a line of precedent allowing experienced drug investigators to suggest that a large amount of drugs and/or a weapon was more than just personal possession; it was possession with intent to distribute. While Judge Tashima's dissent makes this point clear, it bears repeating that words and beliefs, while in certain contexts no doubt dangerous, cannot be analogized to actual, tangible narcotics or weapons. Referring to a poll that found that 66 percent of Americans knew little to nothing about Islam, the dissent summarized the effect of Mohammed's testimony: "The jurors in Hayat's trial, therefore, were particularly susceptible to deferring to Mohammed's 'expert' testimony not only as to the translation and meaning of the supplication, but also as to the ultimate question of whether the supplication proved that Hayat was a 'jihadist' (i.e., a terrorist)—the kind of person who would carry such a prayer."[161]

But the development with the greatest cause for concern comes from the HLF prosecution referenced above. The government asserted a link between Hamas and the charitable entities the defendants sent money to in the West Bank and Gaza Strip, known as zakat committees. To make the connection between the zakat committees and Hamas, the district court allowed two Israeli witnesses to testify anonymously at trial, one of whom was qualified as an expert.[162] Referred to only as "Avi," he testified in his capacity as a legal adviser to the Israel Security Agency (the main Israeli internal security apparatus)[163] that Hamas controlled the zakat committees.[164] The Fifth Circuit upheld the district court's ruling, holding that the anonymous testimony did not violate the defendants' Sixth Amendment confrontation rights.[165] The Supreme Court refused to take up the defendants' appeal on the issue of anonymous expert testimony, leaving the court of appeals' ruling intact.[166]

Initially, the Fifth Circuit's Sixth Amendment discussion dismissed the applicability of a 1968 Supreme Court decision finding reversible error where the sole witness/participant in a drug transaction with the defendant testified anonymously.[167] Despite containing language that denying a defendant information about a witness's identity "effectively ... emasculate[s] the right of cross-examination itself," the Fifth Circuit found the Supreme Court case inapposite, as it dealt with a contested recollection of a drug sale, as opposed to "classified information or issues of witness safety" in the instant case.[168] The court of appeals also reasoned that anonymous testimony was permissible due to the witnesses' identity being classified and the fact that no one who actually knew the witnesses would or could be in a position to talk about them, a point that led one scholar to note: "On what basis the court reached this speculative conclusion is left unstated."[169]

The ruling allowing an anonymous expert witness sends several deeply troubling messages over and above the confrontation clause point. First, it tells the jury that the defendants are so dangerous that they will harm the witness unless his identity is protected. Second, an intelligence officer with a classified identity reinforces the notion that he is an active participant in a war on terrorism that demands secrecy, lest the terrorists' schemes succeed. Third, the jury is told that the expert has specialized knowledge about a terrorist organization that is indecipherable and/or inaccessible to most people, and therefore should be kept secret. All of these messages are somewhat incongruous with the HLF prosecution, as there were no allegations that the defendants were connected to the FTO's violent acts.

Given this state of affairs, the defense was left in the position of being unable to challenge Avi's credentials, methodology, or own past experiences and biases, except in the most general sense; that he worked for the Israeli government, served in the military, and testified anonymously.[170] In those rare cases where courts have allowed an expert witness to testify anonymously, a key factor justifying the decision is the fact that the expert was to testify about the criminal organization in a general sense without factual testimony involving the defendants.[171] The HLF case was just the opposite. Avi's testimony was offered to make the crucial link between the FTO and the defendants' fundraising. The Fifth Circuit justified its holding with a conclusory statement: "[W]hen the national security and safety concerns are balanced against the defendants' ability to conduct meaningful cross-examination, the scale tips in favor of maintaining the secrecy of the witnesses' names."[172] So here, therefore, is the terrorism prosecution's strongest statement on the extent of the loosening of the rules of evidence: an anonymous foreign intelligence agent testifying as an expert while relying on hearsay sources to give opinions on the defendants' guilt. Perhaps this type of testimony is appropriate for a closed congressional briefing, but not a criminal prosecution in which the Fifth Circuit effectively conflated the national security function of an intelligence agent (and a foreign agent at that) with the public nature of a criminal trial.

When viewed in the light of all the other evidentiary exceptions discussed in this chapter, we are left with a picture of the federal courts' acquiescence in the government's terrorism prosecution strategy: highlight the exceptional nature of terrorism and the secretive and classified work needed to stop it. To be fair, there are examples here and there of courts that buck this trend by recognizing the damage to the rule of law it may cause, but they are few and far between. In the meantime, more exceptions and anomalous situations, prompting a further weakening of the evidentiary protections a defendant enjoys, loom.

4

THE IMPLICATIONS AND BROAD HORIZONS OF THE

TERRORISM PROSECUTION

THE PREVIOUS CHAPTERS have focused on the terrorism prosecution as it proceeds in a linear manner: from spying and investigations peppered with informants, to charges underpinned by material support laws that continue to reach farther and farther away from violent activity and even terrorist associations, and then to a trial regime that allows evidence of questionable relevance based on dubious methodologies. Before a discussion of what happens once a defendant is convicted and sentenced to prison—the final stop on the terrorism prosecution train—this chapter serves as a vehicle to investigate the implications of the terrorism prosecution through a few high-profile examples. As opposed to the previous chapters' exploration of trends, laws, and practices that raise the specter of the government creating both crimes and criminals, the cases discussed here fall under the category of what the average person would consider politically motivated violence. That the government chose to pursue charges should not come as a surprise.

Yet the examples below reveal a kind of limitless patience and understanding shown by the courts to the government when it brings criminal charges against individuals suspected of ties to violent groups and/or attacks. This is true even where the government overreaches in terms of interrogating or treating harshly a terrorist suspect, to the point where their statements under interrogation would be constitutionally barred from admission at trial. In addition to new, thinly disguised national security exceptions to basic precepts of constitutional criminal procedure, as well as the controversies over the standards and nature of the evidence used for conviction, the terrorism prosecution also provides an insight into how terrorism itself is constructed and perceived. Going beyond mere links to violent groups, one high-profile prosecution has presented a theory so broad that it borders on outlawing any expressions of solidarity with oppressed populations, no matter how just the cause. It is through this prism that we can understand the idea of a war on terrorism as a war on an abstract concept, as opposed to something more concrete with a fixed address or organizational structure. If a terrorism prosecution can be based on such a theory, it is not difficult to imagine other cases where national security exceptions trump basic procedural rights and even rest on such unlikely factual scenarios as to strain credulity. What follows is a discussion of the cases that exemplify these trends.

THE SAGA OF JOSE PADILLA

The first and most important example here centers on the case of American citizen Jose Padilla, the suspected al-Qaeda "dirty bomber" who was apprehended by the FBI at Chicago's O'Hare International Airport in May 2002 upon arrival from abroad. After being questioned by FBI agents, Padilla was arrested and detained, with the government ultimately choosing to hold him as an "enemy combatant" to whom the traditional rights of criminal defendants would be denied. While he was housed in isolation at a military prison in Charleston, South Carolina, and subjected to aggressive, "enhanced" interrogation techniques, which may have resulted in him being rendered insane, his lawyers pushed for relief in the courts.[1] After several legal twists and turns, which included the Supreme Court initially dodging the question of the constitutionality of his detention on procedural grounds, by late 2005, the Court was set to rule on the matter. Rather than risk an adverse ruling, the government had Padilla indicted on criminal charges stemming from a terrorism investigation in the Southern District of Florida and transferred him to civilian custody in early 2006 to face those charges, which were unrelated to the alleged "dirty bomb" plot. Numerous courts criticized the government's repeated legal maneuverings in the case, which gave the impression that it was seeking to avoid judicial review.[2]

The criminal indictment and subsequent prosecution presents a whole host of issues. Previously, Chapter 3 addressed the specific matter of the dubious expert testimony admitted in Padilla's criminal case, which purported to show the defendants speaking in code to mask their terroristic intent. The Eleventh Circuit's ruling on Padilla's initial seventeen-year prison sentence as being too lenient is covered in the next chapter of this book. And Padilla's attempt to have the charges against him dismissed owing to "outrageous government conduct" as a result of the government's harsh treatment of him while in military custody failed, because such relief is rarely, if ever, granted. In the unlikely event of a court granting relief, the proper remedy is generally the exclusion of any evidence derived from such mistreatment.[3] Even leaving these matters to one side, the prosecution itself raises serious concerns regarding the nature of the criminal counts and the proof used to support them, as they reveal a theory of terrorism and terrorist groups that is sweeping in its scope.

Initially, it bears repeating that the indictment did not involve the dirty bombing charges in any way and seemed designed to avoid the possibility that the saga of Padilla's military detention would be brought up. The charges themselves were quite circular, bordering on the tautological. Along with two other defendants—Adham Hassoun, a Lebanese-born Palestinian, and Kifah Jayyousi, a Jordanian national—Padilla was charged with one count of conspiring to murder, kidnap, or maim people abroad in violation of 18 U.S.C. § 956(a)(1) (§ 956); one count of conspiring to provide material support and resources "or concealing or disguising the nature, source, or ownership of material support or resources, knowing or intending that they are to be used in preparation for, or in carrying out, . . . a conspiracy to murder, kidnap or maim overseas," in violation of 18 U.S.C. § 2339A (§ 2339A);[4] and one substantive § 2339A material support count in support of that same conspiracy to murder, kidnap, or maim abroad.[5] The men were accused of sending money to various parts of the Muslim world under the auspices of an Islamic charity to fund "violent jihad." When they discussed the donations over phone, the government alleged the men spoke in code to conceal the true purpose behind those donations. There were seventy-four overt acts related to the conspiracy that spanned the period between 1993 and 2001, with only one occurring after September 11, 2001.[6] Tellingly, there were no charges brought under § 2339B, the ban on providing material support to a designated FTO. Also, two other individuals were indicted but remained at large during the pendency of the proceedings. There were several other lesser charges levied only against Hassoun, mostly as a result of what the government considered perjured testimony he gave in an immigration court hearing.[7] In August 2007, a federal jury in Miami found the three guilty on all charges, and they were subsequently sentenced to lengthy prison terms.[8]

As opposed to § 2339B, which criminalizes the provision of material support or resources to a designated FTO, § 2339A outlaws the provision of such support in service of any one of several dozen specifically enumerated felonies, without the need to delineate a particular terrorist group as the recipient. However, § 2339A theoretically needs to be linked with violent activity, whereas § 2339B does not, but the government does not have to highlight specific attacks to properly deploy the statute. Frequently, the government will bring § 2339A charges in conjunction with a § 956 conspiracy to murder, kidnap, or maim abroad, as the latter statute is a useful predicate offense for establishing liability in a terrorism prosecution.[9] The three main terrorism charges in the indictment all hinged on demonstrating that the defendants joined a conspiracy as a basis for conviction, meaning that no link to any particular act of violence was necessary, just that the defendants were part of the criminal agreement, although the indictment did specify a host of overt acts the defendants carried out.

The conspiracy was composed of several radical Islamist groups, including but not limited to al-Qaeda, the Egyptian Islamic Jihad, and the Egyptian Islamic Group, "dedicated to the establishment of a pure Islamic state ('Caliphate') governed by strict Islamic law ('Sharia')." The members of this conspiracy were adherents of a radical Salafist interpretation of Islam "that encouraged and promoted 'violent jihad' to be waged by 'mujahideen' using physical force and violence to oppose governments, institutions, and individuals that did not share their view of Islam."[10] The "mujahideen" fought in conflict-ridden countries like Afghanistan, Algeria, Bosnia, Chechnya, Lebanon, Libya, and Somalia, thereby constituting the murder, maiming, kidnapping, and hostage-taking at the heart of the government's theory of conspiracy liability. The government alleged that the defendants functioned as the conspiracy's "North American Support Cell" and sought to prove that "they sent money, physical assets, and mujahideen recruits to these overseas conflicts for the purpose of fighting violent jihad."[11]

When the defense moved for the government to clarify the scope of the conspiracy and its targets by providing more specificity with respect to the allegations, the government responded by offering more detail. It is worth citing the government's own words at length to understand the scope of the conspiracy:

> The defendants herein were part of a larger radical Islamic fundamentalist movement that waged "violent jihad" by opposing governments, institutions, and individuals that did not share their view of Islam or their goal of reestablishing a Caliphate. As it pertains to this case, these defendants supported violence, including murder, maiming and kidnappings, committed by mujahideen groups operating in various jihad theaters around the world. Specifically, the violent Islamist groups in Egypt, Algeria, Tunisia, Libya, Somalia, Afghanistan, Tajikistan, Chechnya, Bosnia and Lebanon.
>
> In some of these theaters, such as Afghanistan, Bosnia and Chechnya, and Tajikistan their violence was directed mainly towards existing central government regimes they believed were oppressing Muslims and resisting the establishment of strict Islamic states. Therefore, they engaged in armed confrontations, including murders, maiming, and kidnappings, against Serbian and Croat forces in Bosnia, Russian forces in Chechnya and Tajikistan, and

opposing Muslim forces in Afghanistan during the civil strife that ensued after the Russian forces withdrew in 1989. In other theaters such as Egypt, Algeria, Libya, Somalia, and Tunisia, they supported the violent Islamist groups and factions committing acts of murder, maiming, and kidnapping against leaders, members, and supporters of what they viewed as apostate regimes, including other Muslims.[12]

What is described is a staggeringly broad conspiracy that transcends boundaries, languages, and cultures, all in service of a common goal of "reestablishing a Caliphate," which is subject to multiple interpretations. The scope of activity covered by reducing the phenomenon of Islamic fundamentalist movements into a sort of monolith is large, indeed. It is axiomatic in the criminal law that for someone to join a conspiracy with others, the individual must agree to join with another, and then agree to the plan being carried out. With the description offered above, there is the very real danger that individuals can be held liable for activities that they never would have contemplated carrying out, or even agreed to support, in countries and regions they do not know much about, let alone have visited.

According to the indictment, the time frame of the charged conspiracy is October 1993 through November 1, 2001. The ten countries referenced represent at least nine different languages over a vast geographic area spanning the southwest Mediterranean, the Balkans, and reaching all the way to Central Asia. In those eight years, every single country had a system of nonrepresentative government—maybe with the exception of Lebanon. But all of the named regimes used repressive means with its enemies and/or were in a state of active violent conflict. It is not a stretch to say that no one actor, governmental or otherwise, had entirely clean hands at any point in the respective conflicts. To target the worldwide jihad movement, to the extent that one even exists, instead of individual terrorist organizations exposes the government's theory to a series of counterpoints and narratives that may be uncomfortable to confront. For example, during the conspiracy's existence, the militia of the breakaway Bosnian Serb republic committed numerous atrocities against Bosnian Muslims, who were represented by the internationally recognized government of Bosnia-Herzegovina. The most notorious of these atrocities was the 1995 Srebrenica massacre, still the largest and only act of genocide in post-World War II Europe, in which some eight thousand Bosnian men and boys were killed after being captured. The Russian military engaged in an exceedingly violent crackdown on Chechen rebels in that breakaway republic, twice sacking the Chechen capital Grozny, in 1994 and 1999. Egypt, Algeria, Tunisia, and Libya all had governments that engaged in violent repression of political dissidents—Islamists as well as others—whether armed or not, and

Somalia featured violations by all sides in a civil war. (It is not clear from this theory what the conflict in Lebanon was during the time period in question, as the country had already emerged from its civil war, and it is hard to conceive of entities in the global Salafist jihad movement supporting the Shiite movement Hizballah in its fight against the Israeli army then occupying southern Lebanon.) These details merely scratch the surface of the complexity involved in charging a worldwide jihad movement with conspiring to murder, maim, kidnap, and so on.

The implication of the government's stance is that no amount of solidarity with oppressed populations will be allowed if the vehicle for delivery is considered suspicious. There is no need to make out a link to an act of violence, or even a particular group, as long as the government can allege a kind of theoretical framework to tie all individuals, dangerous or otherwise, with the belief system in question. Recall that the government potentially has the ability to declare all nonstate political violence terrorism and prohibit material support to groups practicing such violence. Section 2339B, as previously noted, is a flawed statute that sweeps too far in criminalizing what should be protected speech and association. But at the very least, it requires that the government designate a group as an FTO before material support can be banned. Much like the radicalization thesis, the conspiracy at the heart of the Padilla prosecution sweeps up all of those who support "violent jihad" against regimes that oppress Muslims and regards them as equivalent. Is support for the besieged Bosnian Muslims in the face of Serb ethnic cleansing the same as support for al-Qaeda? Does solidarity with Chechen rebel groups—even their violent activities—indicate approval of the 9/11 attacks?

The message behind the indictment is to effectively criminalize the transmission of aid by religious Muslims wishing to alleviate the plight of their religious brethren suffering under objectively dire conditions of violent oppression, even when the groups receiving the aid have not been designated as terrorists. Where the earlier chapter on § 2339B argues that that statute does the same thing, the designation process demands a specific inquiry into more particularized activity. While the government may believe that Padilla and his co-defendants were engaged in something more nefarious than charity, the conspiracy as formulated reaches even ostensibly innocuous conduct. Drawing a conspiracy in such broad terms allows the government to elide the humanitarian/political solidarity element by highlighting shared doctrinal or political similarities between the defendants and members of al-Qaeda with respect to a given individual conflict. It therefore allows the introduction of forms of proof that are likely to be highly inflammatory while of questionable relevance. As noted in the previous chapter, in this case, the government relied on a non-Arabic-speaking expert witness to decipher alleged code words in Arabic and also had played for the jury a 1997 CNN interview with Osama Bin Laden, all because two of the defendants discussed the interview in an intercepted phone call.

Although the trial judge gave a limiting instruction to the effect that the defendants were not in any way involved with the 9/11 attacks, the outcome was clear.[13] At one point, the chief investigatory FBI agent was even allowed to testify that one of the indicted but not present defendants was referring to Bin Laden when he mentioned that he was "over at [O]sama's."[14] Again, note the sweeping nature of this important link the government was allowed to draw between the world's most notorious terrorist, on the flimsiest of bases, running roughshod over established cultural norms. Osama is an exceedingly common Arabic name—the author, of Arab Christian background, has no less than three cousins with that appellation. How then can an FBI agent untrained in the Arabic language and culture draw such a damning conclusion from the intercepted telephone call? Regardless, that did not stop the government from arguing that the defendants spoke in code when referring to Bin Laden, except when they didn't; expert witness Rohan Gunaratna testified that the defendants referring to Bin Laden by his code name was evidence of an affiliation, yet in another call Bin Laden is referred to by name.

None of the above is meant to imply that the defendants did not have religious leanings or political affiliations that may be of legitimate concern to the government. But the procedural posture of the prosecution is important to highlight. When the government could not or would not prosecute Padilla on the dirty bomb charges, after holding him incommunicado for years, the answer was to have him charged criminally in an unrelated investigation. In the course of the case, the government made arguments that drew links between the defendants and al-Qaeda on a theory of conspiracy so broad as to confound even those more sympathetic to its legal counterterrorism approach. National security law experts Robert Chesney and Peter Margulies, both of whom urged the Supreme Court to uphold § 2339B's constitutionality in the *Holder v. Humanitarian Law Project* litigation,[15] have written critically of the government's theory in the *Padilla* case as being needlessly overbroad.[16] Construing the actions of the defendants as inherently suspicious and inculpatory goes too far in their view. When defendant Kifah Jayyousi sent satellite telephones to Chechnya, was it for terrorism or humanitarian purposes? The government could not say, and under its theory, it did not have to, leaving the jury to consider Jayyousi's "general disposition," which reflected his Islamist leanings and political views that were framed in light of evidence that Osama Bin Laden was somehow involved in the case.[17] Even the government's most powerful evidence—an application form to attend a terrorist training camp in Afghanistan allegedly filled out by Padilla—does not necessarily add up to membership in a terrorist conspiracy. As Margulies notes:

First, submission of an application did not necessarily lead to attendance. Second, many attendees at the camps did not follow up on their training, because they became disillusioned, discovered other priorities, or followed prudent counsel to refrain from further activity. Third, even those who did not fall away from Al Qaeda did not necessarily collaborate in schemes to commit violent acts. Viewed in this light, the scope of Padilla's agreement—at best, an agreement to attend a camp—does not match the agreement to facilitate murder, mayhem, or kidnapping that is required under § 956.[18]

If the government had evidence that the defendants were supporting violence against a sovereign government with which the United States was not at war, it could have charged them with violations of the Neutrality Act.[19] If they were suspected of materially supporting a designated FTO, even in the form of speech, they could have been charged with violating § 2339B's strictures. But the *Padilla* prosecution shows something different. When the indefinite detention of a U.S. citizen proclaimed an enemy combatant failed to produce the desired level of deference to the government's position, he was charged with terrorist crimes. As a result, the courts allowed theories of conspiracy liability, already highly amenable to the prosecution, to be shaped even further to criminalize all forms of political solidarity and humanitarian aid, provided they could be somehow linked to the wrong kind of jihad. The criminal terrorism prosecution was allowed to function as a kind of catch-all safety valve of last resort to rescue the government from its initial overreach. In the words of Canadian legal scholar Kent Roach, the *Padilla* case "illustrates that the [criminal terrorist prosecution] remains accommodating in the United States, even in cases where specific terrorist plots are not alleged and the accused claims to have been severely mistreated in custody."[20] Maybe the jury's verdict is a win for the government's desire to hold someone in preventive detention and then prosecute them for a crime defined in the broadest of terms.[21] However, given that at least one juror had basically decided on a guilty verdict before beginning deliberations,[22] there is a real question of whether the victory is worth the cost of expanding criminal liability and its concomitant weakening of procedural protections.

THE *GHAILANI* PROSECUTION: THE COURTS RESCUE THE GOVERNMENT FROM A CRISIS IT CREATED

The pattern of the civilian courts being utilized to save the administration from its war on terror missteps has repeated itself in other cases, even when the price is a significant loosening of procedural protections for criminal defendants. In May 2009, President Obama announced the transfer of several high-profile detainees from the military detention camp at Guantanamo Bay, Cuba, to the United States.[23] This announcement was the opening salvo in the Obama administration's effort to shut down the prison camp, in accordance with the President's statements on the campaign trail, by demonstrating the effectiveness of civilian criminal trials as a method for holding the detainees accountable for any acts of terrorism they were suspected of committing. The next month, Ahmed Khalfan Ghailani, a citizen of Tanzania, was transferred to the Southern District of New York to face criminal charges stemming from his role in the August 1998 bombings of the U.S. Embassy buildings in Nairobi, Kenya, and Dar es Salaam, Tanzania by al-Qaeda, which killed 224 people.[24] The political fallout that began with the President's announcement ensured that Ghailani would end up being the only Guantanamo detainee to be tried in federal court.[25]

The CIA captured Ghailani in Pakistan in 2004 and held him for two years in secret prisons before moving him to the custody of the Department of Defense, which had him transferred to Guantanamo. In 2008, Ghailani was charged with violations of the laws of war and brought before a military tribunal, but those charges were dismissed prior to final adjudication upon his transfer to civilian custody in 2009.[26] The transition to a criminal prosecution was not totally fruitless for the defense, at least in terms of procedural protections, as the government had to suffer some consequences for its conduct. Since Ghailani was subjected to "enhanced" interrogation techniques while in CIA custody, the district court ruled that any information Ghailani divulged as a result would be inadmissible at his criminal trial. This included even the statements of a witness identified as a result of Ghailani's confessions in CIA custody, who was prepared to testify that he sold Ghailani the TNT used in the Dar es Salaam bomb.[27] The case proceeded to trial without the jury hearing of the critical link between him and the bombings, and, in November 2010, he was subsequently acquitted on 281 of the 282 counts against him.[28]

While the result generated criticism from members of Congress, the jury did find Ghailani guilty of one count of conspiring to destroy government property and made a specific finding that his conduct led to the deaths of individuals not connected to the conspiracy.[29] Despite the impression that this criminal prosecution hampered the government's counterterrorism efforts and engendered a ruling that coerced statements cannot be admitted at trial, the district court used the verdict to impose a life sentence, which Ghailani was to serve in solitary confinement at the most restrictive prison run by the Federal Bureau of Prisons.[30] Ghailani was unsuccessful in pursuing legal relief through the courts, and the verdict and sentence were upheld on appeal.[31] Like Jose Padilla, Ghailani's argument that the charges should have been dismissed due to outrageous government conduct—his harsh interrogation by the CIA—was dismissed. Unlike Padilla, however, Ghailani had a viable claim that his right to a speedy trial had been violated since he was indicted in federal court on essentially the same charges he faced in a military commission. Padilla's criminal charges did not in any way relate to any of the violent plots he was suspected of and detained on, so there was no speedy trial issue.

Ghailani made his argument under the Speedy Trial Clause of the Sixth Amendment, because of the five-year delay between the government's gaining custody of him in 2004 and his first appearance before the court in 2009.[32] As the constitutional language governing the speedy trial right is rather undefined, the Supreme Court has articulated a legal test for evaluating claims that is quite flexible, so as to respond to the vagaries of each individual case.[33] Over and above any legal test, in a situation where the government held an individual for five years in CIA and military custody before indicting him on criminal charges in federal court, ostensibly the claim looks to have had a fair chance of success, at least at first blush. But the stakes were quite high. The remedy for a violation of an individual's speedy trial right is ordinarily dismissal of the criminal charges, at least in theory. Both the district court and the court of appeals needed to confront the political reality that a dismissal would force the administration to release Ghailani or return him to military custody. Either choice would severely hamper the Obama administration's efforts to shut down the Guantanamo/military commission process and promote federal criminal adjudication as the answer, not to mention the possibility, that an individual responsible for a horrendously violent act might go free.

The Second Circuit's opinion upholding the denial of speedy trial relief to Ghailani must be read in light of this dynamic. Regarding the delay in bringing the defendant to trial, the Supreme Court's 1972 opinion in *Barker v. Wingo* asks courts to consider the length of the delay, the reason behind it, and whether the defendant is responsible, and to evaluate if the defendant was prejudiced as a result.[34] This is not an exhaustive list, as a court may take into account any other relevant factors.[35] According to the Second Circuit, Ghailani was not prejudiced by any delay due to the significant national security interests of the government in holding him before charging him criminally.[36] The logic employed by the court in concluding that his speedy trial right was not violated was shaky and susceptible to a critique on multiple levels. As observed by legal scholar Anthony O'Rourke, perhaps most noteworthy was the fact that the *Barker* opinion and all the other precedents cited by the Second Circuit concerned cases in which the reason for the delay was intrinsic to the criminal prosecution, that is, the delay was designed to enhance the government's chances of success by, for instance, compelling the testimony of an additional witness.[37] Ghailani's case was different in that the delay was for a reason extrinsic to the criminal prosecution—procuring information from him on al-Qaeda for intelligence purposes. In a similar vein, the court also glossed over Ghailani's argument that the CIA's harsh treatment prejudiced his ability to receive a fair trial, as it found that he would have been held and detained for the separate purpose of interrogation, the criminal charges notwithstanding.[38]

Regardless of this and other leaps of logic, the court was at pains to deny that it created a general national security exception for violations of a defendant's speedy trial right. As with many of the prosecutions discussed in this book, it is hard to imagine what other conclusion could be drawn from such a decision, however. The government held Ghailani for five years before transferring him to civilian custody, and it brought him before a military tribunal some four years after his capture. What the Second Circuit's opinion accomplishes is to set a remarkable precedent that cannot be contained doctrinally. It seems as if the government will not be held accountable for violating a defendant's speedy trial rights if it can show that the defendant was a sufficient threat to national security. It will not be faced with a real choice between criminal prosecution or detention for intelligence/military purposes. Given Ghailani's role in a violent terrorist attack whose political overtones go hand-in-hand with its deadly aftereffects, it is unlikely that the court's decision will generate a great deal of controversy. Yet it relaxes the pressure on the government and provides another example, in addition to that of the Jose Padilla prosecution, of how the criminal model has been employed to let the government off the hook for its national security stumbles. The decision also serves as a kind of corollary to the public safety exception to *Miranda* in national security cases discussed in the previous chapter. The length of detention does not affect whether any confession will be suppressed. So long as there is a valid need for interrogation without warnings or counsel, the government can detain an individual indefinitely without offending the constitutionally mandated right to a speedy trial. The Second Circuit opinion also portends the extension of such logic outside the national security realm. In an article advocating the use of a military tribunal for Ghailani, former Attorney General Michael Mukasey notes the stakes of criminal prosecution: "[T]he law that is created is going to be a law that is applicable straight across the board—in all criminal cases—and it could do a lot of damage. Once the rules are created, it is nearly impossible to confine those rules solely to terrorist cases."[39] While this book is in no way intended as a justification for the use of military tribunals either as originally envisioned or as currently operating, *Ghailani* demonstrates the dangers of simply arguing that the criminal courts are the answer, without further study or scrutiny of the impact of such decisions on criminal law and procedure generally.

OTHER USES OF THE CRIMINAL TERRORIST PROSECUTION—
IMPROBABILITIES AND POLITICAL EXCEPTIONALISM

The criminal prosecution has also played the role of a kind of deus ex machina in cases with seemingly improbable or unbelievable facts that implicate an individual seen as a long-standing threat. When that particular individual suspected of involvement with terrorism seems beyond the reach of American prosecutors, miraculously, she appears to carry out an attack that renders her subject to prosecution. Consider the case of Aafia Siddiqui, a Pakistani national and former green card holder in the United States. During her time in America, where she obtained a master's degree from M.I.T. and a Ph.D. in neuroscience from Brandeis University, her activities on behalf of various Muslim groups caught the attention of the FBI.[40] After meeting with the Bureau's agents on one occasion in 2001, she returned to Pakistan with her family in 2002, skipping a second interview the FBI had requested as a follow-up.[41] In 2003, based on allegations of her involvement with an al-Qaeda financier as well as her rumored marriage to Khaled Sheik Mohammed's nephew—himself also an al-Qaeda operative—the FBI placed Siddiqui on a wanted list and issued a global alert for her, at which point she disappeared.[42]

She later resurfaced in Afghanistan in 2008, where she was detained by Afghani security forces who suspected her of trying to attack the governor of Ghazni Province. The day after her arrest, a team of American military and FBI personnel went to the Afghan police facility to interview her, with an eye toward taking her into custody. Siddiqui, who was being held unrestrained in a dimly lit room behind a curtain partition, reached out beyond the curtain to grab a machine gun left unattended by one of the American soldiers. In the struggle over the gun that ensued, the soldier who had left his machine gun out shot and wounded Siddiqui with his pistol. As she was arrested, she uttered a stream of anti-American sentiments. Later, while being treated for her injuries, she made a series of allegedly incriminating statements to the FBI agents guarding her in the hospital.[43]

Siddiqui was convicted in the Southern District of New York of numerous crimes, including attempted murder, stemming from her thwarted attack. The prosecution made sure to highlight the political dimension of her crime by noting her repeated anti-American statements and the fact that when captured, she had documents in her possession that indicated the possibility of an attack on landmarks in New York City. On appeal, the Second Circuit affirmed her convictions and eighty-six-year prison sentence without too much controversy, at least from a legal standpoint.[44] But questions immediately cropped up regarding her competence to face the accusations against her. The court-ordered psychologist who examined her initially found her incompetent to stand trial, only to later revise the assessment and state that Siddiqui was malingering.[45] Her behavior during the proceedings was erratic, as she feuded with her lawyers, and then decided, against their advice, to testify in her own defense. They viewed her decision as tactically disastrous and lodged a formal objection with the court, which allowed the testimony regardless.[46] Siddiqui testified in full head covering, with only her eyes visible to the jury, and was subjected to a thorough cross-examination by the government. She also stated that during the years before the attack attempt, she had been subjected to torture in secret prisons by a "group of people pretending to be Americans doing bad things in America's name."[47]

The case also raised serious questions about Siddiqui herself. The first related to her whereabouts during the five years between her disappearing from view in Pakistan and resurfacing in Afghanistan and behaving in a suspicious manner. As she alluded to in her testimony, family members and prominent Pakistani figures raised the possibility in the press that she had been held in a secret American prison for that period, while also speculating that she may have been held in the custody of Pakistani intelligence.[48] Her prosecution never answered this question with any certainty, leading to continued speculation on the whereabouts for five years of someone whom the American government considered a dangerous al-Qaeda member, going so far as to place her on a list of al-Qaeda terrorists the CIA was authorized to "kill or capture."[49] Finally, there was the second question, which related the details of the 2008 attempted attack itself. What was a woman with a Ph.D. and three young children doing in war-torn Afghanistan looking to carry out a violent attack on her own? Surely, al-Qaeda had other, less-skilled operatives to use in such circumstances? None of these questions were answered, but the government used the flexibility of a criminal terrorism prosecution to enable Siddiqui's incarceration for what looks like the rest of her life.

DEFINING AND PROSECUTING TERRORISM: THE GOVERNMENT'S EXCLUSIVE DOMAIN

The criminal prosecution has made clear that only the government is authorized to define and combat the terrorist threat; outside actors can have no role. When defendants in the *Abu Marzook* prosecution argued that the government's designation of Hamas as a RICO enterprise was an improper basis for RICO conspiracy charges, the district court dismissed the claim without much discussion. Further attempts to inject Hamas's political status into the case were rejected, as was the notion that the prosecution raised a nonjusticiable political question.[50] When the government says that a group is a terrorist organization, facts or arguments that the group's political status should counteract that designation are not valid, as Chapter 2 (on material support) makes clear. Yet beyond arguments about material support and the status of any given movement is the question of which entities are entitled to take action to stop political violence.

As the case of various Cuban intelligence agents active in southern Florida in the late 1990s demonstrates, even where a foreign intelligence service has solid information about politically violent plots against Cuba emanating from the United States, it risks having its members criminally prosecuted if it takes action to stop the source of that violence. The agents, whose profiles ranged from professional intelligence officers to lower-level assets who provided information on what they observed while working as clerical staff at U.S. military bases, came to be known as the Cuban Five. They worked as part of group called La Red Avispa (the Wasp Network) that spied on Cuban exile groups active in South Florida that had been responsible for several acts of violent terrorism in Cuba, including an attack that left one Italian Canadian businessman dead. They also spied on an exile group called Brothers to the Rescue, which flew small airplanes as part of an effort to help people flee Cuba. In February 1996, information from the men led to the Cuban military's shooting down of two planes dispatched by the organization, resulting in the death of the two pilots.[51] The work of the men was not a secret to U.S. law enforcement. In June 1998, FBI agents met in Havana with their Cuban counterparts, who offered information that La Red Avispa had collected, with a specific focus on a plot to blow up an airplane of tourists coming to Cuba from either Europe or Latin America. While no one was ever arrested in connection with that proposed attack, three months later, the FBI arrested the members of La Red Avispa and charged them with various crimes of espionage, with the leader of the group receiving an additional charge of conspiracy to commit murder stemming from the downing of the Brothers to the Rescue plane.[52]

In 2001, the men were convicted in federal court in Miami of various offenses and sentenced to terms ranging from fifteen years in prison at the low end to two consecutive life terms for the Network's leader.[53] Surprisingly, a 2005 panel of the Eleventh Circuit threw out their convictions on the basis that they were tried in an implacably hostile environment in south Florida, as the community there constituted too biased a jury pool to provide a fair and impartial trial to Cuban intelligence agents.[54] The full court of appeals later overturned that verdict and reinstated their convictions.[55]

Despite some pointed criticism of the case in the media and of the fairness of the trial expressed by the United Nations, however, the essential message of the entire Cuban Five prosecution is that the concept of fighting terrorism and/or taking counterterrorist action remains the exclusive domain of the U.S. government. It alone defines what types of terrorism can be fought and identifies the specific personnel authorized to carry out that task. This was true even before the 9/11 attacks. It remains even more salient now that counterterrorist activity is construed broadly, as evidenced by the prominent role played by the material support ban, operating in a preventive mindset. The construction of terrorism is also broad, as witnessed by the over-reliance on informants to drive prosecutions of plots that would have never existed but for the informants' own machinations. However, in a case where nonstate groups located in the United States actively plotted to attack and undermine the Cuban government—activity that narrowly and uncontrovertibly tracks the understanding of what constitutes terrorism under American law—Cuban agents were prosecuted and imprisoned for attempting to stop those attacks. The foreign agents passed on information to the FBI on the threats it had detected but that did not lead to any arrests or prosecutions, other than their own. While it is true that there are very clear laws against unauthorized espionage by foreign agents in the United States, as in many other countries, one wonders if the existence of such laws abroad would deter American law enforcement or military personnel from taking action abroad to stop politically motivated violence against Americans. To the extent that political preferences and questions of foreign policy influenced the decision to prosecute the Cuban agents, consider the fact that roughly contemporaneous with the case making its way through the courts the government paid ten journalists to submit reports critical of Fidel Castro on Cuban opposition media outlets based in Miami.[56]

Therefore, the terrorism prosecution exists solely for the government to define, at its discretion, what the terrorist threat is that must be combated, even where other countries can point to actual violence that emanates from the United States. And when viewed in combination with the post-9/11 examples of Jose Padilla, Ahmed Khalfan Ghailani, and Aafia Siddiqui, that type of discretion covers the most expansive theories of what represent terrorist threats, regardless of how a lack of factual specificity can criminalize what may be legitimate political activity. The terrorism prosecution also serves as a stop-gap measure of last resort when the government wishes to eschew the military commission model, even in cases with suspicious or mysterious facts. Likewise, decisions such as submitting an individual to harsh interrogation and incommunicado detention need not stand in the way of a criminal prosecution. Understanding these dynamics allows the reader to appreciate the depth of discretion the government retains in bringing criminal terrorist prosecutions and how the criminal model has paved the way for expansive theories of terrorism that cover far too much protected inchoate activity.

5

THE FINAL STOP: SENTENCING AND CONFINEMENT

GIVEN THE ROUGHLY chronological approach this volume takes to terrorism prosecutions, this final chapter explores what transpires at the end of process by examining the unique context of criminal sentencing in the shadow of a terrorism conviction. Specifically, the existence of a special sentencing enhancement, which empowers the court to issue a dramatically higher sentence warranted by the underlying crime in cases linked to terrorism, cements and reinforces the notion of terrorism exceptionalism in the criminal realm. In handing down stiffer sentences in terrorism prosecutions than in ordinary criminal cases, courts run headlong into the Supreme Court's recent sentencing jurisprudence, which in general requires higher levels of proof for longer prison terms as well as urges greater deference to a district court's decision. And in its most extreme form, courts of appeal overturning district court sentences in terrorism cases as too lenient expose the thinly supported theories at the heart of terrorism exceptionalism. Unfortunately, exceptionalism does not end with a criminal sentence, but continues on to plague the terrorism prisoner through special restrictions and units within the federal prison system that severely restrict visitation and communication rights.

As the vast majority of criminal cases in federal court end in a conviction, whether by guilty plea or through a trial, the issue of determining a proper sentence is one of particular significance. Over the past fifteen years, as a result of a relatively high number of decisions throughout that time period, the Supreme Court has radically altered the legal architecture of the sentencing universe. Previously, the facts of each individual defendant's crime(s) were plugged into a set of formulae determined by the United States Sentencing Guidelines (Guidelines), resulting in a mandatory sentence a court could only alter in truly unusual circumstances. In 2005, however, the Supreme Court decided *United States v. Booker*, which held that the Guidelines were advisory, not mandatory, and that a court was free to depart from them provided it issued a "reasonable" sentence.[1]

The Court, building on and reemphasizing a series of recent decisions, relied on the following logic to ensure a sentence complies with the Sixth Amendment: "Any fact (other than a prior conviction) which is necessary to support a sentence exceeding the maximum authorized by the facts established by a plea of guilty or a jury verdict must be admitted by the defendant or proved to a jury beyond a reasonable doubt."[2] Where before courts could rely on facts outside a jury verdict or guilty plea to enhance a sentence, under the lower preponderance of the evidence standard, *Booker* ended that practice. Subsequent decisions provided more of a framework to assess properly what exactly constitutes a "reasonable" sentence. In 2007, the Court noted in *Gall v. United States* that as long as the district court commits no "procedural" error—such as, for example, treating the Guidelines as mandatory, relying on erroneous facts, or failing to properly explain the sentence it issues—a court of appeals can review a sentence for "substantive" reasons, but with a proviso.[3] Substantive review of a district court's sentence must show "due deference," as "[t]he fact that the appellate court might reasonably have concluded that a different sentence was appropriate is insufficient to justify reversal of the district court."[4] A court of appeals therefore may not overrule a sentence determined by the district court based on a disagreement over what the proper sentence should be, as long as the original sentence falls within the contours of what can be considered reasonable.

As will be explored below, the concept of what represents a reasonable sentence holds particular salience in the terrorism context, where courts can be moved to express strong opinions on the nature of terrorism and the appropriateness of a given sentence. This is perhaps a natural outgrowth in an area in which a special sentencing enhancement exists for terrorist crimes. Traditionally, when crimes of terrorism were adjudicated in federal court, they involved an act of violence with a political component, so any sentence, severe as it might be, corresponded to normal practices for violent crimes.[5] Even where a specific crime like aircraft hijacking engendered a heightened government response and harsher penalties, it retained the common characteristic of being a crime of politically motivated violence.[6] The legal underpinning of the criminal model of sentencing functioned without issue when applied to a terrorism case involving violence.

THE TERRORISM ENHANCEMENT—U.S.S.G. § 3A1.4

Yet in the wake of the 1993 World Trade Center bombings, in 1994, Congress requested that the United States Sentencing Commission (Sentencing Commission) amend the Guidelines to provide for heightened penalties for any crime involving international terrorism. The result was U.S. SENTENCING GUIDELINES MANUAL § 3A1.4 (§ 3A1.4), which dramatically increases the sentence of an individual convicted of terrorist crimes.[7] The enhancement applies "[i]f the offense is a felony that involved, or was intended to promote, a federal crime of terrorism," and triggers a massive increase in the minimum sentence.[8] A federal crime of terrorism is defined according to a two-prong test in 18 U.S.C. § 2332b(g)(5) as (1) "an offense that is calculated to influence or affect the conduct of government by intimidation or coercion, or to retaliate against government conduct," and (2) any one of a whole host of specifically enumerated statutes.[9] The Patriot Act of 2001 significantly expanded the scope of activity that could warrant the application of the enhancement. Most pertinent to the issue of the length of a custodial sentence, under § 3A1.4, a convicted defendant is automatically entered into criminal history Category VI, the most extreme classification, which is usually reserved for career criminals. This classification holds regardless of whether the individual being sentenced has ever committed a crime.[10] Thus, if a court finds that § 3A1.4 applies, the minimum sentencing range a convicted defendant faces is 210 to 262 months.[11]

The application of the enhancement is quite severe, which reflects the shared belief of Congress and the Sentencing Commission that terrorist offenses are the type of heinous crimes that require heightened punishment. Without the enhancement, there is a marked difference between the penalties for ordinary crimes of violence and terrorist-specific offenses not involving violence. According to one study, the Guideline ranges for federal crimes of terrorism reveal a clear disparity between the lengthy penalties for run-of-the-mill violent crimes and the lesser sanctions for crimes of supporting or financing terrorism.[12] When § 3A1.4 is applied, however, the distinction between sentences for violent and nonviolent crimes narrows, exposing a fundamental inconsistency between the penalties Congress has promulgated and the actual sentencing levels terrorism defendants are exposed to, irrespective of violent conduct.

Statistics issued by the Sentencing Commission show that the enhancement has been applied 241 times since 1996, the first year it was in force, through 2013, the last year for which figures are available.[13] While initially § 3A1.4 was rarely applied, in the post-*Booker* world, the enhancement has been in greater evidence, with the last two years posting record numbers.[14] While there were thirty-nine instances of § 3A1.4 being applied in 2012, by 2013, the count reached forty-four.[15] However, despite this rise in prevalence, the enhancement does not represent any statistically significant trend in sentencing, because those forty-four cases constituted some 0.1 percent of the 70,982 federal cases in which the courts issued a criminal sentence in 2013.[16]

Once a court rules in favor of applying the enhancement, it is more than likely to be upheld on appeal. Of the 44 opinions issued by the federal courts of appeal since the passage of § 3A1.4, there are only three instances of a court of appeals upholding a district court's refusal to apply it or to issue a much lower sentence than prescribed by the enhancement in clear and final terms; in all other cases, the court ruled in favor of applying it.[17] This amounts to a rate of affirmance of around 93 percent. Compare this ratio to the most recent data on sentencing appeals, which for 2013 revealed that 77.2 percent of criminal sentences were upheld on appeal, an increase from the 73.5 percent ratio in 2012.[18]

Section 3A1.4 can be advantageous to sentencing courts when faced with the stark choice between a shorter Guidelines sentence without the enhancement and a much more lengthy sentence with the enhancement. In those instances, if the sentencing court finds § 3A1.4 applicable, it can opt to issue a sentence in the middle of the individualized Guidelines calculations with and without the enhancement. *United States v. Ashqar* serves as an example of this trend.[19] The defendant, a co-defendant of Muhammad Salah (see Chapter 3), was convicted of obstruction of justice and criminal contempt for refusing to answer questions at a grand jury empaneled to investigate Hamas activity the United States; Ashqar was acquitted on the RICO count, which likened the group to organized crime.[20] His Guidelines calculation without the enhancement was twenty-four to thirty months on the contempt count, but jumped to the 210 to 262 month range when § 3A1.4 was found applicable.[21] The district court chose a middle-of-the-road solution and issued a 135-month sentence, which the Seventh Circuit upheld as reasonable under *Rita*.[22]

At first blush, it appears as if the courts are acting prudently by finding a compromise position in between two extremes.[23] But consider the type of conduct being punished when evaluating the "reasonableness" of any of these sentences. As previously discussed, the main statute undergirding most terrorism prosecutions is § 2339B, the ban on providing material support to a designated FTO, which criminalizes nonviolent activity on behalf of foreign groups. Additionally, the statute is specifically mentioned as a precursor felony for "federal crime of terrorism" purposes under § 3A1.4,[24] meaning that materially supporting an FTO can generate very high sentences for what would otherwise be innocuous and constitutionally protected activity. By way of contrast, in reported decisions of the courts of appeal involving purely domestic terrorist crimes, the cases all reflect some form of violent activity or conspiracy to commit violence, without exception.[25]

Two § 2339B prosecutions demonstrate this trend in action. The first example comes from the Fourth Circuit's 2004 decision upholding the conviction and 155-year sentence of Muhammad Hammoud, a Lebanese national prosecuted for running a cigarette smuggling ring between North Carolina, where the sales tax on cigarettes was low, and Michigan, where the tax was much higher (see Chapter 3).[26] The scheme encompassed over $3 million in fraud, and the jury also convicted Hammoud of conspiracy to provide material support to the FTO Hizballah, as well as one count of substantive material support in the amount of $3,500, based on the government's theory that the proceeds of the smuggling were sent to the FTO.[27] That single transaction served as the basis for the application of § 3A1.4.[28] As *Booker* had yet to be decided, the court of appeals was not troubled by the numerous enhancements the district court had applied to Hammoud's sentence.[29]

With § 2339B's status as a predicate felony for "federal crime of terrorism" purposes per § 3A1.4, once the Fourth Circuit upheld the district court's finding that Hammoud had attempted to coerce or intimidate a government through his support to Hizballah, it upheld the enhancement's application as well.[30] The Fourth Circuit affirmed the convictions and 155-year prison sentence even though the original Guidelines sentence, based on facts found by the jury, would have been fifty-seven months.[31] This remarkably long sentence was overturned by the Supreme Court in the wake of *Booker*, prompting the Fourth Circuit to remand the case to the district court for resentencing, without disturbing Hammoud's convictions and Guidelines level calculation.[32] After being re-sentenced by the district court to thirty years in prison, Hammoud's second appeal was again rejected by the Fourth Circuit.[33] Specifically, the court of appeals noted that applying the enhancement, with its criminal history category of VI—even when dealing with a first-time offender—was reasonable because Congress had made findings justifying such a harsh classification on the basis of a terrorist's supposedly undeterrable nature.[34] In light of Hammoud's allegedly long-standing links with Hizballah, the court reasoned that the application of § 3A1.4 rests on the assumption that recidivism in terrorists is more likely than in cases of ordinary criminals.[35]

Here, we must bear in mind that the conduct Hammoud was accused of was entirely nonviolent in nature. He was not linked to any act of violence, not to mention plots to blow up government buildings, hostage situations, or murders and kidnapping aboard hijacked airplanes. There is also the issue of the proof the government produced in support of the charges. Hammoud's conviction on one count of substantive material support and one count of conspiracy to provide material support to an FTO were based on the testimony of a co-defendant who had reached a deal with the government. In his dissent to the original Court of Appeals opinion upholding the convictions and 155-year sentencing, Fourth Circuit Judge Roger Gregory commented on the issue of material support:

> It is further worth noting that not only did the government fail to connect Hammoud's purported $3,500 donation to [alleged Hizballah figure] Sheik Abbas Harake to any illegal purpose, or concededly criminal act, but the government could barely connect the funds to Harake *to any degree whatsoever.* The government admits that the only source of information indicating that Hammoud was sending money to Hizballah was Said Harb. Harb was described throughout the trial as untrustworthy, manipulative, a liar and an exaggerator. With reference to the alleged $3,500 in "material support" provided to Hizballah, Harb testified that he had once carried money to Harake for Hammoud. He testified that the money he carried was in an envelope which Hammoud said had two checks totaling $3,500. Harb testified that he spoke with Harake by telephone while in Lebanon, but never met with him and did not deliver money to him. Instead, Harb stated he "g[a]ve [the envelope] to my mom and, you know, told her to make sure it gets to [Hammoud's] mom." Ostensibly, under the government's theory, Hammoud's mother gave the money to Harake, although I have found no testimony in the record completing this chain that allegedly stretched from Hammoud to Harake. Indeed, Harb never explained how the money got to Harake, nor did he state that he even spoke with Hammoud's mother to make sure she received the envelope, let alone spoke to Harake to assure that he received the envelope from Hammoud's mother. Despite these facts, the $3,500 transfer was the sole transaction offered by the government in support of Count 78 against Hammoud.[36]

Hammoud's case was the first post-9/11 terrorism conviction under the material support ban, which may partially explain the harshness of the second sentence.[37] A disputed $3,500 donation transformed a trial on ordinary—even if high in volume—fraud charges to a symbolic strike against terrorism in the name of national security less than a year after the traumatic attacks of September 11, 2001. The material support ban, when coupled with § 3A1.4, produced a shockingly high sentence for a financial donation that would have been legal before 1996. Though the 155-year term was later reduced to 30, Hammoud's sentence served as a statement that the government considers terrorist offenders different and worthy of harsher punishment.

Whatever one's position on *Hammoud*, however, at least it falls under § 2339B's "money-is-fungible" rhetoric, which Congress expressly adopted. In the government's view, the $3,500 Hammoud was convicted of sending to a Hizballah figure could free up money to use for violence. Such logic justifies the imposition of a sentencing enhancement, which uses the prospect of a heightened criminal penalty to deter surreptitious terrorism financing. Much like a § 2339B charge itself, the logic of § 3A1.4's application based on a material support conviction unravels when there is no actual link to violent activity.

Regarding the second example, recall again the Holy Land Foundation (HLF) prosecution, with its shaky material support charges and controversial methods of proof (see Chapters 2 and 3). The convictions generated enhanced sentences when § 3A1.4 was ruled applicable; fifteen years for two defendants, twenty years for one defendant, and sixty-five years for the remaining two, all of which were upheld on appeal by the Fifth Circuit.[38] With the material support ban listed as an offense for "federal crime of terrorism" purposes, the defendants challenged § 3A1.4's application on the basis that their conduct was "calculated to influence or affect the conduct of government by intimidation or coercion."[39] In affirming the sentences, the Fifth Circuit supported the district court's conclusion "that the evidence established that HLF's purpose was to support Hamas as a fundraising arm, and that videotapes, wiretaps, and seized documents interlinked the defendants, HLF, and Hamas, and demonstrated the defendants' support of Hamas's mission of terrorism."[40]

By way of recapitulation, note that the defendants were convicted of materially supporting an FTO, not because charitable donations freed up money for weapons but through their support of religious charities allegedly affiliated with Hamas, even though they had a separate financing structure and might not have been financially linked at all. The government did not dispute that the support was legitimate charity in a conflict-rife region of the world, but argued that it enhanced Hamas's reputation in the West Bank and Gaza Strip, given the link it tried to draw between the committees and the FTO.[41] Recall also that the government relied in significant part on anonymous foreign intelligence agents testifying as experts to draw these conclusions. Incidentally, the committees were never designated as part of, or a front for, the FTO Hamas, despite those allegations first being made in 2004, several years before the final verdict.[42]

After the verdicts, the district court ruled that the HLF defendants were trying "to influence or affect the conduct of government by intimidation or coercion," based on their own personal political beliefs and statements in support of an FTO, and found § 3A1.4 applicable. The court made this ruling under the lower preponderance of the evidence standard. Critically, this stands in marked contrast with the requirements for conviction under § 2339B: that the government prove beyond a reasonable doubt—a much higher evidentiary standard—that the defendants know that what they are providing is material support and that they know the support is for a banned FTO. Many litigants in a large number of material support prosecutions have attempted—without much success—to argue that under the statute, the government must prove that a defendant had the specific intent to further the illegal goals of the FTO.[43] The application of § 3A1.4 in the HLF prosecution turns this argument entirely on its head; the government can obtain a conviction under the lesser knowledge mens rea, but for sentencing purposes a court can find the specific intent to pressure a government by intimidation or coercion—that is, the illegal goals of the FTO—under the significantly lower preponderance of the evidence standard.

After § 3A1.4 was applied, the sentences in HLF ranged from fifteen to sixty-five years in prison, although the rationale seems particularly punitive; it seemed as though the defendants were given harsh sentences for engaging in legitimate charity and having unpopular political beliefs. Other than retributive punishment, it was not clear what purpose the application of the enhancement served. There was no real issue of the sentence serving as deterrence, since the HLF had tried to coordinate with an unresponsive government to avoid funding terrorist groups upon § 2339B's passage in 1996.[44] The Fifth Circuit recognized that the bulk of the allegations at trial concerned activity that occurred before Hamas's designation in 1997, so the passage of the law did have a clear deterrent effect.[45] Further, the government shut down the HLF shortly after 9/11, and both the corporate entity and individual defendants ceased all fundraising activity for a period of at least two years before the initial indictment was handed down.[46]

With the terrorism enhancement's applicability on deterrence grounds essentially mooted, what is left is the retributive-inspired view that the type of support the HLF defendants provided demands sentences in excess of those meted out for many ordinary violent crimes, because of the connection to terrorism.[47] This is another way of saying that the harsh sentences in this case only make sense if we view the defendants' conduct—rooted as it was in their religious obligation—as causing so much harm that it justified enhanced punishment. Tying the conduct to the sentence, the material support at issue sounded in the nebulous concept of enhancing an FTO's legitimacy, and construing the level of harm as so great as to warrant a heavy sentence requires much more of an explanation than the record provides. Unless one takes the view that anyone convicted of a material support crime is an inveterate terrorist who must be punished severely, what is the purpose of sentencing the HLF defendants to up to sixty-five years in prison, given the undisputed fact that their activities were in no way linked to violence?

Although not discussed here, there are other problems with § 3A1.4's application that may or may not be resolved as part of the Supreme Court's *Booker*-inspired review of sentencing practices for their fidelity to the Sixth Amendment's requirements.[48] In addition to any legal issues is the statement the government and courts are making on the irredeemable nature of convicted terrorist defendants by deploying the enhancement. In and of itself, § 3A1.4 tells us that terrorism is different and worthy of greater punishment, reflecting society's heightened concern about terrorists operating in its midst. In that vein, applying the enhancement includes an expressive component; it allows a court to state its condemnation of terrorism in a general sense. While this is a potentially hazardous function, in that the application of § 3A1.4 can dramatically increase a sentence with limited oversight, at least the district courts doing the sentencing have the benefit of a full hearing of all the relevant facts before making any decisions. With respect to the courts of appeals, however, there is the recent phenomenon of their overturning the sentence below as unreasonably lenient, almost as a kind of commentary on the heightened blameworthiness of the terrorist offender.[49] This is turn raises the real question of whether the courts of appeals, in reviewing sentences in high-profile terrorism prosecutions, faithfully adhere to the deferential standards of *Booker* and its progeny.

UNITED STATES V. ABU ALI

The first example of this phenomenon is that of Ahmed Omar Abu Ali, an American student at a university in Saudi Arabia who was arrested in the wake of a terrorist bombing in Riyadh on suspicion of belonging to a local al-Qaeda cell, and whose case was discussed earlier in Chapter 3.[50] After the district court upheld the voluntariness of the confession Abu Ali gave to the Saudi authorities, he was convicted by a jury of multiple terrorist crimes, which included providing material support to an FTO, conspiracy to commit air piracy, and conspiracy to assassinate the President of the United States.[51] His Guidelines calculation called for life in prison, but the district court decided on a thirty-year prison sentence, followed by thirty years of supervised release.[52] The district court justified its downward variance on the basis of a careful consideration of statutorily mandated factors, such as Abu Ali's own personal characteristics and history, the need for just punishment, adequate deterrence, protection of the public, and rehabilitation.[53] To avoid the possibility of a disparate sentence, the district court engaged in a comparison between Abu Ali and other individuals sentenced for serious terrorist crimes. It reasoned that his case was closer to that of John Walker Lindh, the "American Taliban" who received a twenty-year sentence for fighting with the group in Afghanistan, than those of Timothy McVeigh and Terry Nichols, who received the death penalty and life in prison, respectively, for killing 168 people in the 1995 bombing of the Oklahoma City federal building.[54]

Over Judge Diana Gribbon Motz's dissent, which took the position that the majority failed to respect the *Booker* line of cases regarding appellate review of a sentence and improperly overrode the district court's specific findings,[55] the Fourth Circuit rejected the sentence as unreasonable and remanded for resentencing, offering the strong suggestion that a life sentence was warranted.[56] The majority disagreed with the district court's likening of Abu Ali's sentence to that of Lindh in contrast to those of McVeigh and Nichols, as it deemed that comparison "the driving force behind [the district court's] ultimate [sentencing] determination."[57] The district court took the hint and gave Abu Ali a life term at resentencing. The second time around, the district court expressed its concern for public safety were Abu Ali to be released after thirty years—based on his failure to express any remorse for his crimes—as justification for the heightened punishment. Not surprisingly, the newer, harsher sentence survived appellate review and was deemed reasonable.[58]

The initial Fourth Circuit majority minimized the importance of the fact that Abu Ali's convictions were for crimes still in the highly inchoate planning stages, a factor relied upon by the district court originally to justify its variance from the Guidelines.[59] Judge Motz took the opposite view—namely, that lack of actual harm was a valid factor to consider in assessing the reasonableness of a sentence. This was in line with her critique that "[t]he majority's approach in this case reflects a fundamental misunderstanding of the shift in sentencing jurisprudence that has occurred since the Supreme Court issued its landmark decision in *Booker*."[60] Rejecting all attempts to humanize Abu Ali or even consider the economic benefits to the public of the thirty-year sentence, the Fourth Circuit did not hide its outrage over the intractable threat that all terrorist defendants—as personified by Abu Ali—represented.[61] It noted:

> We are similarly unmoved by the district court's (and dissent's) references to letters describing Abu Ali's "general decent reputation as a young man" and his overall "good character." What person of "decent reputation" seeks to assassinate leaders of countries? What person of "good character" aims to destroy thousands of fellow human beings who are innocent of any transgressions against him? This is not good character as we understand it, and to allow letters of this sort to provide the basis for such a substantial variance would be to deprive "good character" of all its content.[62]

Operating according to such logic, it was hardly a surprise that the majority dismissed the potential of a thirty-year sentence's to rehabilitate a youthful Abu Ali and was not deterred by the fact that a life term meant that the public would pay for his medical care in advanced age.[63]

UNITED STATES V. LYNNE STEWART

This type of dispute over the proper nature of appellate review in a terrorism case is not limited to *Abu Ali*. In *Stewart*, while the Second Circuit panel unanimously agreed to remand the issue of sentencing for the district court to consider more fully the matter of what it deemed Lynne Stewart's perjury,[64] two judges issued separate opinions to clarify their positions.[65] Judge John M. Walker, Jr. wrote that the district court should have imposed a sentence far closer to the Guidelines recommendation of 360 months, which reflected the application of § 3A1.4, than the 28 months initially levied.[66] In his concurrence, Judge Guido Calabresi specially commended the district court for its careful handling of the prosecution and stressed the high level of deference due its role as a sentencing court.[67] Judge Walker specifically invoked the terrorism enhancement as evidence of Congress's view that terrorist and material support crimes are qualitatively different and call out for more severe sentencing.[68] Judge Calabresi disagreed and argued that because those crimes cover such a wide swath of activity, appellate courts must respect the broad discretion that district courts have in sentencing defendants in terrorism prosecutions.[69]

Judges Walker and Calabresi also differed regarding the role that actual harm plays in determining a sentence, reprising the dispute between the majority opinion and Judge Motz's dissent in *Abu Ali*. Judge Walker took the position that a lack of harm should not serve as a basis for a downward deviation when a defendant has been convicted of material support conspiracy, which does not require a direct relation to any violence, and cited the *Abu Ali* majority's reasoning in support.[70] Judge Calabresi remarked on the role actual harm has played in the sentencing process historically, and cited recent judicial opinions in which the court ordered a downward variance in terrorism cases. He also pointed out that Congress had implicitly recognized the role harm played in material support cases by raising the penalty for a conviction to life in prison when the support resulted directly in death.[71] The disagreement between the two judges seemed to come down to the perceived essence of the terrorist crime. Judge Calabresi intimated that he did not fully agree with Judge Walker's position that terrorism, as an extraordinary type of crime, fundamentally affects the sentencing process.[72] Describing Stewart's case as involving conduct that fell into the "heartland"[73] of terrorism crimes, Judge Walker stressed again that a downward variance was not warranted.[74]

Judge Walker's opinion scarcely concealed his outrage at Stewart's conduct. But he did not elaborate on his contention that Stewart's crimes fell into the "heartland" of material support for terrorism. For example, to the extent possible, "heartland" material support might be described as providing money to carry out murder abroad, in accordance with Stewart's conviction under 18 U.S.C. § 2339A. As a longtime criminal defense lawyer, she was convicted, however, of facilitating her client's—an imprisoned foreign terrorist leader—statement of opposition to his militant organization's ceasefire with the Egyptian government, in violation of federal prison authorities' restrictions on his communicating publicly.[75] The government recognized that no one was harmed as a result of Stewart's actions.[76] Without delving further into the merits of the case,[77] we can recognize the potential danger in such activity. But to assume outright that it falls into a "heartland" of terrorist support crime, without more,[78] reflects a type of visceral outrage at all conduct linked to terrorists that has the potential to affect negatively the individualized and careful process that is criminal sentencing. In other words, we might ask how Stewart's crimes constitute "heartland" terrorist support when there has been no case like hers before or since. Given the lack of authority on what constitutes a "heartland" material support crime in *Stewart*, Judge Walker's opinion does not provide a well-reasoned basis to impose harsher penalties.

THE JOSE PADILLA PROSECUTION

Speculating about the nature of terrorist crimes brings us back to the supposedly irredeemable nature of a terrorist, a phenomenon well represented by the Eleventh Circuit's decision overturning as substantively unreasonable Jose Padilla's sentence on material support charges.[79] As discussed previously in Chapter 4, the jury ultimately convicted him on criminal charges entirely unrelated to the "dirty bomb" allegations.[80] Although the district court found § 3A1.4 applicable, which put Padilla's Guidelines range at 360 months to life in the criminal history VI category, it first reduced his sentencing exposure after considering the § 3553(a) factors, and then took off another forty-two months, in recognition of the harsh and lengthy nature of his confinement in military detention.[81] Ultimately, he received a sentence of 208 months in prison.[82]

The Eleventh Circuit overturned the sentence as too lenient because it did not adequately consider Padilla's extensive criminal history as a youth in Chicago.[83] The court of appeals highlighted Padilla's career offender status, which featured seventeen prior arrests, including one for murder, as a reason for rejecting his sentence. It also remarked on the continuing nature of the threat he represented:

> "[T]errorists[,] [even those] with no prior criminal behavior[,] are unique among criminals in the likelihood of recidivism, the difficulty of rehabilitation, and the need for incapacitation." Padilla poses a heightened risk of future dangerousness due to his al-Qaeda training. He is far more sophisticated than an individual convicted of an ordinary street crime.[84]

The Eleventh Circuit drew further inspiration from *Abu Ali* to justify the reversal of Padilla's sentence on two grounds.[85] First, the court of appeals rejected the district court's comparison of Padilla's sentence to those of other terrorist defendants not similarly situated. In the Eleventh Circuit's words, they, unlike Padilla, "either [were] convicted of less serious offenses, lacked extensive criminal histories, or had pleaded guilty."[86] The court likened Padilla's case more to those of 9/11 co-conspirator Zacarias Moussaoui and Oklahoma City bomb plotter Terry Nichols and seemed to recommend that the district court consider a life sentence upon remand, although that message was not entirely clear from the opinion.[87] Second, the court of appeals more or less rejected out of hand as immaterial the district court's lowering the sentence in reliance on both the lack of actual harm caused by Padilla and the fact that his criminal conduct did not target the United States.[88] Finally, the Eleventh Circuit majority opinion concluded by noting that the district court's downward variance based on the length and nature of Padilla's pretrial confinement was excessive.[89] In the district court's knocking 152 months off of Padilla's Guideline sentence calculation, the court of appeals found improper the crediting of Padilla's time already served at a rate of three and one-half times his actual time detained.[90]

As with the two other cases discussed above, the majority opinion provoked a strong dissent, in this instance by Judge Rosemary Barkett.[91] She characterized the majority's position on the district court's consideration of Padilla's criminal history and pretrial confinement in crafting a sentence as a violation of *Booker* and its progeny. In particular, she highlighted *Gall*'s admonition that "'[t]he fact that the appellate court might reasonably have concluded that a different sentence was appropriate is insufficient to justify reversal of the district court.'"[92] Similarly, she argued that the district court was correct in relying on the lack of actual harm caused by Padilla and the fact that he did not target the United States to calculate his sentence.[93] Under current Supreme Court and Eleventh Circuit precedent, a district court's sentencing discretion deserves "due deference," a point she believed the majority had ignored.[94] Judge Barkett also characterized the majority's opinion as a simple disagreement with the district court regarding which terrorist defendants were similarly situated for sentencing purposes. In her view, the district court properly adhered to 18 U.S.C. § 3553(a) in conducting its analysis.[95]

Over and above her general criticism that the Eleventh Circuit majority failed to afford proper deference to the district court's sentencing discretion stood Judge Barkett's more specific criticism of the majority's logic regarding Padilla's future dangerousness.[96] In her view, the majority's opinion rejected not only the idea that Padilla's likelihood of recidivism might decrease with age but also that such a presumption must necessarily pertain in the case of every terrorist defendant.[97] She faulted the majority for coming to this conclusion without citing any evidence and in spite of the government's not challenging the district court's finding on Padilla's threat of recidivism.[98] The lack of evidence was particularly telling. For a start, the majority justified its position by likening terrorists to sex offenders in their potential to recidivate.[99] This comparison was inapt, however, as the case cited by the majority in support of this position referenced the multiplicity of judicial opinions and statistical studies that demonstrated the likelihood of recidivism for sex offenders.[100] In contrast, the terrorism case cited by the majority—*United States v. Meskini*, a Second Circuit opinion—contained no such evidence to support its conclusion that terrorist defendants constituted a greater threat to recidivate.[101] Further, Judge Barkett wrote that even *Meskini*, with its conclusory language, made sure to recognize the district court's sentencing discretion when applying the § 3553(a) factors, which allow for individualized determinations of a terrorist defendant's future dangerousness, something the Eleventh Circuit majority disregarded.[102] In conclusion, Judge Barkett rounded off her opinion by noting that the "old adage that 'hard facts make bad law' is clearly evident here."[103] In any event, on re-sentencing, the district court added four years to Padilla's original sentence, resulting in a term of twenty-one years.[104]

It seems clear that what the above examples speak to is a sense that terrorism is different, exceptional, and worthy of greater punishment. The fact that there exists a congressionally mandated terrorism enhancement only serves to bolster this view. But the Supreme Court has been clear in its rulings post-*Booker* than a district court's sentencing decision is to be accorded a high degree of deference. Neither Congress nor the courts (nor, for that matter, the Sentencing Commission) have authorized an exception to the rule on sentencing discretion in terrorism cases.[105] A review of *Meskini*'s language—"even terrorists with no prior criminal behavior are unique among criminals in the likelihood of recidivism, the difficulty of rehabilitation, and the need for incapacitation"—could be accurate (or not), but surely now, in the more than thirteen years following the September 11, 2001, attacks, we might expect the government to produce some empirical evidence in support of this statement.[106] *Meskini* leaves us with more questions than answers as well. Is it true in all situations? Or does its validity depend on the cause of a terrorist, that is, someone willing to use violence for political purposes? Posited differently, does this statement apply different standards, depending on the popularity of a given cause? Does it allow courts to distinguish between terrorism defendants based on the likelihood that they will engage in violent acts?[107] There is also the issue of *Meskini's* relationship to the purpose of criminal sentencing. From a utilitarian perspective, can we not imagine a defendant charged with terrorist crimes changing his ways without the imposition of a heavy sentence? And from a retributive angle, how can we properly evaluate a sentence for the type of harm caused, especially where terrorism prosecutions spring from a preventive model and often touch on inchoate activity or broadly defined material support? The decisions above brush past these questions, which must seem immaterial, to offer a resounding answer on the inveterate obduracy of the terrorist convict, whose threat to society never wanes. So normal review of the sentencing function must make way for terrorist exceptionalism once again.

Ironically, the trend toward harsh punishment for terrorism defendants stands in contrast to the growing realization at the federal level that long prison sentences, particularly for low-level drug crimes, should be eliminated. In 2013, Attorney General Holder announced a "Smart on Crime" initiative, which is designed to explore alternatives to incarceration as a sentencing strategy for individuals convicted of crimes. The initiative is motivated in part by "the shameful racial and ethnic disparities that too often plague the criminal justice process."[108] In 2014, the Sentencing Commision voted first to reduce the penalties for most drug-trafficking crimes, and then opted to make the application of those lesser sanctions retroactive.[109] Terrorism defendants, even when convicted of lower-level crimes, seem to be exempt from this trend, given the fear and suspicion the charges against them can provoke.

POSTSCRIPT: CONFINEMENT—EVEN WHEN IMPRISONED, THE TERRORIST PRISONER IS EXCEPTIONAL

At this point, it should come as no surprise that a criminal defendant convicted and sentenced under the terrorism rubric can often end up separated and categorized differently than other prisoners. The separate status includes restrictions on the prisoner's ability to communicate with the outside world, placement in solitary confinement, denial of access to a whole host of privileges and materials, and even assignment to one specific prison, regardless of security status or proximity to family members. It is important to note that the type of classification discussed here exists apart from the normal status a prisoner is assigned after sentencing, such as minimum, medium, or maximum security. There are two main classifications, both of which impact a terrorism defendant's experience in different ways from that of an ordinary prisoner. The first involves the imposition of Special Administrative Measures (SAMs) that the federal Bureau of Prisons (BOP) can employ in situations implicating national security and/or particularly dangerous prisoners. The second concerns the assignment of terrorism prisoners to a specific prison within the prison system known as the Communications Management Unit (CMU).

SAMs can be applied in two different situations.[110] The first involves restrictions imposed "to prevent disclosure of classified information that would pose a threat to the national security if the inmate disclosed such information."[111] The conditions "include, but are not limited to, placing an inmate in administrative detention and restricting social visits, mail privileges, phone calls, access to other inmates and to the media."[112] Under the direction of the Attorney General, the BOP Director sets the SAMs term, although it cannot exceed one year.[113] However, the Director is authorized to extend the SAMs indefinitely in up to one-year increments, provided "the Attorney General receives certification from the intelligence community that there is a danger that the inmate will disclose classified information and that the unauthorized disclosure would pose a threat to the national security."[114] The second involves SAMs "that are reasonably necessary to protect persons against the risk of death or serious bodily injury."[115] Specifically, this type of SAM "may be implemented when there is a substantial risk that an inmate's communications or contacts with persons could result in death or serious bodily injury to persons, or substantial damage to property that would entail the risk of death or serious bodily injury to persons."[116] As with the first situation, this type of SAM cannot be initially imposed for more than a year.[117] The Director can extend the SAMs period in increments not exceeding one year if the Attorney General attests to the prisoner's ongoing threat to cause serious injury or death.[118]

In the non-terrorism context, SAM-type restrictions on communications and solitary confinement go hand-in-hand, with the paradigmatic case being that of the gang leader who continues to run his criminal organization's affairs from prison. Perhaps the most notorious example is that of Luis Felipe, the head of the Latin Kings street gang, who ordered the commission of several gang-related killings while he was incarcerated in New York State prison. After being convicted of federal RICO charges related to the killings, he was placed under highly restrictive conditions and sent to the BOP's most secure supermax prison in Colorado, where inmates are confined to their cells for twenty-three hours a day, as part of his highly unusual life sentence to be served in solitary confinement. In Felipe's situation, the courts upheld the denial of access to the outside world (except to communications with his lawyer) to deal with a situation of ongoing extreme violence, which did not stop even after incarceration in state prison.[119] Putting aside the very legitimate questions about the morality, legality, and effectiveness of holding someone in long-term solitary confinement,[120] Felipe's situation represented a kind of foundational case for the application of SAMs in high-profile prosecutions.

As of 2011, there were fewer than fifty prisoners subject to SAMs in BOP custody, many of whom were convicted in terrorism cases.[121] For example, notorious prisoners like Ramzi Ahmed Yousef, convicted for his role in setting off a bomb at the World Trade Center in 1993 and a later plot to blow up commercial aircraft while in flight, were subject to SAMs and often could not find relief from their harsh strictures.[122] Lynne Stewart's prosecution stemmed from the violation of SAMs imposed on her client, "Blind Sheik" Omar Abdel Rahman, the leader of the Egyptian FTO, al-Gama'a al-Islamiyya.[123] The imposition of SAMs has been criticized by noted defense lawyer Joshua Dratel as "reflexively" applied in national security cases in the Southern District of New York, the main locus of the government's most prominent terrorism prosecutions.[124] While certainly a valid criticism, as a review of reported case law does not provide many instances of relief from SAMs, courts have begun to scrutinize them somewhat more closely, even when applied to prisoners convicted of deadly attacks.

For example, in 2012, although the Tenth Circuit had dismissed convicted Nairobi Embassy bomber Mohamed al-'Owhali's challenge to the SAMs imposed on him, it questioned the penological goals advanced by some of the restrictions, such as denying him the right to receive former President Jimmy Carter's book, PALESTINE: PEACE NOT APARTHEID.[125] Although the court remarked that "[w]e cannot imagine how this book could have raised safety concerns or facilitated terrorist activity," it nonetheless denied al-'Owhali's challenge as improperly pled.[126] More recently, in 2014, the federal district court in Colorado with jurisdiction over the BOP's supermax prison found fault with several of the SAMs imposed on convicted Dar es Salaam Embassy bomber Khalfan Khamis Mohammed. Specifically, the court ruled that the denial of contact with his brother, the authorities' failure to provide a response to his request to add thirty-two individuals to his contact list, and the rejection of his request to route his mail through his attorney after review by the FBI (which coordinated with the BOP in applying the SAMs) were arbitrary and capricious. Rather than order the relief Mohammed requested, however, the court remanded the matter to the FBI for the opportunity to reevaluate the requests.[127]

Despite the ruling in *Mohammed*, and as with many of the national security measures discussed in this volume, SAMs have consequences that go beyond their stated aim of stopping terrorism. Post-9/11, the government began using the restrictions more frequently in the pretrial context.[128] Discussing the case of Syed Fahad Hashmi, scholars Laura Rovner and Jeanne Theoharis detail how Hashmi, a Muslim American citizen and outspoken student activist, was charged with various material support crimes stemming from what appeared to be a tangential connection to an al-Qaeda operative. Specifically, the allegations of material support arose from his allowing an acquaintance to stay in his apartment while carrying suitcases filled with socks and rain gear destined for al-Qaeda. Although initially detained in solitary confinement, Hashmi was allowed to have visitors, a radio, and access to newspapers and magazines, and his lawyer was permitted to report on their conversations to third parties. After five months, Hashmi was moved to a more restrictive unit where he was held in complete isolation, monitored round the clock, and initially allowed contact with only his lawyer. While later his parents and brother were added to his list of permitted visitors, Hashmi spent the remaining two and a half years of pretrial detention under these strictures, up until his guilty plea to one material support charge. And in any case, his limited visitors could not reveal the contents of their conversations with him outside prison.[129] Rovner and Theoharis raise the question of why SAMs were imposed in Hashmi's case, given his lack of criminal record and seeming inability to effect terrorism outside of prison (he had no criminal record and was never linked or charged with an act of violence) and posit that the government was simply trying to get Hashmi to either cooperate or plead guilty under the weight of the oppressive pretrial conditions.[130] Needless to say, nothing in the regulations governing the imposition of SAMs authorizes their use for coercive purposes. Finally, there is the troubling effect of SAMs on the attorney-client privilege, specifically with respect to the monitoring of inmate mail, making the defense of individuals charged with terrorism that much harder.[131] The example of accused Boston Marathon Bomber Dzhokhar Tsarnaev is only the latest example of the government applying pretrial SAMs, much to the chagrin of his defense attorneys, who live in fear of violating the restrictions while trying to mount a mitigation defense to charges that carry the death penalty.[132]

Extensive monitoring and control under SAMs is clearly not an option to be used in very many cases, as it would be highly impractical to deploy individualized restrictions on even a small percentage of the hundreds of thousands of prisoners in BOP custody. The BOP has therefore devised another method for maximizing control over prisoners convicted of terrorism offenses. Over the last several years, it has established and maintained a special unit mainly for terrorism-convicted prisoners—thereby reinforcing their exceptional status—while employing strategies to immunize the unit from legal challenge. In 2006, the Department of Justice's Inspector General found fault with the BOP for allowing three of the imprisoned

1993 World Trade Center bombers to send around ninety letters to suspected terrorists abroad, apparently due to inadequate staff to monitor and translate the correspondence in question.[133] In response, the BOP responded by creating a special facility called the Communications Management Unit (CMU).[134] At the outset, it should be noted that the need for a special unit is questionable in and of itself. As much of this book shows, the number of actual dangerous terrorism convicts is quite small. The BOP tends to house terrorist prisoners with convictions for violent activity in its supermax facility in Colorado. Many of those sent to the CMU tend to have been classified in a low-security status by the BOP, and have been convicted of inchoate offenses such as material support or ensnared in a sting operation.[135]

The CMU's stated purpose is "to house inmates who, due to their current offense of conviction, offense conduct, or other verified information, require increased monitoring of communication between inmates and persons in the community in order to protect the safety, security, and orderly operation of Bureau facilities, and protect the public."[136] The BOP describes a CMU as "a self-contained general population housing unit where inmates reside, eat, and participate in all educational, recreational, religious, visiting, unit management, and work programming...."[137] The central aspect of a CMU is its thorough monitoring of an inmate's communications with the outside world, whether through written correspondence or telephone conversation, as well as enhanced monitoring of inmate visitation.[138] For CMU inmates, all written mail must be reviewed and approved by prison staff before it is either sent out or received. [139] An inmate is only entitled to one three-minute phone call per month, and telephonic communications are live-monitored and recorded by staff.[140] Crucially for individuals of foreign background, the inmate and the call recipient must converse solely in English, unless the call is subjected to simultaneous translation monitoring, which must be arranged in advance.[141] If either the inmate or the call recipient breaks the English-only rule, the call is to be terminated immediately, with the risk that further punishment might ensue; "inmates may be subject to disciplinary action, and the [call recipient] may be removed from the inmate's approved telephone list."

Visitation with CMU inmates is noncontact, with sessions taking place in secure partitioned rooms and communication occurring through telephone voice contact.[142] As with telephone conversations, visits are live-monitored by staff and subject to recording; the English-only rule applies in visitations as well.[143] Even communication between inmates and "religious service providers from the community" is monitored according to rules that greatly resemble those governing written communications, telephone communications, and visitation—depending on how the inmate corresponds with the religious figure.[144] By way of comparison between the CMU and regular BOP custody, consider that a normal federal inmate is allowed many more hours of visitation, can mingle with prisoners from other units, can enjoy contact visits, and is not monitored in cell block conversations. Further, the communications of federal inmates in general are subject only to sporadic monitoring, as opposed to the complete and total review of all inmate communications in the CMU.[145]

There are currently two CMUs—one in Terre Haute, Indiana, the other in Marion, Illinois.[146] Both of these locations are relatively near each other in the Midwest, leaving CMU inmates far removed from family if they happen to hail from different parts of the country.* As opposed to the general trend of courts acceding to the government's terrorist exceptionalism, perhaps because the individuals held in CMUs are already convicted and sentenced, courts have been less reluctant to examine the BOP's administration of the units with a more critical eye. John Walker Lindh, who was sentenced to twenty years in prison after pleading guilty to charges related to his fighting with the Taliban in Afghanistan, successfully sued the BOP for its denial of group prayer rights to Muslim inmates held in the CMU.[147] The court ruled that the practice violated the Religious Freedom Restoration Act and ordered the BOP to allow group prayer, whose denial the court found inexplicable, especially in light of the fact that "playing basketball, watching television and movies, playing cards, discussing current events, and watching religious videos in Arabic" were all permitted.[148]

More significantly, how someone actually is assigned to a CMU remains a bit of a mystery. As a result of a lawsuit brought by the Center for Constitutional Rights (CCR) on behalf of, among others, Jose Padilla's co-defendant Kifah Jayyousi and FBI sting target Yassin Aref, it emerged that the BOP has yet to issue a written document regarding its policy on CMU designation.[149] It was only in 2009, several years after the CMU was established, that the BOP finally produced a document laying out the criteria—not the policy—for designation.[150] The idea that BOP inmates were subjected to such a harsh fate for several years with no written frame of reference is telling. And even when the criteria for designation were reduced to

---

* This dynamic played out in the case of my former client, Hatem Fariz. After pleading guilty to one count of providing nonviolent services to an terrorist organization, he was sentenced to thirty-seven months in prison in July 2006, with the court agreeing to request that the BOP allow him to serve his time at the federal prison complex in Coleman, Florida, around seventy-five miles from his home in Tampa. Duly classified as a minimum security prisoner, he began serving his sentence in Coleman, only to be transferred after a few months to the CMU in Terre Haute without explanation. Aside from the obvious difficulties of moving him some one thousand miles from his wife and children to a restrictive and isolated unit, the CMU created a particularly insurmountable obstacle toward communication with his mother, who speaks almost no English. When I inquired with a friend then working as an attorney with the BOP about his status and the reason for the transfer, she expressed surprise and promised to look into the matter, as she was not previously aware of the existence of the CMU. I never got a response to my query.

writing, they were highly generalized and not of much use.[151] Further, the lawsuit revealed that inmates were being assigned to the CMU, with its highly restrictive environment, on the basis of unwritten understandings, which could differ within the BOP from office to office. Prisoners are only told the reasons for being sent to the CMU after their transfer, and even then the explanation is—in CCR's words— "frequently vague, incomplete, inaccurate, and/or completely false," so they have no meaningful method for challenging their stay in the unit.[152] Needless to say, there is no record of an inmate successfully petitioning to leave the CMU under the BOP's administrative appeal procedures.[153]

Unfortunately, this lack of standards and cavalier attitude characterize the BOP's approach to individuals it can single out as terrorists. Randall Todd Royer, a federal inmate who had been sentenced to twenty years in prison on terrorism charges, challenged the BOP's policy instituted in 2006 for designating terrorism inmates by filing a federal lawsuit. Royer alleged that the BOP uses such designations to send a prisoner to administrative segregation, such as in the federal supermax prison or the CMU. The BOP responded to the lawsuit by denying it had a terrorist inmate policy, even after it had previously admitted that it had housed Royer in various segregated units, including the CMU, on the basis that he was linked to international terrorism. The court noted that it was "perplexed" that the BOP would take such a position in litigation.[154] Unfortunately, the BOP's perplexing behavior in the lawsuit continued. In January 2014, after it had missed several discovery deadlines, the court expressed its frustration with the BOP:

> Defendant's [BOP] sneering argument that plaintiff is not prejudiced by all this delay by defendant because he remains incarcerated is beyond the Court's comprehension. The whole point of this litigation is whether defendant can continue to single out plaintiff for special treatment as a terrorist during his continued period of incarceration. Did any supervising attorney ever read this nonsense that is being argued to this Court? I regret that I am away, sitting by designation on another court with a terrible backlog, or I would hold a hearing in open court to hold the government attorneys accountable for their misconduct here. Plaintiff's discovery efforts should not be further delayed, and requiring payment of attorney's fees will make clear that the Court totally and categorically rejects the practice of the government in this case.[155]

Maybe this is the point at which federal court indulgence with the government's approach to those implicated in terrorist crimes finally ends. Once an individual is well and truly incapacitated, he cannot be simply shut off from the outside world absent some sort of acceptable due process.

But there is one aspect of the CMU program that seems designed to survive judicial scrutiny—the makeup of its population. When the CMU's existence first came to light in late 2006/early 2007, the BOP's stated goal was to monitor comprehensively the communications of the then over two hundred terrorism inmates in the federal system. In keeping with the government's view of which demographic represents the terrorist threat, when the first batch of seventeen prisoners was sent to Terre Haute, only two were non-Muslim.[156] By 2014, the lawsuit in *Aref* revealed that 101 of the 178 prisoners who are or have been held in a CMU are Muslim, which represents around 57 percent of the total population of the unit.[157] Given that only 6 percent of federal prisoners are Muslim, this figure represents an overrepresentation of Muslim prisoners in the CMU by nearly 1,000 percent. The *Aref* court has already ruled that the ethnic makeup of the CMUs does not constitute a violation of the inmate's constitutional rights to equal protection, something it seemed the BOP worked to consciously avoid.[158] This has not stopped the BOP from introducing non-Muslim inmates dubbed "balancers," that is, individuals who "balance" out the CMU's heavily Muslim population and alleviate somewhat its discriminatory appearance.[159] According to CCR attorneys, to help "balance" out the CMU, the BOP has used the unit as a method to silence and punish "political prisoners and others who the Bureau of Prisons wants to silence—so jailhouse lawyers, prisoners who advocate for themselves and for other prisoners behind bars end up in these units as well."[160] For example, one of the co-plaintiffs in the *Aref* lawsuit is Daniel McGowan, whom the BOP described as a "member and leader in the Earth Liberation Front (ELF) and Animal Liberation Front (ALF), groups considered domestic terrorist organizations."[161] Another, Andy Stepanian, an animal rights activist, was comforted by guards within the CMU, who told him "[y]ou're nothing like these Muslims. You're just here for balance. You're going to go home soon."[162]

Confinement in the CMU has left inmates and their families devastated in its wake, as noted in several critical journalistic reports. While the BOP enjoys a high level of deference from courts regarding its decisions on prison management and inmate unit assignment, the CMU is noteworthy in its offhand characterization of the terrorist threat and the loose and haphazard criteria governing designation there. By way of comparison, while designation to the most severe facility in the BOP system—the federal supermax prison in Florence, Colorado—is, in many ways, a harsher fate, the decision to designate is governed by a much more transparent and clear procedure than that used for the CMU.[163] However, even though the judicial record so far reveals courts being more willing to subject the administration of the CMU to greater scrutiny, this development must be viewed through the operative lens of terrorist exceptionalism running throughout this chapter and entire volume.

What does the existence and current operation of the CMU signify? Courts have not criticized the harshness of the conditions or the rationale behind the existence of a restrictive and severely monitored unit, but rather its administration. If the BOP were to regularize the criteria governing the CMU by providing more uniform review and standards, it would most probably operate unhindered. While that may provide relief in a few cases—pending the outcome in the *Aref* litigation—it might actually signal the acceptance of this practice, much like the others post-conviction, from sentencing through to conditions of confinement. Although this would come as no surprise, it would nevertheless not limit the depth of the tragedy for the sentenced terrorism inmate.

CONCLUSION

SINCE 9/11, THE "war on terror" has come to symbolize broad, extensive, and opaque efforts—abroad and domestically—toward stopping further attacks. We have seen these efforts break new ground in the expansion of executive power, with the creation of an internationally condemned torture regime, extensive surveillance on a global scale, and the creation and maintenance of detention facilities at Guantanamo Bay, Cuba, and other sites around the world. Another area impacted by the wide swath of these policies has been in the realm of criminal terrorism prosecutions; the goal of this book has been to document this phenomenon.

The mentality that we are in a nebulous and continuous war on terror has produced a preventive approach for the criminal prosecution model, with a focus on stopping suspected plots before they come to fruition. Such a mindset encourages law enforcement to perceive threats broadly, even if those threats are vague and poorly defined. The ban on providing material support to FTOs offers the perfect statutory complement to these preventive efforts, as it allows for the criminalization of material support in the form of speech, in addition to material support that bolsters an FTO's legitimacy, far removed from any attacks or violent activity. The preventive focus has also engendered widespread spying programs targeting Muslim communities in their entirety, undergirded by a radicalization thesis that assumes the terrorist threat lurks within the heart of the practitioners of that misunderstood faith. According to such logic, deploying informants to provocatively stir up violent plots is an essential tactic, despite the fact that the targets of those informants exhibit no legally cognizable basis to otherwise justify an investigation. Exceptions to normal rules of evidence gathering are also created, as evidenced by the FBI's memorandum suspending the applicability of *Miranda* in the national security context. Viewing the inchoate threat of terrorism broadly has also led courts to admit evidence whose relevance and reliability is both shaky and tangential. This is true whether we consider lay or expert evidence and testimony. And once a defendant has been convicted, a special sentencing enhancement encourages lengthy prison terms, even for activity whose link to violence is disputed and tenuous, at best. Finally, the preventive mindset follows convicted defendants into the conditions of their confinement, where the authorities can severely restrict their communications with the outside world and general prison population, even when their disciplinary records do not warrant such treatment, on the theory that these convicted terrorists pose a special threat. That the methods and metrics for placing someone in such a status are murky and ever-shifting has not stopped the operation of special terrorism units so far.

As noted at the outset of this volume, rectifying this state of affairs could be a relatively straightforward task. But because of the nature of the term "terrorism" and all it evokes politically and societally, it is unlikely that the solutions proposed at the beginning of this book to the problems posed by terrorism prosecutions would be adopted without, at the very least, a more widespread understanding of the general impact of such prosecutions on our criminal justice system. Specifically, the existence of an unrecognized terrorism exception in criminal cases has no built-in barrier restricting that exception to prosecutions in which terrorism-related crimes are charged. While the author has engaged in an analysis assuredly at odds with many of the views of former Attorney General Mukasey, the latter certainly had it right when he noted, in the context of the speedy trial issue at the heart of the *Ghailani* prosecution, that once courts recognize an exception in a terrorism case, it is very hard to prevent its migration to ordinary criminal actions. Also, the jurisprudential record to date has not fully considered how the government's terrorism prosecutions augur for certain critical constitutional rights, particularly the right of association. Courts ruling on First Amendment challenges to § 2339B, for example, have tended to dismiss arguments invoking constitutional principles that protect association, which lie at the heart of American democracy, thereby undermining the rule of law.[1]

Implicit in the much more involved and extensive national debate surrounding the United States' reaction to the 9/11 attacks—whether regarding torture, Guantanamo, NSA surveillance, and the like—is the understanding that all of these measures are exceptional, extraordinary, and unique to a particular moment in time or specific threat. Even those who defend the application of these measures tailor their reasoning to the type of threat the country faces. The same cannot be said of the legal innovations generated by the criminal prosecution with its very real, yet not-fully-articulated terrorist exceptionalism. The cases and rulings discussed here have left a precedential trail that has begun to affect the normal course of criminal law enforcement in the United States, as well as having transformed terrorism into a legal trigger for departures from normal rules and constitutional protections. Juxtaposing the criminal terrorism prosecution with the exceptional tactics represented by Guantanamo, torture, etc., which have been much more prevalent in public discourse and media coverage, allows us to understand how those extraordinary methods have shaped law enforcement's counterterrorist response.

In particular, the common thread of terrorist exceptionalism running through the military and criminal justice models has influenced law enforcement practices, which continue to evolve and build on what has come before, in turn expanding the counterterrorism framework and preventive mindset. The Drug Enforcement Agency and Bureau of Alcohol, Tobacco, and Firearms have increased their use of sting operations whereby an informant, usually to mitigate his own criminal charges, entices armed targets to rob imaginary stash houses in the false hope that they contain large amounts of drugs and cash.[2] Even though courts have refused to dismiss these tactics as outrageous government conduct, they have raised questions about the wisdom and risk to the public of allowing armed men, many with a criminal background, to engage in such activity.[3] Concerns about police officers going undercover have resurfaced in the wake of popular demonstrations against police brutality, with a December 2014 incident involving an undercover officer pointing his gun at protestors in Oakland, California, being only the latest example.[4] And, as a result of extensive terrorism investigations, the use of undercover operatives and informants has expanded exponentially, now reaching entities like the Supreme Court Police Force and even government agencies like the Department of Agriculture, NASA, and the Small Business Administration.[5]

Perhaps by and large, the American public is comfortable with courts granting their imprimatur to the above legal regime on the basis that it is necessary to combat the terrorist threat. But while the number of federal terrorism prosecutions since 9/11 has been miniscule when compared to the vastly greater prevalence of ordinary criminal cases, their impact has been disproportionately influential. Only a very small percentage of terrorism prosecutions have reflected an actual security threat, due to the prevalence of the preventive use of § 2339B and relying in great part on the work of informants. But the small numbers have not stopped the government, with the judiciary's assent, from radically reassessing basic tenets of criminal law and procedure for all, under the umbrella of fighting terrorism.

As noted extensively in this volume, in relying on the radicalization theory to drive these prosecutions, the government has embraced a mentality that views individuals from a particular religious minority as akin to an existential threat. Additionally, the radicalization theory also zeroes in on those individuals willing to act on their own, or in smaller groupings, who are often unconnected to any specific organization. Unaffiliated individuals are normally not able to avail themselves of the benefit of outside governments or authorities to take up their plight. This is in contrast to the Cuban 5, the last three of whom were freed in December 2014 pursuant to a prisoner exchange between the United States and Cuba, as part of a historic rapprochement between the two nations.[6] The vast majority of terrorism defendants, like sting target Yassin Aref or the directors of the Holy Land Foundation, are not able to call on a foreign government to negotiate a prisoner exchange on their behalf. These unaffiliated individuals, from a religious community viewed with suspicion by the public at large, represent an ideal vehicle for the government's largely unimpeded campaign to expand its discretion to proactively investigate and prosecute.

Finally, a careful investigation of the criminal prosecution model is critical in that it has been lauded as the alternative to the Guantanamo-based military tribunal model. However, the either/or choice between the two systems is largely a false one. Trying to compare the plight of the detainees—many of whom have been held without any legal basis and ultimately cleared for release—with those brought before the federal courts pursuant to criminal charges reviewed and authorized by a grand jury might well be impossible. The former regime exists wholly outside and in contravention of well-established and understood norms. It is an exceptional process, while the latter operates according to clearly delineated rules and procedures. But as this book documents, those clear rules and procedures, and the constitutional protections under which they function, have come under sustained attack in the name of prosecuting terrorism, all the while advocates of the criminal model tout its reliability in garnering convictions. Drawing parallels between the two systems seems particularly inapt in the wake of the public release of a summary of a Senate report on the CIA's use of torture to obtain information from terrorist suspects.[7] Given the exceedingly brutal methods employed by the CIA that ultimately produced very little in the way of valuable information on terrorist activities, the critique here might seem misplaced. After all, at the time of writing, in December 2014, 127 individuals remain in detention in Guantanamo, 59 of whom have been approved for release.[8] Surely, their fate, especially that of the latter group, is cruel when juxtaposed with that of those properly indicted and prosecuted. Additionally, there does not seem to be any legal constraint on the government's sending or returning a criminal defendant in a terrorism prosecution to military detention in the event of his being acquitted or receiving a short sentence.[9] But as this book hopefully demonstrates, mere trumpeting of the criminal model as the best method for trying terrorism suspects is inaccurate and incomplete at best.

In the meantime, as the country continues to grapple with the repercussions of the extended war on terror, serious questions about the criminal process touted as the optimal vehicle for ensuring justice in cases of terrorism endure. It is time for more convincing answers than those the courts and the government have already offered.

Notes

INTRODUCTION

1. This exercise also allows for consideration of the adjudicative processes at work in a criminal terrorism prosecution, in light of the fact that indefinite detention at Guantanamo is the greater deprivation of detainee rights, while military commissions have been seen as less objectionable. *See, e.g.*, Ramzi Kassem, *A View from Gitmo*, Opinion, N.Y. TIMES, June 8, 2014, at SR7 (calling Guantanamo "at its core a lawless place" and noting "[i]n the absurd history of the detention camp, it is not uncommon for inmates among the handful who have been convicted by the military commissions to be the ones who are released. Questionable though their legitimacy and fairness may be, the military commissions can at least determine a finite term for internment at Guantánamo, one that the American government has chosen to honor so far").

2. *About the Center for American Progress*, CTR. FOR AM. PROGRESS (2014), http://www.americanprogress.org/about/mission/; *CAP Board of Directors*, CTR. FOR AM. PROGRESS (2014) http://www.americanprogress.org/about/c3-board/.

3. Ken Gude, *Criminal Courts Are Tougher on Terrorists than Military Detention*, CTR. FOR AM. PROGRESS, Jan. 20, 2010, http://www.americanprogress.org/issues/security/news/2010/01/20/7207/criminal-courts-are-tougher-on-terrorists-than-military-detention/ (also noting that military commissions are "unreliable and soft on terrorists").

4. David S. Kris, *Law Enforcement as a Counterterrorism Tool*, 5 J. NAT. SEC. L. & POL. 1 (2011) (former Assistant Attorney General for National Security making the case for criminal model); Kelly Anne Moore, Opinion, *Take Al-Qaeda to Court*, N.Y. TIMES, Aug. 21, 2007, at A19 (former lead prosecutor of terrorism suspects advocating criminal model).

5. Morris Davis, *No to Guantanamo for Ahmed Abu Khattala*, Op-Ed., N.Y. TIMES, June 20, 2014; Morris Davis, *Khalid Sheikh Mohammed Gets His Way*, SALON.COM (May 2, 2012), http://www.salon.com/2012/05/02/khalid_sheikh_mohammed_gets_ his_way.

6. Benjamin Weiser, *Holder, in New York City, Calls Terror Trials Safe*, N.Y. TIMES, Apr. 2, 2014, at A22.

7. Tina Susman, *Sulaiman Abu Ghaith Guilty Verdict Revives Terror Trial Venue Debate*, L.A. TIMES, Mar. 26, 2014.

8. Benjamin Weiser, *Cleric Convicted of All Terrorism Charges*, N.Y. TIMES, May 20, 2014, at A17.

9. *See* Aziz Z. Huq, *Forum Choice for Terrorism Suspects*, 61 DUKE L.J. 1415, 1474 (2012).

10. Matt Apuzzo, *A Holder Legacy: Shifting Terror Cases to the Civilian Courts, and Winning*, N.Y. TIMES, Oct. 21, 2014, at A17 ("But as Mr. Holder prepares to leave office, his success in reversing the Bush administration's emphasis on trying terrorism suspects in secret prisons or at offshore military tribunals may be one of his most significant achievements").

11. GABRIELLA BLUM & PHILIP B. HEYMANN, LAWS, OUTLAWS, AND TERRORISTS: LESSONS FROM THE WAR ON TERRORISM 105 (2010) ("By placing overall control in the hands of judges, we would be displaying our belief in the rule of law."); Daphne Eviatar, *The Abu Ghaith Trial: How Terrorism Prosecutions Are Supposed to Happen*, JUST SECURITY BLOG (Mar. 26, 2014, 11:50 AM), http://justsecurity.org/8600/abu-ghaith-trial-u-s-terrorism-prosecutions-supposed-happen (blog posting by Senior Counsel of Human Rights First in support of federal prosecution); *Detention*, ACLU (2014), https://www.aclu.org/national-security/detention ("If there is reliable evidence against a detainee, he should be prosecuted in our federal courts, which are well-equipped to handle sensitive national security evidence while protecting fundamental rights."); *see also* Jeanne Theoharis & Laura Rovner, *Preferring Order to Justice*, 61 AM. U. L. REV. 1331, 1333–35 nn.8–12 (2012) (collecting sources).

12. Kim Lane Scheppele, *Law in a Time of Emergency: States of Exception and the Temptations of 9/11*, 6 U. PA. J. CONST. L. 1001, 1025 n.84 (2004).

13. James Forman, Jr., *Exporting Harshness: How the War on Crime Helped Make the War on Terror Possible*, 33 N.Y.U. REV. L. & SOC. CHANGE 331, 338 (2009).

14. Theoharis & Rovner, *supra* note 11, at 1336. *But see* Wadie E. Said, Humanitarian Law Project *and the Supreme Court's Construction of Terrorism*, (2011 BYU L. REV. 1455, 1479 (citing articles)).

15. ACLU, BLOCKING FAITH, FREEZING CHARITY: CHILLING MUSLIM CHARITABLE GIVING IN THE "WAR ON TERRORISM FINANCING" (June 2009), https://www.aclu.org/files/pdfs/humanrights/blockingfaith.pdf.

16. CTR. FOR HUMAN RIGHTS & GLOBAL JUSTICE, TARGETED AND ENTRAPPED: MANUFACTURING THE "HOMEGROWN THREAT" IN THE UNITED STATES (May 18, 2011), http://chrgj.org/wp-content/uploads/2012/07/targetedandentrapped.pdf.

17. *See* DIALA SHAMAS & NERMEEN ARASTU, MAPPING MUSLIMS: NYPD SPYING AND ITS IMPACT ON AMERICAN MUSLIMS (last visited Nov. 22, 2014), http://www.law.cuny.edu/academics/clinics/immigration/clear/Mapping-Muslims.pdf.

18. HUMAN RIGHTS WATCH & HUMAN RIGHTS INSTITUTE, COLUMBIA LAW SCHOOL, ILLUSION OF JUSTICE: HUMAN RIGHTS ABUSES IN US TERRORISM PROSECUTIONS (July 2014), http://www.hrw.org/sites/default/files/reports/usterrorism0714_ForUpload_1.pdf; STEPHEN

Downs & Kathy Manley, Project Salam, Inventing Terrorists: The Lawfare of Preemptive Prosecutions (May 2014), http://www.projectsalam.org/inventing-terrorists-study.pdf.

19. Said, *supra* note 14, at 1479 (citing sources).

20. *See* Wadie E. Said, *The Material Support Prosecution and Foreign Policy*, 86 Ind. L.J. 543, 555 (2011).

21. Downs & Manley, *supra* note 18, at 2.

22. Holder v. Humanitarian Law Project, 561 U.S. 1, 130 S. Ct. 2705 (2010).

23. In the period between 1980 and 1990, federal courts denied several extradition requests by the British government for individuals suspected of direct involvement in violent attacks against British forces in Northern Ireland, as political offenses that could not serve as the basis for extradition. *See* Said, *supra* note 20, at 574–75 n.191 (discussing examples and noting courts' different approach to British attempts to extradite Irish Republican Army members with Israeli efforts to extradite Palestinians suspected of politically motivated attacks).

24. Joshua Holland, *Only 1 Percent of "Terrorists" Caught by the FBI Are Real: "The Terror Factory" Author Trevor Aaronson Exposes the Bureau's Undercover Sting Operations for the Farce They Are*, Salon.com (July 10, 2013), http://www.salon.com/2013/07/10/only_1_percent_of_ terrorists_caught_by_fbi_are_real_partner/.

25. Jesse J. Norris & Hanna Grol-Prokopczyk, *Estimating the Prevalence of Entrapment in Post-9/11 Terrorism Cases*, J. Crim. L. & Criminology (forthcoming 2015).

26. I should also mention that I have stated these recommendations before in various law review articles over the past several years. *See* Wadie E. Said, *The Terrorist Informant,* 85 Wash L. Rev. 687, 736 (2010) (arguing for a halt to the use of informants without the use of an articulable suspicion that terrorism-related activity is afoot); (Said, *supra* note 14, at 1507–08 (urging the Supreme Court to change its ban on material support in the form of speech on behalf of an FTO)); (Said, *supra* note 20, at 591 (arguing that government needs to show specific intent to further illegal goals of FTO when material support is for humanitarian purposes)); *Constructing the Threat and the Role of the Expert Witness: A Response to Aziz Rana's* Who Decides on Security?, 44 Conn. L. Rev. 1545, 1560–61 (2012) (urging courts to scrutinize more rigorously the credentials, methodology, and proposed testimony of the government's expert witnesses in terrorism cases); Wadie E. Said, *Sentencing Terrorist Crimes*, 75 Ohio St. L.J. 477 (2014) (arguing that the application of the terrorism sentencing enhancement raises questions about its constitutionality and questioning the need for such an enhancement).

27. *See, e.g.,* Robert Ferguson, Inferno (2014); Jonathan Simon, Mass Incarceration on Trial (2014); Michelle Alexander, The New Jim Crow (2012); William Stuntz, The Collapse of American Criminal Justice (2011); Alexandra Natapoff, Snitching (2009); Angela Davis, Arbitrary Justice (2007); David Cole & Jules Lobel, Less Safe, Less Free (2007).

CHAPTER I

1. U.S. Dep't of State, Bureau of Counterterrorism, *Foreign Terrorist Organizations,* http://www.state.gov/j/ct/rls/other/des/123085.htm (last visited Nov. 23, 2014).

2. *Id.*

3. U.S. Dep't of State, Off. of the Coordinator for Counterterrorism, *State Sponsors of Terrorism*, http://www.state.gov/j/ct/list/c14151.htm (last visited Nov. 23, 2014) (listing Cuba, Iran, Sudan, and Syria).

4. Muneer I. Ahmad, *Resisting Guantanamo: Rights at the Brink of Dehumanization*, 103 Nw. U. L. Rev. 1683, 1697 (2009).

5. John Tehranian, Whitewashed: America's Invisible Middle Eastern Minority 121 (2009); Susan M. Akram & Kevin R. Johnson, *Race and Civil Rights Pre-September 11, 2001: The Targeting of Arabs and Muslims, in* Civil Rights in Peril: The Targeting of Arabs and Muslims 18 (Elaine C. Hagopian ed., 2004); Yvonne Yazbeck Haddad, Not Quite American? The Shaping of Arab and Muslim Identity in the United States 21 (2004).

6. Natsu Taylor Saito, *Symbolism Under Siege: Japanese American Redress and the "Racing" of Arab Americans as "Terrorists,"* 8 Asian L.J. 1, 12 (2001); Jack G. Shaheen, Guilty: Hollywood's Verdict on Arabs after 9/11 (2008); Jack G. Shaheen, Reel Bad Arabs: How Hollywood Vilifies a People (2001); Edward W. Said, Covering Islam: How the Media and the Experts Determine How We See the Rest of the World (1997).

7. Susan M. Akram & Maritza Karmely, *Immigration and Constitutional Consequences of Post-9/11 Policies Involving Arabs and Muslims in the United States: Is Alienage a Distinction Without a Difference?*, 38 U.C. Davis L. Rev. 609, 624–31 (2005); *see also* U.S. Dep't of Just., Off. of the Inspector Gen., *The September 11 Detainees: A Review of the Treatment of Aliens Held on Immigration Charges in Connection with the Investigation of the September 11 Attacks* (June 2003), http://www.justice.gov/oig/special/0306/ (documenting violations of Muslim and Arab immigrants' civil rights while detained by the authorities in the wake of 9/11); Susan M. Akram, *Scheherezade Meets Kafka: Two Dozen Sordid Tales of Ideological Exclusion*, 14 Geo. Immigr. L.J. 51 (1999) (detailing cases and the practice of using secret evidence against Arab and Muslim noncitizens suspected of involvement with terrorist groups).

8. Leti Volpp, *The Boston Bombers*, 82 Fordham L. Rev. 2209, 2215 (2014) (noting "that whatever a Muslim person does will potentially be perceived as a terrorist act; a person who appears Arab, Muslim, or Middle Eastern is presumptively a terrorist; mass killing is presumptively an act of Muslim terrorists"); Wadie E. Said, *The Terrorist Informant*, 85 Wash. L. Rev. 687, 706–07 (2010) (collecting examples); *see generally* Stephen Sheehi, Islamophobia: The Ideological Campaign Against Muslims (2011). Mahmood Mamdani, Good Muslim, Bad Muslim (2004).

9. FBI Counterterrorism Div., The Radicalization Process: From Conversion to Jihad 2 (2006), http://cryptome.org/fbi-jihad.pdf.

10. *Id.* at 4.

11. *Id.* at 10.

12. *Id.* at 7.

13. *Id.* at 10.

14. *Id.* at 8.

15. *Id.* at 10.

16. *Id.* at 8.

17. *Id.* at 9.

18. *Id.* at 10.

19. *See* Amna Akbar, *Policing "Radicalization,"* 3 U.C. Irvine L. Rev. 801, 827 n.51 (2014) (collecting sources).

20. *Id.* at 119–20.

21. Press Release, U.S. Dep't of Just., Off. of Public Affairs, Attorney General Holder Announces Pilot Program to Counter Violent Extremists (Sept. 15, 2014), http://www.justice.gov/opa/pr/attorney-general-holder-announces-pilot-program-counter-violent-extremists.

22. *Id.*; Naureen Shah, *Terrorist . . . or Teenager,* SLATE.COM (Nov. 12, 2014, 3:15 PM), http://www.slate.com/articles/news_and_politics/politics/2014/11/justice_department_s_countering_violent_extremism_program_ripe_for_abuse.html.

23. *Id.*

24. Spencer Ackerman, *FBI Teaches Agents: "Mainstream" Muslims Are "Violent, Radical,"* WIRED (Sept. 14, 2011, 8:45 PM), http://www.wired.com/dangerroom/2011/09/fbi-muslims-radical/all.

25. Spencer Ackerman, *FBI Purges Hundreds of Documents in Islamophobia Probe,* WIRED (Feb. 15, 2012, 6:30 AM), http://www.wired.com/2012/02/hundreds-fbi-documents-muslims/.

26. Glenn Greenwald & Murtaza Hussain, *Meet the Muslim-American Leaders the FBI and NSA Have Been Spying On,* THE INTERCEPT (July 9, 2014), https://firstlook.org/theintercept/article/2014/07/09/under-surveillance/

27. Paul Vitello & Kirk Semple, *Muslims Say F.B.I. Tactics Sow Anger and Fear,* N.Y. TIMES, Dec. 18, 2009, at A1 ("[There are] differing views within the bureau about the effectiveness of community outreach, said Michael Rolince, a former director of counterterrorism in the F.B.I.'s Washington field office. Some factions within the agency, he said, have always been leery of Islamic and Arab-American organizations, considering their loyalties to be divided. 'There are some people in the bureau who believe, as I do, that the relationship with the Muslim community is crucial and must be developed with consistency,' Mr. Rolince said. 'And there are those who don't.'").

28. Neil MacFarquhar, *Muslim Groups Oppose a List of "Co-Conspirators,"* N.Y. TIMES, Aug. 16, 2007, at A19.

29. ACLU, BLOCKING FAITH, FREEZING CHARITY: CHILLING MUSLIM CHARITABLE GIVING IN THE "WAR ON TERRORISM FINANCING" 53–55 (2009), http://www.aclu.org/files/pdfs/humanrights/blockingfaith.pdf.

30. Matt Apuzzo, *Profiling Rules Said to Give F.B.I. Tactical Leeway,* N.Y. TIMES, Apr. 10, 2014, at A1 ("Senior agents speak at mosques and meet regularly with imams and leaders of Muslim nonprofit groups, but suspicions remain.").

31. MITCHELL D. SILBER & ARVIN BHATT, NYPD INTELLIGENCE DIV., RADICALIZATION IN THE WEST: THE HOMEGROWN THREAT (2007) ("Radicalization in the West"), http://www.nypdshield.org/public/sitefiles/documents/nypd_report-radicalization_in_the_west.pdf. Incidentally, "jihadi-Salafi" is one of only four terms defined in the report's glossary; the others are "Salafi," "mujahedeen," and "takfir." No citation or reference is provided in support of the definitions given. *See id.* at 86. Additionally, the definitions themselves have been criticized as inaccurate and truncated. *See* DIALA SHAMAS & NERMEEN ARASTU, MAPPING MUSLIMS: NYPD SPYING AND ITS IMPACT ON AMERICAN MUSLIMS 16 (last visited Nov. 22, 2014), http://www.law.cuny.edu/academics/clinics/immigration/clear/Mapping-Muslims.pdf (pointing out the inaccuracies in the definition of "Salafi").

32. SILBER & BHATT, *supra* note 31, at 5–6.

33. *Profile of Mitchell D. Silber,* K2 INTELLIGENCE, http://www.k2intelligence.com/person/mitchell-silber/ (last visited Nov. 24, 2014).

34. Matt Apuzzo & Adam Goldman, Enemies Within: Inside the NYPD's Secret Spying Unit and Bin Laden's Final Plot Against America 74–76 (2013) (discussing the recruitment of officers from the Muslim community to spy on their own).

35. Silber & Bhatt, *supra* note 31, at 6.

36. *Id.* at 10.

37. *Id.* at 22.

38. *Id.* at 30.

39. *Id.* at 31.

40. *Id.* at 36.

41. *Id.* at 38.

42. *Id.* at 43.

43. *Id.* at 44.

44. *Id.* at 45.

45. *Id.* at 21–54.

46. *Id.* at 55–75.

47. *Id.* at 56.

48. *Id.*

49. *See* Akbar, *supra* note 19, at 837–40.

50. *Id.* at 838.

51. *See* Said, *supra* note 8, at 715–18; *see also* Chapter 3 on evidence, *infra*.

52. *See* Akbar, *supra* note 19, at 840.

53. Silber & Bhatt, *supra* note 31, at 76–80.

54. Apuzzo & Goldman, *supra* note 34, at 39–40.

55. *Id.* at 66–69.

56. *Id.* at 45; Editorial, *Spying at the N.Y.P.D.*, N.Y. Times, Apr. 17, 2014, at A22 (noting "the Police Department's longstanding tendency to trample on people's rights during investigations of groups engaged in political activities").

57. Apuzzo & Goldman, *supra* note 34, at 43–49.

58. Handschu v. Special Servs. Div., 288 F. Supp. 2d 411, 422–31 (S.D.N.Y. 2003).

59. Handschu v. Special Servs. Div., 273 F. Supp. 2d 327, 348 (S.D.N.Y. 2003).

60. *Handschu*, 288 F. Supp. 2d at 422 (emphasis added).

61. Apuzzo & Goldman, *supra* note 34, at 125.

62. *Id.* at 72, 74–78; Shamas & Arastu, *supra* note 31, at 10.

63. Apuzzo & Goldman, *supra* note 34 at 75; Shamas & Arastu, *supra* note 31, at 7–11.

64. NYPD Intelligence Div., Demographics Unit, N.Y.P.D. Secret: Newark, New Jersey, Demographics Report (Sept. 25, 2007), http://hosted.ap.org/specials/interactives/documents/nypd/nypd_newark.pdf.

65. Apuzzo & Goldman, *supra* note 34, at 140–41. The first indication that the NYPD was spying on student groups at colleges and universities outside the city came when a building inspector entered an apartment at a housing complex near Rutgers University in New Brunswick, New Jersey, in June 2009, and found it was empty except for some NYPD gear and the walls plastered with pictures of terrorists. When the inspector called 911, the operator dispatched New Brunswick police officers and the FBI, who had no idea that the NYPD had rented the apartment under a false name for the purpose of spying on students. *See* Matt Apuzzo

& Adam Goldman, *NYPD Spying: How a 911 Caller Outed NYPD Surveillance of Muslims in New Jersey*, Associated Press, July 25, 2012, http://www.huffingtonpost.com/2012/07/25/nypd-spying-new-brunswick-muslim-surveillance-new-jersey_n_1701340.html.

66. Matt Apuzzo & Adam Goldman, *Documents Show NY Police Watched Devout Muslims*, Associated Press, Sept. 6, 2011, http://www.ap.org/Content/AP-In-The-News/2011/Documents-show-NY-police-watched-devout-Muslims.

67. Apuzzo & Goldman, *supra* note 34, at 78.

68. *Id.* at 180.

69. *Handschu*, 288 F. Supp. 2d at 424–28.

70. For a comprehensive discussion of RICO enterprise liability, see Gerard E. Lynch, *RICO: The Crime of Being a Criminal, Parts III & IV*, 87 Colum. L. Rev. 920, 937–45 (1987).

71. *See* United States v. Marzook, 426 F. Supp. 2d 820, 824–26 (N.D. Ill. 2006) (upholding the designation of FTO Hamas as a RICO enterprise in the face of a political question challenge); United States v. Al-Arian, 308 F. Supp. 2d 1322, 1349–50 (M.D. Fl. 2004) (same regarding FTO the Palestinian Islamic Jihad); *see also* Lynch, *supra* note 70, at 931–32; Meg Laughlin, Jennifer Liberto & Justin George, *8 Times, al-Arian Hears "Not Guilty,"* Tampa Bay Times, Dec. 7, 2005; Lolly Bowean & Gerry Doyle, *Bridgeview Mosque Cheers Salah Verdict*, Chi. Trib., Feb. 2, 2007, http://articles.chicagotribune.com/2007-02-02/news/0702020186_1_muhammad-salah-verdict-salah-family; Jimmy Gurule, Unfunding Terror: The Legal Response to the Financing of Global Terrorism 380 (2008).

72. The "terrorism enterprise" concept first appeared in then Attorney General John Ashcroft's guidelines governing FBI criminal investigations. *See* John Ashcroft, The Attorney General's Guidelines on General Crimes, Racketeering Enterprise, and Terrorism Enterprise Investigations 15–18, May 30, 2002, http://www.hermes-press.com/generalcrimes2.pdf ("Like the section [of the guidelines] addressing racketeering enterprise investigations, [the section on terrorism enterprise investigations] is concerned with the investigation of entire enterprises, rather than just individual participants and specific criminal acts, and authorizes investigations to determine the structure and scope of the enterprise as well as the relationship of the members").

73. *Handschu*, 288 F. Supp. 2d at 427.

74. *Id.* at 425.

75. *Id.* at 427–28.

76. United States v. Ivic, 700 F.2d 51, 61 (2d Cir. 1983).

77. Shamas & Arastu, *supra* note 31, at 32–33.

78. *See* Akbar, *supra* note 19 at 844 (collecting sources).

79. Matt Apuzzo & Adam Goldman, *NYPD Keeps Files on Muslims Who Change Their Names*, Associated Press, Oct. 26, 2011, http://www.ap.org/Content/AP-In-The-News/2011/NYPD-keeps-files-on-Muslims-who-change-their-names.

80. Apuzzo & Goldman, *supra* note 34, at 230.

81. Handschu v. Special Servs. Div., No. 71 Civ. 2203 (S.D.N.Y.), Galati Dep. 124 (June 28, 2012), http://www.nyclu.org/files/releases/Galati_EBT_6.28.12.pdf.

82. Apuzzo & Goldman, *supra* note 34, at 280.

83. Editorial, *More Overreach by the N.Y.P.D.*, N.Y. Times, June 24, 2013, at A20.

84. Quoted in Apuzzo & Goldman, *supra* note 34, at 277.

85. Hassan v. City of N.Y., No. 2:12-CV-3401, 2014 WL 654604 (D.N.J. Feb. 20, 2014) (granting the City's motion to dismiss amended complaint); Raza v. City of N.Y., CV 13-3448 (E.D.N.Y filed June 18, 2013); *see also* ACLU, Raza v. City of New York: *Legal Challenge to NYPD Muslim Surveillance Program,* https://www.aclu.org/national-security/raza-v-city-new-york-legal-challenge-nypd-muslim-surveillance-program.

86. Matt Apuzzo & Joseph Goldstein, *New York Drops Unit That Spied on Muslims,* N.Y. TIMES, Apr. 16, 2014, at A1.

87. APUZZO & GOLDMAN, *supra* note 34, at 283.

88. Anna Lekas Miller, *The NYPD Has Disbanded Its Most Notorious Spy Unit, but Is the Age of Muslim Surveillance Really Over?,* THE NATION, Apr. 23, 2014, http://www.thenation.com/article/179504/nypd-has-disbanded-its-most-notorious-spy-unit-age-muslim-surveillance-really-over.

89. Apuzzo & Goldstein, *supra* note 86.

90. Editorial, *Muslims and the N.Y.P.D.,* N.Y. TIMES, May 26, 2014, at A18; Joseph Goldstein, *New York Police Recruit Muslims to Be Informers,* N.Y. TIMES, May 11, 2014, at A1.

91. U.S. DEP'T OF JUST., THE ATTORNEY GENERAL'S GUIDELINES FOR DOMESTIC FBI OPERATIONS 17 (Oct. 3, 2008), http://www.justice.gov/ag/readingroom/guidelines.pdf.

92. *Id.* at 20.

93. Charlie Savage, *F.B.I. Focusing on Security Over Ordinary Crime,* N.Y. TIMES, Aug. 24, 2011, at A16.

94. FED. BUREAU OF INVESTIGATION, DOMESTIC INVESTIGATIONS AND OPERATIONS GUIDE § 4.3.3.2.5 (Oct. 15, 2011), http://vault.fbi.gov/FBI%20Domestic%20Investigations%20and%20Operations%20Guide%20%28DIOG%29/fbi-domestic-investigations-and-operations-guide-diog-2011-version/fbi-domestic-investigations-and-operations-guide-diog-october-15-2011-part-01-of-03/view.

95. Apuzzo, *supra* note 30.

96. U.S. DEP'T OF JUST., THE ATTORNEY GENERAL'S GUIDELINES REGARDING THE USE OF FBI CONFIDENTIAL HUMAN RESOURCES (Dec. 13, 2006), https://www.fas.org/irp/agency/doj/fbi/chs-guidelines.pdf.

97. U.S. DEP'T OF JUST., THE ATTORNEY GENERAL'S GUIDELINES ON FEDERAL BUREAU OF INVESTIGATION UNDERCOVER OPERATIONS § VII (May 30, 2002), http://www.fas.org/irp/agency/doj/fbi/fbiundercover.pdf ("These Guidelines are set forth solely for the purpose of internal DOJ guidance. They are not intended to, do not, and may not be relied upon to create any rights, substantive or procedural, enforceable by law by any party in any matter, civil or criminal, nor do they place any limitations on otherwise lawful investigative or litigative prerogatives of the Department of Justice.").

98. TREVOR AARONSON, THE TERROR FACTORY: INSIDE THE FBI'S MANUFACTURED WAR ON TERRORISM 44–45 (2013) (noting how the number of informants rose from 6,000 in the mid-1980s to the present levels); FED. BUREAU OF INVESTIGATION, FY 2008 AUTHORIZATION AND BUDGET REQUEST TO CONGRESS 4-23–4-24, https://s3.amazonaws.com/s3.documentcloud.org/documents/238034/33-fbi-se-2.pdf.

99. *Terror Trials by the Numbers,* MOTHER JONES, Sept./Oct. 2011, http://www.motherjones.com/politics/2011/08/terror-trials-numbers.

100. ALEXANDRA NATAPOFF, SNITCHING: CRIMINAL INFORMANTS AND THE EROSION OF AMERICAN JUSTICE 27–29 (2009).

101. *See* PAUL BUTLER, LET'S GET FREE: A HIP-HOP THEORY OF JUSTICE 79–100 (2009) (advocating noncooperation with the police in most situations when they request that someone become a "snitch" because of the negative role informants play in underprivileged communities); NATAPOFF, *supra* note 100, at 101–19 (detailing how the use of "snitches" can lead to more distrust and violence in inner-city communities, leading to an unwillingness to cooperate with the police); Andrea L. Dennis, *Collateral Damage? Juvenile Snitches in America's "Wars" on Drugs, Crime, and Gangs*, 46 AM. CRIM. L. REV. 1145, 1170–76 (2009) (highlighting the particular danger of using juvenile informants because of their youth and susceptibility to retaliatory violence); Alexandra Natapoff, *Snitching: The Institutional and Communal Consequences*, 73 U. CIN. L. REV., 645, 683–96 (2004) (analyzing the various harms informants wreak on disadvantaged communities).

102. NATAPOFF, *supra* note 100 at 29–30.

103. United States v. Russell, 411 U.S. 423, 433, 440 (1973); *see also* Said, *supra* note 8, at 692–94.

104. Said, *supra* note 8, at 693–94 (also discussing the existence of the theoretically possible test for proving outrageous government conduct in the informant context, although the barriers for such a showing are exceedingly high).

105. Jacobson v. United States, 503 U.S. 540, 542–47, 552 (1992); *see also* Gabriel J. Chin, *The Story of* Jacobson v. United States: *Catching Criminals or Creating Crime, in* CRIMINAL LAW STORIES (Donna K. Coker & Robert Weisberg eds., 2012).

106. *Jacobson*, 503 U.S. at 548–49; Paul Marcus, *Presenting, Back from the [Almost] Dead, the Entrapment Defense*, 47 FLA. L. REV. 205, 228–33 (1995); *but see* United States v. Cromitie, 727 F.3d 194, 208 (2d Cir. 2013) (commenting that *Jacobson* misstated the correct standard at the time it was decided, which was that predisposition should be gauged prior to the government's inducement to commit the crime, not the initial contact with the target, but nevertheless applying *Jacobson*'s standard as written).

107. *See, e.g.,* T. Ward Frampton, *Predisposition and Positivism: The Forgotten Foundations of the Entrapment Doctrine*, 103 J. CRIM. L. & CRIMINOLOGY 111 (2013); Kevin A. Smith, Note, *Psychology, Factfinding, and Entrapment*, 103 MICH. L. REV. 759, 761 (2005).

108. *See* Said, *supra* note 8, at 696–97.

109. *See* FED. R. EVID. 404(b) ("Evidence of a crime, wrong, or other act is not admissible to prove a person's character in order to show that on a particular occasion the person acted in accordance with the character.").

110. Jonathan C. Carlson, *The Act Requirement and the Foundations of the Entrapment Defense*, 73 VA. L. REV. 1011, 1039 (1987).

111. *See* Said, *supra* note 8, at 712–13 (discussing *United States v. Duggan*, 743 F.2d 59 (2d Cir. 1984)); *see also* Robert D. McFadden, *5 Are Acquitted in Brooklyn in Plot to Run Guns to I.R.A.*, N.Y. TIMES, Nov. 6, 1982, at L31; Joyce Wadler, *Unbowed, and Unashamed of His I.R.A Role*, N.Y. TIMES, Mar. 16, 2000, at B2 ("T[his] is the legend of Mr. Harrison. At his 1982 trial on weapons charges, when the prosecutor asserts that he has been running guns for six months, Mr. Harrison, in a grand heroic stance, orders his lawyer to set the record straight. 'Mr. Harrison is insulted,' his lawyer says. 'He wants the court to know that there has not been a weapon sent to Northern Ireland in the last 25 years without Mr. Harrison.'").

112. *See* Said, *supra* note 8, at 713–14 (discussing Salem and both terrorism prosecutions).

113. *See* United States v. Khalil, 214 F.3d 111 (2d Cir. 2000) (affirming convictions of two Palestinian men convicted of conspiring to detonate pipe bombs in the New York subway

system after police were tipped off by their roommate); John Kifner, *Arrested Men Often Seen, Little Known in Park Slope*, N.Y. TIMES, Aug. 1, 1997, at B4.

114. Nick Baumann, *This American Refused to Become an FBI Informant. Then the Government Made His Family's Life Hell*, MOTHER JONES, May/June 2014, http://www.motherjones.com/politics/2014/05/sudan-fbi-informant-naji-mansour-terrorism ("'The problem for many American Muslims who have been approached by the FBI to become informants is that they aren't involved in criminal conspiracies and don't have relationships with criminals,' says Mike German, an ex-FBI agent who now works at the Brennan Center for Justice at New York University. 'Instead, they are being asked to spy broadly against their religious community. That creates a conundrum because the person may be perfectly willing to help the FBI fight terrorism but simply has no information to provide'").

115. For details about both cases, see AARONSON, *supra* note 98, at 91–102.

116. For a discussion of the problems in this approach, see Emily Stabile, *Recruiting Terrorism Informants: The Problems with Immigration Incentives and the S-6 Visa*, 102 CAL. L. REV. 235 (2014).

117. See AARONSON, *supra* note 98, at 107–11; *see also* Chapter 2, *infra*, on material support prosecutions for a longer discussion of Mehanna's case.

118. Tanvir v. Holder, No. 13-CV-6951 (S.D.N.Y. filed Oct. 1, 2013); Latif v. Holder, No. 10-CV-750-BR (D. Or. filed June 29, 2010); *see also* Press Release, Ctr. for Constitutional Rights, Lawsuit Exposes FBI Abuse of No Fly List to Coerce Individuals to Become Informants (Apr. 23, 2014), http://ccrjustice.org/newsroom/press-releases/lawsuit-exposes-fbi-abuse-of-no-fly-list-coerce-individuals-become-informants; Press Release, ACLU, Federal Court Sides with ACLU in No Fly List Lawsuit (Aug. 29, 2013), https://www.aclu.org/national-security/federal-court-sides-aclu-no-fly-list-lawsuit.

119. Nick Baumann, *Meet the American Citizens Who Allege the US Had Them Locked Up Abroad*, MOTHER JONES (May 1, 2014, 5:00 AM), http://www.motherjones.com/politics/2014/05/list-alleged-proxy-detainees.

120. Baumann, *supra* note 114.

121. Nick Baumann, *Listen to a Secret Tape of FBI Agents Interviewing—and Threatening—a Potential Informant*, MOTHER JONES (May 1, 2014, 5:00 AM), http://www.motherjones.com/politics/2014/05/naji-mansour-fbi-audio-transcript.

122. Baumann, *supra* note 114.

123. United States v. Duka, 671 F.3d 329, 333, 335 (3rd Cir. 2011).

124. The details above are drawn from Said, *supra* note 8, at 722–24, and AARONSON, *supra* note 98, at 163–68.

125. *Duka*, 671 F.3d at 334, 351–52.

126. The details are drawn from Said, *supra* note 8, at 726–28, and AARONSON, *supra* note 98, at 115–35.

127. United States v. Aref, No. 04-CR-402, 2007 WL 603508, at *2–4 (N.D.N.Y. Feb. 22, 2007), *aff'd*, 285 F. App'x 784 (2d Cir. 2008) (upholding conviction and denying motion for a new trial); Michael Wilson, *Jury Convicts 2 Albany Men in Missile Sting*, N.Y. TIMES, Oct. 11, 2006, at B1.

128. See United States v. Cromitie, 727 F.3d 194 (2d Cir. 2013).

129. The pertinent facts are taken from Said, *supra* note 8, at 728–29; and *Cromitie*, 727 F.3d at 199–204.

130. A.G. Sulzberger, *Defense Cites Entrapment in Terror Case*, N.Y. TIMES, Mar. 18, 2010, at A22 ("'But for government's money and supplies and Hussain's indefatigable efforts, there is not the slightest chance that the crimes charged would or even could have occurred,' Susanne Brody, a federal defender, wrote in one of two filings in United States District Court.").

131. *Cromitie*, 727 F.3d at 211.

132. Graham Rayman, *The Alarming Record of the F.B.I.'s Informant in the Bronx Bomb Plot*, VILLAGE VOICE (July 8, 2009), http://www.villagevoice.com/2009-07-08/news/the-alarming-record-of-the-f-b-i-s-informant-in-the-bronx-bomb-plot/.

133. *Cromitie*, 727 F.3d at 216 (internal citation omitted).

134. *Id*. at 211 n.13(internal citation omitted).

135. Sting targets can also elect to argue that they have been subject to outrageous government conduct, in that the informant has behaved in such an extreme manner in pushing the plot that he has violated their constitutional rights. In contrast to an entrapment defense, this claim places the conduct of the government actor under scrutiny. However, a litigant's chance of succeeding in proving outrageous government conduct is remote, bordering on the theoretical. United States v. Augustin, 661 F.3d 1105, 1122–23 (11th Cir. 2011) (quoting United States v. Edenfield, 995 F.2d 197, 200 (11th Cir. 1993) (rejecting claim of outrageous government conduct, which can be granted in only "'the rarest and most outrageous circumstances,'" in case where informants participated in a scheme to blow up buildings, such as the FBI's Miami headquarters and the Chicago Sears Tower).

136. AARONSON, *supra* note 98, at 219–24.

137. The details are drawn from *Smadi v. United States*, Nos. 3:12-CV-4154-M-BK, 3:09-CR-0294-M-01, 2013 WL 2145591 (N.D. Tex. May 16, 2013); Jason Trahan, *Dallas Bomb Plotter Hosam Smadi Sentenced to 24 Years in Prison*, DALLAS MORNING NEWS (Oct. 20, 2010, 7:05 AM), http://www.dallasnews.com/news/community-news/dallas/headlines/2010 1019-Dallas-bombing-plotter-Hosam-Smadi-sentenced-2540.ece (last updated Nov. 26, 2010); James C. McKinley, Jr., *Friends' Portrait of Texas Bomb Plot Suspect at Odds with F.B.I.*, N.Y. TIMES, Sept. 28, 2009, at A12.

138. William Glaberson, *New York: Brooklyn: FBI Informer Sentenced*, N.Y. TIMES, Apr. 19, 2005, at B2.

139. AARONSON, *supra* note 98, at 171–79.

140. For an in-depth discussion of this issue, see AARONSON, *supra* note 98, at 181–90 ("If you take a close look at all the terrorism stings the FBI has engaged in since 9/11, you'll find missing recordings in nearly every one.").

141. *Id*. at 182–88; Kirk Johnson, *Oregon Man Convicted in Holiday Bombing Plot*, N.Y. TIMES, Feb. 1, 2013, at A19; United States v. Mohamud, 941 F. Supp.2d 1303 (D. Or. 2013).

142. AARONSON, *supra* note 98, at 189.

143. Tricia Bishop, *Would-Be Catonsville Bomber Sentenced to 25 Years in Prison*, BALT. SUN, Apr. 6, 2012.

144. Eric Lichtblau & William M. Arkin, *More Federal Agencies Are Using Undercover Operatives*, N.Y. TIMES, Nov. 16, 2014, at A1("In terrorism cases—the area in which the F.B.I. has used undercover stings most aggressively—prosecutors have a perfect record in claims of entrapment"); CTR. ON LAW & SEC., N.Y.U. SCH. OF LAW, TEN YEARS LATER: TERRORIST TRIAL REPORT CARD: SEPTEMBER 11, 2001–SEPTEMBER 11, 2011 26 (2011), http://www.lawandsecurity.org/Portals/0/Documents/TTRC%20Ten%20Year%20Issue.pdf.

145. Sabrina Siddiqui, *Americans' Attitudes Toward Arabs and Muslims Are Getting Worse, Poll Finds*, HUFFINGTON POST (July 29, 2014, 10:00 AM), http://www.huffingtonpost. com/2014/07/29/arab-muslim-poll_n_5628919.html (last updated July 29, 2014, 5:59 PM) (noting 42 percent of Americans support law enforcement profiling of Arab and Muslim Americans, with 36 percent having a favorable view of Arab Americans and only 27 percent having a favorable view of Muslim Americans).

146. *Cromitie*, 727 F.3d at 209–16.

147. 503 U.S. 540, 542 (1992).

148. United States v. al-Moayad, 545 F.3d 139 (2d Cir. 2008). For a longer discussion of the rulings in the *al-Moayad* case, see Chapter 3, *infra*, on evidence.

149. *al-Moayad*, 545 F.3d at 146.

150. Benjamin Weiser, *Softer View of Suspect in U.S. Case on Terror*, N.Y. TIMES, Apr. 30, 2014, at A20.

151. Denny Walsh, *Lodi-Area Terrorism Suspect Nearly Released on Bail*, SACRAMENTO BEE (May 7, 2014, 5:43 PM), www.sacbee.comnews/local/crime/article2598262.html (last updated Oct. 8, 2014, 12:15 PM). At the time of writing, Teausant's case remained pending after the court granted a defense request for a continuance in order to review the extensive evidential record, much of which was subject to security restictions. United States v. Teausant, *Stipulation and Order to Continue Status Conference*, 2:14-cr-00087-JAM, Oct. 2, 2014 (E.D. Ca.).

152. Samer Hijazi, *FBI Arrests Local Man for Alleged Hizbullah Ties, Family Speaks Out*, ARAB AMERICAN NEWS, Mar. 21, 2014, http://www.arabamericannews.com/news/news/id_8464/ FBI-arrests-local-man-for-alleged-Hizbullah-ties,-family-speaks-out.html.

153. *Id.*

154. United States v. Hamdan, *Order Granting Motion for Competency Evaluation*, 2:14-cr-20232-GER-DRG (E.D. Mich. June 12, 2014).

155. AARONSON, *supra* note 98, at 234.

156. FED. BUREAU OF INVESTIGATION, FY 2014 BUDGET REQUEST SUMMARY (Jan. 28, 2014), http://www.justice.gov/jmd/2014summary/pdf/fbi.pdf.

157. *See, e.g.*, Akbar Ahmed, Op-Ed., *Fair to Muslims?*, N.Y. TIMES, Mar. 9, 2011, at A27; Malia Wollan & Charlie Savage, *Holder Calls Terrorism Stings "Essential*," N.Y. TIMES, Dec. 12, 2010, at A34.

158. *See, e.g.*, Petra Bartosiewicz, *Deploying Informants, the FBI Stings Muslims*, NATION (July 2–9, 2012), http://www.thenation.com/article/168380/deploying- informants-fbi-stings-muslims#; David K. Shipler, Op-Ed., *Terrorist Plots, Hatched by the F.B.I.*, N.Y. TIMES, Apr. 29, 2012, at SR4; Rick Perlstein, *How FBI Entrapment Is Inventing "Terrorists"—and Letting Bad Guys Off the Hook*, ROLLING STONE, May 15, 2012; Glenn Greenwald, *The FBI Again Thwarts Its Own Terror Plot*, SALON.COM (Sept. 29, 2011, 2:30 PM), http://www.salon.com/2011/09/29/ fbi_terror/.

159. Coleen Rowley, Letter to the Editor, *Fear, Terror, and the Mosques*, L.A. TIMES, Mar. 7, 2009, at A28 (criticizing the practice of spying on mosques as lacking "factual justification"). During her tenure as an FBI agent, Rowley criticized the Bureau's handling of the pre-9/11 investigation of the suspected "20th hijacker," Zacarias Moussaoui. *Id.; see also* Memorandum from Coleen Rowley to FBI Director Robert Mueller (May 21, 2002) (edited version), http://www. apfn.org/apfn/wtc_whistleblower1.htm.

160. Erik Love, *The FBI's War on Fake Terrorism*, JADALIYYA, July 30, 2014, http://www. jadaliyya.com/pages/index/18720/the-fbi's-war-on-fake-terrorism.

161. Associated Press, *FBI Chief Defends Use of Informants in Mosques*, MSNB.COM (June 8, 2009), http://www.msnbc.msn.com/id/31177049/.

162. Wollan & Savage, *supra* note 157.

163. Ali Soufan, *Enemies Domestic*, WALL ST. J., Jan. 23, 2013.

164. APUZZO & GOLDMAN, *supra* note 34, at 280 n.3 (citing Justin Elliott, Fact-Check: *How the NYPD Overstated Its Counterterrorism Record*, PROPUBLICA (July 10, 2012, 9:33 AM), http://www.propublica.org/article/fact-check-how-the-nypd-overstated-its-counterterrorism-record).

165. Aziz Z. Huq, *The Signaling Function of Religious Speech in Domestic Counterterrorism*, 89 TEX. L. REV. 833 (2011) (criticizing the phenomenon of using religious speech as a predictor of terrorist intent). This is also reflective of the more general phenomenon of selectively blaming the perceived bad acts of an individual from a minority group on his or her culture. *See* Leti Volpp, *Blaming Culture for Bad Behavior*, 12 YALE J. L. & HUMAN. 89 (2000).

166. CTR. ON LAW & SEC., *supra* note 144.

167. U.S. SENTENCING COMM'N, 2013 SOURCEBOOK OF FEDERAL SENTENCING STATISTICS, Introduction, http://www.ussc.gov/research-and-publications/annual-reports-sourcebooks/2013/sourcebook-2013 (last visited Nov. 23, 2014).

168. APUZZO & GOLDMAN, *supra* note 34, at 142–45.

169. Additionally, the reemergence of the sting operation has not been limited to the political context. A recent report by *USA Today* reveals that the Bureau of Alcohol, Tobacco, and Firearms (ATF) has used stings extensively over the last decade to target minorities. Some 91 percent of the targets were African American or Latino men, raising a real question of bias in cases where the ATF constructed the crimes, which involved large-scale drug or weapons transactions, that resulted in high prison sentences. As with terrorism stings targeting Muslims, these drug stings focus on politically marginalized groups that are hard-pressed to force law enforcement to change its tactics. *See* Brad Heath, *Investigation: ATF Drug Stings Targeted Minorities*, USA TODAY (July 20, 2014, 10:19 PM), http://www.usatoday.com/story/news/nation/2014/07/20/atf-stash-house-stings-racial-profiling/12800195/.

170. *See Synopsis*, BETTER THIS WORLD, http://betterthisworld.com/film.html; PBS, *Film Description*, BETTER THIS WORLD, http://www.pbs.org/pov/betterthisworld/film_description.php.

171. United States v. McDavid, 396 F. App'x 365, 367, 372 (9th Cir. 2010) (upholding conviction on crimes related to a plot to bomb "a federal facility for tree genetics, a federal dam and fish hatchery, and cell phone towers"); *The New Political Prisoners: Leakers, Hackers, and Activists: Eric McDavid*, ROLLING STONE, http://www.rollingstone.com/politics/lists/the-new-political-prisoners-leakers-hackers-and-activists-20130301/eric-mcdavid-19691231; Colin Moynihan, *Man Convicted of Environmental Terrorism Is Freed*, N.Y. TIMES, Jan. 9, 2015, at A13.

172. *The FBI vs. Occupy: Secret Docs Reveal "Counterterrorism" Monitoring of OWS from Its Earliest Days*, DEMOCRACY NOW!, Dec. 27, 2012, http://www.democracynow.org/2012/12/27/the_fbi_vs_occupy_secret_docs; Naomi Wolf, Opinion, *Revealed: How the FBI Coordinated the Crackdown on Occupy*, GUARDIAN, Dec. 29, 2012, http://www.theguardian.com/commentisfree/2012/dec/29/fbi-coordinated-crackdown-occupy.

173. United States v. Wright, 747 F.3d 399 (6th Cir. 2014); Arun Gupta, *Cleveland Anarchist Bomb Plot Aided and Abetted by the FBI*, GUARDIAN, Nov. 28, 2012, http://www.theguardian.com/commentisfree/2012/nov/28/cleveland-anarchist-bomb-plot-fbi; *Unmasked: Meet the FBI's Bridge Bomb Plot Snitch*, SMOKING GUN (May 2, 2012), http://www.thesmokinggun.com/documents/fbi-informant-shaquille-azir-756123.

174. Jordan Smith, *APD Undercover Officers Outed in Occupy Austin Case*, AUSTIN CHRONICLE, Nov. 6, 2012, http://www.austinchronicle.com/daily/news/2012-11-06/apd-undercover-officers-outed-in-occupy-austin-court-case/; James Pinkerton, *Undercover Austin Police Officers Aided Houston Occupy Protestors*, HOUSTON CHRONICLE, Sept. 5, 2012, http://www.chron.com/news/houston-texas/article/Undercover-Austin-police-officers-ai ded-Houston-3841846.php (last updated Sept. 5, 2012, 10:20 PM).

175. Eric Lichtblau & William M. Arkin, *More Federal Agencies Are Using Undercover Operatives*, N.Y. TIMES, Nov. 16, 2014, at A1.

176. *Id.*

177. Sheryl Gay Stolberg & Laurie Goodstein, *Domestic Terrorism Hearing Opens with Contrasting Views on Dangers*, N.Y. TIMES, Mar. 11, 2011, at A15.

178. Kathleen Belew, Op-Ed., *Veterans and White Supremacy*, N.Y. TIMES, Apr. 16, 2014, at A25; Ginger Thompson, *Extremist Report Draws Criticism: Prompts Apology*, CAUCUS BLOG, N.Y. TIMES (Apr. 16, 2009, 3:03 PM), http://thecaucus.blogs.nytimes.com/2009/04/16/extremist-report-draws-criticism-prompts-apology/.

179. ARIE PERLIGER, CHALLENGERS FROM THE SIDELINES: UNDERSTANDING AMERICA'S VIOLENT FAR-RIGHT, COMBATING TERRORISM CTR. (Nov. 2012), https://www.ctc.usma.edu/wp-content/uploads/2013/01/ChallengersFromtheSidelines.pdf.

180. Michael S. Schmidt, *At F.B.I., Change in Leaders Didn't Change Focus on Terror*, N.Y. TIMES, May 19, 2014, at A1.

181. CHARLES KURZMAN, MUSLIM-AMERICAN TERRORISM IN 2013 (Feb. 5, 2014), http://sites.duke.edu/tcths/files/2013/06/Kurzman_Muslim-American_Terrorism_in_2013.pdf.

182. David Schanzer & Charles Kurzman, Opinion, *Year After Boston Bombing, It's Clear That Threat of Homegrown Terrorism Overhyped*, NEWSOBSERVER.COM, Apr. 14, 2014, http://www.newsobserver.com/2014/04/14/3784842/year-after-boston-bombing-its.html; Mike German, *Debunked NYPD Radicalism Report Just Won't Die*, BLOG OF RIGHTS, ACLU (Feb. 11, 2013, 12:51 PM), https://www.aclu.org/blog/national-security-religion-belief/debunked-n ypd-radicalization-report-just-wont-die.

183. This mindset permeates the government's terrorist watch lists, which have a disproportionate focus on Arab and Muslim Americans. *See, e.g.*, Jeremy Scahill & Ryan Devereaux, *Barack Obama's Secret Terrorist Tracking System, by the Numbers*, INTERCEPT, Aug. 5, 2014, https://firstlook.org/theintercept/article/2014/08/05/watch-commander/ ("The top five U.S. cities represented on the main watchlist for 'known or suspected terrorists' are New York; Dearborn, Mich.; Houston; San Diego; and Chicago. At 96,000 residents, Dearborn is much smaller than the other cities in the top five, suggesting that its significant Muslim population—40 percent of its population is of Arab descent, according to the U.S. Census Bureau—has been disproportionately targeted for watchlisting," even though, in the words of a local Muslim American leader, " 'To my knowledge, there have been no Muslims in Dearborn who have committed acts of terrorism against our country.' ").

CHAPTER 2

1. *See* CTR. ON LAW & SEC., N.Y. UNIV. SCH. OF LAW, TERRORIST TRIAL REPORT CARD: SEPTEMBER 11, 2001–SEPTEMBER 11, 2011 13–14 (2011), http://www.lawandsecurity.org/Portals/0/Documents/TTRC%20Ten%20Year%20Issue.pdf.

2. David Cole, Enemy Aliens: Double Standards and Constitutional Freedoms in the War on Terror 75–76 (2003); *see also* David Cole & Jules Lobel, Less Safe, Less Free: Why America Is Losing the War on Terror 49–50 (2007).

3. Norman Abrams, *The Material Support Terrorism Offenses: Perspectives Derived from the (Early) Model Penal Code*, 1 J. Nat'l Sec. & Pol'y 5, 7 (2005).

4. *See* United States v. Afshari, 426 F.3d 1150 (9th Cir. 2005).

5. *Id.* at 1152–53; Julie Cart, *Fundraisers Plead Guilty to Helping Terrorists*, L.A. Times, Apr. 30, 2009; Jessica Garrison & David Rosenzweig, *Terror Funding Charges Rejected*, L.A. Times, June 22, 2002.

6. United States v. Assi, 414 F. Supp. 2d 707, 709–11 (E.D. Mich. 2006).

7. *Id.* at 715.

8. The discussion in this section is largely taken from my previous work. *See, e.g.*, Wadie E. Said, *The Material Support Prosecution and Foreign Policy*, 86 Ind. L.J. 543, 556–60 (Winter 2011).

9. 18 U.S.C. § 2339A(b)(1).

10. Antiterrorism and Effective Death Penalty Act, Pub. L. No. 104-132, 110 Stat. 1214, 1247, § 301 (finding that, inter alia, certain foreign terrorist groups raised funds in the United States for violence under humanitarian pretenses). This finding has been cited with approval by many courts reviewing the statute, including the Supreme Court. *See* Said, *supra* note 8, at 577 n.200 (citing cases).

11. *See* David Cole, *The New McCarythyism: Repeating History in the War on Terrorism*, 38 Harv. C.R.-C.L. L. Rev. 1, 12 (2003) ("The legislative history of the material support law contains not one word of testimony about even a single terrorist organization's finances, much less all 'foreign organizations that engage in terrorist activity.' A congressional 'finding' that 'domestic political parties that engage in illegal conduct are so tainted by their criminal conduct that any contribution facilitates that conduct' surely would not authorize imposing guilt by association on support of domestic groups.... [I]t simply does not follow that all organizations that use or threaten to use violence will turn any donation that supports their lawful activities into money for terrorism.").

12. 8 U.S.C. § 1189(a)(1), (d)(4).

13. 8 U.S.C. § 1189(d)(2).

14. *See* People's Mojahedin Org. of Iran v. Dep't of State, 182 F.3d 17, 23 (D.C. Cir. 1999); *see also* Said, *supra* note 8, at 562–63.

15. However, it should be noted that the D.C. Circuit Court has remarked that it has yet to decide whether a designation that was based in large part on classified information would comport with due process. *See* People's Mojahedin Org. of Iran v. Dep't of State, 613 F.3d 220, 231 (D.C. Cir. 2010) ("[N]one of the cases [brought pursuant to the statute] decide[] whether an administrative decision relying critically on undisclosed classified material would comport with due process because in none was the classified record essential to uphold an FTO designation.").

16. See generally 8 U.S.C. § 1189 for a description of the designation process and its strictures.

17. *People's Mojahedin Org.*, 613 F.3d at 230–31; Nat'l Council of Resistance of Iran v. Dep't of State, 251 F.3d 192, 209 (D.C. Cir. 2001).

18. *People's Mojahedin Org.*, 613 F.3d at 230–31 (D.C. Cir. 2010); *Nat'l Council of Resistance of Iran*, 251 F.3d at 209.

19. *See id.* at 225 ("It submitted evidence to the Secretary of its changed circumstances, asserting that, since its initial FTO designation in 1997, it had: ceased its military campaign against the Iranian regime and renounced violence in 2001; voluntarily handed over its arms to U.S. forces in Iraq and cooperated with U.S. officials at Camp Ashraf (where all of its members operating in Iraq are consolidated) in 2003; shared intelligence with the U.S. government regarding Iran's nuclear program; in 2004 obtained 'protected person' status under the Fourth Geneva Convention for all PMOI members at Camp Ashraf based on the U.S. investigators' conclusions that none was a combatant or had committed a crime under any U.S. laws; disbanded its military units and disarmed the PMOI members at Ashraf, all of whom signed a document rejecting violence and terror; and obtained delisting as a terrorist organization from the United Kingdom (the Proscribed Organisations Appeal Commission and the Court of Appeal) in 2008 and from the European Union (the European Court of First Instance) in 2009. The PMOI also thrice supplemented its petition with additional information and letters in support from members of the U.S. Congress, members of the UK and European parliaments and retired members of the U.S. military, among others.")

20. *In re* People's Mojahedin of Iran, 680 F.3d 832, 833 (D.C. Cir. 2012).

21. Scott Shane, *Across Party Lines, Lobbying for Iranian Exiles on Terrorist List*, N.Y. Times, Nov. 27, 2011, at A1.

22. Josh Rogin, *Terrorist Group's Supporters Throw Party in U.S. Congress*, Cable (Mar. 22, 2012), http://thecable.foreignpolicy.com/posts/2012/03/22/terrorist_group_s_supporters_throw_party_in_us_congress.

23. Scott Shane, *Star Lobbyists Help Iran Group Escapte Shadow*, N.Y. Times, Sept. 22, 2012, at A1.

24. United States v. Rahmani, 209 F. Supp. 2d 1045, 1053 (C.D. Cal. 2002), *rev'd sub nom.* United States v. Afshari, 392 F.3d 1031 (9th Cir. 2004), *rev'd*, 426 F.3d 1150 (9th Cir. 2005).

25. *Afshari*, 426 F.3d at 1154–55.

26. 426 F.3d at 1158–59.

27. *Id.*

28. *Id.*

29. *Id.* at 1161 (internal citation omitted).

30. United States v. Afshari, 446 F.3d 915, 919–21 (9th Cir. 2006) (Kozinski, J., dissenting).

31. *Id.* at 922.

32. U.S. Dep't of State, Bureau of Counterterrorism, *Foreign Terrorist Organizations*, http://www.state.gov/j/ct/rls/other/des/123085.htm (last visited Nov. 24, 2014).

33. *Id.*

34. Niki Kitsantonis, *Greek Police Hunt for Convicted Terrorist Who Disappeared on Furlough*, N.Y. Times, Jan. 7, 2014; Anthee Carassava, *Greeks Claim Victory over Terrorist Group but Questions About Suspects' Ties Remain*, N.Y. Times, July 19, 2002.

35. Chai v. Dep't of State, 466 F.3d 125, 129–30 (D.C. Cir. 2006) (discussing Kach/Kahane Chai's links to terrorist activity).

36. Dean E. Murphy, *Terror Label No Hindrance to Anti-Arab Jewish Group*, N.Y. Times, Dec. 19, 2000.

37. Dean E. Murphy, *F.B.I. Raids Brooklyn Office of Kahane Followers*, N.Y. Times, Jan. 15, 2001; *News Brief*, Jewish Telegraphic Agency, Jan. 16, 2001, http://www.jta.org/2001/01/16/archive/the-u-s-state-department-revoked-the-visa-of (noting revocation by the United States of a visa for Baruch Marzel, a Kahane Chai leader).

38. Jim Rutenberg, Mike McIntire & Ethan Bronner, *Tax-Exempt Funds Aid Settlement in West Bank*, N.Y. TIMES, July 6, 2010, at A1.

39. *See* United States v. Armstrong, 517 U.S. 456 (1996) (laying out the exceedingly high burden a defendant must make out to state successfully a selective prosecution claim).

40. *See* Ben Saul, *Civilizing the Exception: Universally Defining Terrorism, in* POST 9/11 AND THE STATE OF PERMANENT LEGAL EMERGENCY: SECURITY AND HUMAN RIGHTS IN COUNTERING TERRORISM (Aniceto Masferrer ed., 2012) (discussing the problem of defining terrorism and concluding that there is insufficient evidence of a customary international law definition of terrorism); Sudha Setty, *What's in a Name? How Nations Define Terrorism Ten Years after 9/11*, 33 U. PA. J. INT'L L. 1 (2011) (discussing the myriad problems of defining terrorism domestically and internationally); Karima Bennoune, *Terror/Torture*, 26 BERKELEY J. INT'L L. 1, 19–27 (2008) (noting that an internationally agreed-upon definition exists and that the current debate centers on the exceptions to that definition); George P. Fletcher, *The Indefinable Concept of Terrorism*, 4 J. INT'L CRIM. JUST. 894, 911 (2006) ("A concept like terrorism that lies at the centre of our political life may not lend itself to the discipline of legal thinking. It is probably like the notions of 'democracy' or 'constitutionalism' or 'rule of law'—too important to be settled once and for all in a legislative definition.").

41. *See* 8 U.S.C. § 1189(a)(1)(A)-(C) (2006); 18 U.S.C. § 2331(1) (2006) (defining "international terrorism" as "violent acts or acts dangerous to human life" occurring abroad that are intended "(i) to intimidate or coerce a civilian population; (ii) to influence the policy of a government by intimidation or coercion; or (iii) to affect the conduct of a government by mass destruction, assassination, or kidnapping"); *see also* 22 U.S.C. § 2656f(d)(2) (2006) (defining "terrorism" as "premeditated, politically motivated violence perpetrated against noncombatant targets by subnational groups or clandestine agents").

42. *See* Alison Elizabeth Chase, *Legal Mechanisms of the International Community and the United States Concerning State Sponsorship of Terrorism*, 45 VA. J. INT'L L. 41 (2004).

43. Gerald L. Neuman, *Humanitarian Law and Counter-Terrorist Force*, 14 EUR. J. INT'L L. 283, 288–89 (2003).

44. Gerald L. Neuman, *Terrorism, Selective Deportation and the First Amendment After Reno v. AADC*, 14 GEO. IMMIGR. L.J. 313, 327 (2000) (noting that the definition of "terrorist activity" in the immigration context "also governs the process, created in 1996, for the designation of 'foreign terrorist organizations'").

45. *See* S-K-, 23 I. & N. Dec. 936, 937–38 (BIA 2006) (citing the relevant legislative provisions).

46. Neuman, *supra* note 44, at 327.

> "Terrorist activity" is defined as follows: [T]he term "terrorist activity" means any activity which is unlawful under the laws of the place where it is committed (or which, if it had been committed in the United States, would be unlawful under the laws of the United States or any State) and which involves any of the following:
>
> (I)   The highjacking or sabotage of any conveyance (including an aircraft, vessel, or vehicle).
>
> (II) The seizing or detaining, and threatening to kill, injure, or continue to detain, another individual in order to compel a third person (including a governmental organization) to do or abstain from doing any act as an explicit or implicit condition for the release of the individual seized or detained.

(III) A violent attack upon an internationally protected person (as defined in section 1116(b)(4) of title 18) or upon the liberty of such a person.

or

(IV) An assassination.

(V) The use of any—

(a) biological agent, chemical agent, or nuclear weapon or device,

(b) explosive, firearm, or other weapon or dangerous device (other than for mere personal monetary gain), with intent to endanger, directly or indirectly, the safety of one or more individuals or to cause substantial damage to property.

(VI) A threat, attempt, or conspiracy to do any of the foregoing.

8 U.S.C. § 1182(a)(3)(B)(iii).

47. *In re S-K-*, 23 I. & N. Dec. at 937.

48. *Id.*

49. *Id.* at 938.

50. *Id.* at 941.

51. *Id.*

52. *Id.* at 948 (Osuna, Acting Vice Chairman, concurring).

53. *In re* S-K-, 24 I. & N. Dec. 475, 476 (BIA 2008).

54. *Id.* at 476 & n.3.

55. Editorial, *Long Overdue: Clearing Nelson Mandela's Record*, N.Y. TIMES, Apr. 9, 2008.

56. Caitlin Dewey, *Why Nelson Mandela Was on a Terrorism Watchlist in 2008*, WASH. POST, Dec. 7, 2013; DAVID COLE & JAMES X. DEMPSEY, TERRORISM AND THE CONSTITUTION: SACRIFICING CIVIL LIBERTIES IN THE NAME OF NATIONAL SECURITY 117 (3d ed. 2006).

57. Dewey, *supra* note 56.

58. Press Release, U.S. Dep't of State, Delisting of the Mujahedin-e Khalq (Sept. 28, 2012), http://www.state.gov/r/pa/prs/ps/2012/09/198443.htm.

59. Hannah Allam, *Thinking Helping to Fight ISIS Will Get You Off the Terrorist List? Think Again*, McCLATCHYDC, Nov. 4, 2014, http://www.mcclatchydc.com/2014/11/04/245649_think-helping-to-fight-isis-will.html?rh=1.

60. Jeffrey Gettleman & Nicholas Kulish, *Somali Militants Mixing Business and Terror*, N.Y. TIMES, Oct. 1, 2013, at A1.

61. Special Briefing, Off. of the Spokesperson, U.S. Dep't of State, Background Briefing on Somalia and Delivery of Humanitarian Assistance (Aug. 2, 2011), http://www.state.gov/p/af/rls/spbr/2011/169479.htm.

62. *See, e.g.*, Sam Adelsberg, Freya Pitts & Sirine Shebaya, *The Chilling Effect of "Material Support" Law on Humanitarian Aid: Causes, Consequences, and Proposed Reforms*, 4 HARV. NAT'L SEC. J. 282, 300–18 (2013).

63. *Id.* at 300–02.

64. *See* Said, *supra* note 8, at 582 n.229.

65. Humanitarian Assistance Facilitation Act, H.R. 3526, 113th Cong. (2013), http://beta.congress.gov/bill/113th/house-bill/3526.

66. Humanitarian Assistance Facilitation Act of 2013, *Overview, https*://www.govtrack.us/congress/bills/113/hr3526#overview (last updated Nov. 18, 2014).

67. Paula Mejia, *U.S. Threatened James Foley's Family over ISIS Ransom Demand, His Mother Says*, NEWSWEEK, Sept. 12, 2014, http://www.newsweek.com/us-threatened-james-foleys-family-over-isis-ransom-demand-270151; Graeme Wood, *Ransoms: The Real Cost*, NYR BLOG (Nov. 19, 2014, 10:36 PM), http://www.nybooks.com/blogs/nyrblog/2014/nov/19/ransoms-real-cost/?insrc=hpbl.

68. Humanitarian Law Project v. Reno, 205 F.3d 1130, 1136 (9th Cir. 2000). This passage has been cited favorably over the years by several other courts. *See* United States v. Hammoud, 381 F.3d 316, 381, 329 (4th Cir. 2004), *vacated*, 543 U.S. 1097 (2005); United States v. Marzook, 383 F. Supp. 2d 1056, 1068 (N.D. Ill. 2005). Additionally, this same logic has been followed in civil cases that include material support allegations. *See* Boim v. Holy Land Found. for Relief & Dev., 549 F.3d 685, 698 (7th Cir. 2008) ("If Hamas budgets $2 million for terrorism and $2 million for social services and receives a donation of $100,000 for those services, there is nothing to prevent its using that money for them while at the same time taking $100,000 out of its social services 'account' and depositing it in its terrorism 'account.' . . . Anyone who knowingly contributes to the nonviolent wing of an organization that he knows to engage in terrorism is knowingly contributing to the organization's terrorist activities.").

69. Humanitarian Law Project v. U.S. Dep't of Justice, 352 F.3d 382, 394 n.10 (9th Cir. 2003), *vacated as superseded by statute*, 393 F.3d 902 (9th Cir. 2004) ("While the Fifth Amendment's right to 'personal guilt' is similar to the First Amendment's right to the freedom of association raised by the plaintiffs [previously], the Fifth Amendment claim stands 'independently of the claim made under the First Amendment.' "); *see also* United States v. Al Kassar, 660 F.3d 108, 130 n.4 (2d Cir. 2011) (noting the same logic behind the First and Fifth Amendment challenges to § 2339B).

70. 367 U.S. 203, 211 (1961).

71. *Id.* at 224–25 (emphasis added).

72. The only court opinions to hold that specific intent was required under § 2339B came from the Middle District of Florida in *United States v. Al-Arian*, a prosecution in which the author represented one of the four defendants. United States v. Al-Arian, 308 F. Supp. 2d 1322, 1335–39 (M.D. Fla. 2004); United States v. Al-Arian, 329 F. Supp. 2d 1294, 1298–1300 (M.D. Fla. 2004).

73. *Humanitarian Law Project*, 352 F.3d at 402–03.

74. 18 U.S.C. § 2339B(a)(1) (2006) (as amended by the Intelligence Reform and Terrorism Prevention Act of 2004 (IRTPA), Pub. L. No. 108–458, 118 Stat. 3638) ("[a] person must have knowledge that the organization is a designated terrorist organization. . ., that the organization has engaged or engages in terrorist activity . . . , or that the organization has engaged or engages in terrorism.").

75. Holder v. Humanitarian Law Project, 561 U.S. 1 12 (2010).

76. *Id.* at 8–14.

77. *Id.* at 14.

78. *Id.* at 15–17.

79. *Id.* at 54–60 (Breyer, J., dissenting).

80. *Id.* at 14, 18–24.

81. For a longer discussion and criticism of the Court's vagueness rulings, see Said, *supra* note 8 at 1494–98.

82. 395 U.S. 444, 448–49 (1969) (distinguishing between mere advocacy and unlawful "incitement to imminent lawless action").

83. *Holder*, 561 U.S. at 30.

84. *Id.* at 30–33.

85. *Id.* at 49 (Breyer, J., dissenting).

86. *Id.* at 30–33.

87. Colin R.G. Murray, *The Problems with Proscription: Tackling Terrorist Organizations in the United States and the United Kingdom, in* SATVINDER JUSS & CLIVE WALKER, HUMAN RIGHTS AND THE WAR ON TERRORISM 20 (forthcoming 2015), http://papers.ssrn.com/sol3/papers.cfm?abstract_id=2513326.

88. United States v. El-Mezain, 664 F.3d 467, 485 (5th Cir. 2011).

89. *Id.*; United States v. Holy Land Found. for Relief & Dev., 3:04-CR-240-G, Superseding Indictment at ¶ 4 (N.D. Tex. Nov. 30, 2005) ("'Zakat,' which means 'charity' or 'alms giving' is one of the pillars of Islam and is an act incumbent on all practicing Muslims.").

90. *Id.* ("Additionally, due to HAMAS' substantial expenditures and the fungible nature of money, some of the money collected externally under humanitarian banners is routed to military and operational use, in addition to freeing up other funds for specific terrorist acts. Such uses include the provision of weapons, explosives, transportation services, safehouses, and job salaries for operatives.").

91. For an extended discussion of this issue, see Said, *supra* note 8 at 585–86.

92. *See Holy Land Found. for Relief & Dev.*, Superseding Indictment at ¶ 4.

93. *Id.*

94. Jason Trahan, *Summations Tell Jury: Don't Look at Politics*, DALL. MORNING NEWS, Nov. 11, 2008, at 3B (noting that even after retrying the defendants, the government had not designated the zakat committees); Press Release, U.S. Dep't of Treasury, Treasury Designates Charity Funneling Money to Palestinian Islamic Jihad—Action Marks 400th Designation of a Terrorist or Financier (May 4, 2005), www.treasury.gov/press-center/press-releases/pages/js2426.aspx (designating group implicated as a front group in connection with the prosecution in *United States v. Al-Arian*).

95. ACLU, BLOCKING FAITH, FREEZING CHARITY: CHILLING MUSLIM CHARITABLE GIVING IN THE "WAR ON TERRORISM FINANCING" 61–67 (2009), http://www.aclu.org/files/pdfs/humanrights/blockingfaith.pdf.

96. Mehanna was not the first individual indicted on § 2339B grounds based on activity online. In 2004, the government charged a Saudi graduate student at the University of Idaho with violating § 2339B based on his maintenance of certain websites suspected of terrorist links; a jury acquitted him on all terrorism counts. *No Conviction for Student in Terror Case*, N.Y. TIMES, June 11, 2004; *see also* Susan N. Herman, TAKING LIBERTIES: THE WAR ON TERROR AND THE EROSION OF AMERICAN DEMOCRACY 23–32 (2011).

97. United States v. Mehanna, 735 F.3d 32, 41 (1st Cir. 2013).

98. *Id.* The First Circuit noted that the word *jihad* could refer to both violent and nonviolent activity, but "the defendant used the term to refer to violent jihad—and that is the meaning we ascribe to it throughout the opinion." *See id.* at 41 n.3.

99. Andrew F. March, Op. Ed., *A Dangerous Mind?*, N.Y. TIMES, Apr. 22, 2012, at SR1 (Mehanna's expert witness characterizing the text as "a fairly routine exercise of Islamic jurisprudence explaining to pious Muslims how they can discharge what many of them believe to be a duty to contribute to wars of self-defense").

100. David Cole, *39 Ways to Limit Free Speech*, NYR BLOG (Apr. 19, 2012, 3:15 PM), http://www.nybooks.com/blogs/nyrblog/2012/apr/19/39-ways-limit-free-speech/; Amna Akbar, *How Tarek Mehanna Went to Prison for a Thought Crime*, NATION, Dec. 31, 2013 (the prosecution did not assert "that Mehanna's translations caused harm, or that he intended the translation to incite imminent criminal conduct. Instead, the speech-as-material-support theory appears to have turned largely on his attempts to convince and 'inspire' others to support opinions the United States government finds objectionable").

101. *See, e.g.*, George D. Brown, *Notes on a Terrorism Trial—Preventive Prosecution, "Material Support," and the Role of the Judge After* United States v. Mehanna, 4 HARV. NAT'L SEC. J. 1 (2013); Nikolas Abel, United States v. Mehanna, *The First Amendment, and Material Support in the War on Terror*, 54 B.C. L. REV. 711 (2013); Benjamin Wittes, *David Cole and Peter Margulies: An Exchange on Tarek Mehanna*, LAWFARE BLOG (Apr. 22, 2012, 3:45 PM), http://www.lawfareblog.com/2012/04/david-cole-and-peter-margulies-an-exchange-on-tarek-mehanna/.

102. *Mehanna*, 735 F.3d at 40 (also noting "the fine line between vital national security concerns and forbidden encroachments on constitutionally protected freedoms of speech and association").

103. *Id.* at 51.

104. *See* Marty Lederman, *Avoidance of the First Amendment Questions in the Mehanna Case*, JUST SECURITY BLOG (Nov. 14, 2013, 8:44 AM), http://justsecurity.org/2013/11/14/avoidance-amendment-questions-mehanna-case/.

105. *See* Akbar, *supra* note 97 (the government "conceded that there were no terrorist training camps in Yemen in 2004 and never introduced evidence that Mehanna had found one").

106. *See* Wadie E. Said, *The Terrorist Informant*, 85 WASH. L. REV. 687, 710–11 (2010) (discussing the case of Foad Farhi, an Iranian imam who refused to become an informant and, as a result, was pressured by the FBI to drop his bid for political asylum in the United States and leave the country or else he would be charged with terrorism crimes); *see also* discussion in Chapter 1, *supra*, on informants.

107. Matt Zapotosky, *Craig Baxam, ex-U.S. Soldier, Charged with Trying to Aid Terror Group al-Shabab*, WASH. POST, Jan. 9, 2012.

108. Ian Duncan, *7 Years Prison for Ex-Soldier Accused of Trying to Join Terror Group*, BALT. SUN, Jan. 13, 2014.

109. *See* Al-Bahlul v. United States, 767 F.3d 1, 10–12 (D.C. Cir. 2014); Hamdan v. United States, 696 F.3d 1238 (D.C. Cir. 2012).

110. United States v. Moalin, No. 10-CR-4246-JM, 2013 WL 6079518 (S.D. Cal. Nov. 18, 2013) (denying motion for a new trial); Ellen Nakashima, *NSA Cites Case as Success of Phone Data-Collection Program*, WASH. POST, Aug. 8, 2013.

111. *See, e.g.*, Laura K. Donohue, *U.S. Efforts to Stem the Flow of Funds to Terrorist Organizations: Export Controls, Financial Sanctions, and Material Support, in* DIRTY ASSETS: EMERGING ISSUES IN THE REGULATION OF CRIMINAL AND TERRORIST ASSETS 261–90 (Colin King & Clive Walker eds., 2015). Malick W. Ghachem, *Religious Liberty and the Financial War on Terror*, 12 FIRST AMEND. L. REV. 139 (2013).

CHAPTER 3

1. 561 U.S. 1, 130 S. Ct. 2705 (2010).

2. Americo R. Cinquegrana, *The Walls (and Wires) Have Ears: The Background and First Ten Years of the Foreign Intelligence Surveillance Act of 1978*, 137 U. PA. L. REV. 793, 806–12 (1989).

3. *See* TIM WEINER, ENEMIES: A HISTORY OF THE FBI xv–xvii, 140 (2012).

4. 50 U.S.C. §§ 1801(a) & (b), 1805.

5. *Id.* § 1803.

6. 18 U.S.C. § 2518; *see also* Daniel J. Solove, *Restructuring Electronic Surveillance Law*, 72 GEO. WASH. L. REV. 1264, 1278–82 (2004).

7. 50 U.S.C. § 1804(a)(6)(B).

8. *See* William C. Banks, *The Death of FISA*, 91 MINN. L. REV. 1209, 1262–71 (2007).

9. 50 U.S.C. § 1803(a)(1).

10. *See* Banks, *supra* note 8, at 1266 (discussing *United States v. al-Arian*).

11. *In re* All Matters Submitted to the Foreign Intelligence Surveillance Court, 218 F. Supp. 2d 611, 624 (FISA Ct. Rev. 2002), *abrogated by In re* Sealed Case, 310 F.3d 717 (FISA Ct. Rev. 2002).

12. *In re Sealed Case*, 310 F.3d at 731.

13. James Risen & Eric Lichtblau, *Bush Lets U.S. Spy on Callers Without Courts*, N.Y. TIMES, Dec. 16, 2005, at A1; Press Briefing by Attorney General Alberto Gonzales & General Michael Hayden, Principal Deputy Director for National Intelligence, Dec. 19, 2005, http://georgewbush-whitehouse.archives.gov/news/releases/2005/12/print/20051219-1.html.

14. 50 U.S.C. § 1881a. In February 2013, the Supreme Court rejected a challenge to this section of the FAA by ruling that the plaintiffs—a collection of human rights organizations—lacked standing to sue because their alleged injury was speculative and might never occur. *See* Clapper v. Amnesty Int'l U.S.A., 568 U.S. 398, 133 S. Ct. 1138 (2013).

15. *Clapper*, 133 S.Ct. at 1142-43.

16. Adam Liptak, *A Secret Surveillance Program Proves Challengeable in Theory Only*, N.Y. TIMES, July 16, 2013, at A11.

17. Glenn Greenwald, *NSA Collecting Phone Records of Millions of Verizon Customers Daily*, GUARDIAN, June 5, 2013.

18. United States v. Mohamud, 2014 WL 2866749 (D. Ore. June 24, 2014); United States v. Moalin, 2013 WL 6079518 (S.D. Ca. Nov. 18, 2013).

19. Glenn Greenwald & Ewen MacAskill, *NSA Prism Program Taps into User Data of Apple, Google and Others*, GUARDIAN, June 6, 2013.

20. Glenn Greenwald & Spencer Ackerman, *NSA Collected U.S. Email Records in Bulk for More Than Two Years Under Obama*, GUARDIAN, June 27, 2013.

21. Barton Gellman, *NSA Broke Privacy Rules Thousands of Times a Year, Audit Finds*, WASH. POST, Aug. 15, 2013.

22. Klayman v. Obama, 957 F. Supp. 2d 1, 29–44 (D.D.C. 2013).

23. Am. Civil Liberties Union v. Clapper, 959 F. Supp. 2d 724, 756–57 (S.D.N.Y. 2013).

24. *See* Electronic Privacy Information Center, Foreign Intelligence Surveillance Act Court Orders 1979–2014, http://epic.org/privacy/wiretap/stats/fisa_stats.html.

25. Letter from Peter J. Kadzik, Principal Deputy Assistant Attorney General, to The Honorable Harry Reid, Majority Leader, United States Senate (Apr. 30, 2014), http://fas.org/irp/agency/doj/fisa/2013rept.pdf; Peter J. Kadzik, Principal Deputy Assistant Attorney General,

to The Honorable Harry Reid, Majority Leader, United States Senate (Apr. 30, 2013), http://fas.org/irp/agency/doj/fisa/2012rept.pdf; Letter from Ronald Weich, Assistant Attorney General, to The Honorable Joseph R. Biden, President, United States Senate (Apr. 30, 2012), http://www.fas.org/irp/agency/doj/fisa/2011rept.pdf.

26. *See* United States v. Daoud, 761. F.3d 678, 681-82 (7th Cir. 2014); United States v. Aldawsari, 740 F.3d 1015, 1018-19 (5th Cir. 2014); United States v. Duka, 671 F.3d 329, 336–47 (3d Cir. 2011); United States v. Abu-Jihaad, 630 F.3d 102, 120 (2d Cir. 2010) (listing all cases to date considering and rejecting constitutional challenges to FISA).

The ruling in *United States v. Mehanna* is typical of a court's approach to a defendant's challenging the admission of FISA-derived evidence as illegal; a two-page order noting how the government followed all of the steps detailed by the statute in obtaining the evidence, thereby rendering it legal and properly admissible. 2011 WL 3652524 (D. Mass. Aug. 19, 2011).

27. *Duka*, 671 F.3d at 341–45.

28. Hasbajrami v. United States, 2014 WL 4954596, at *1-5 (E.D.N.Y. Oct. 2, 2014) (allowing withdrawal of guilty plea when government failed to reveal that it made use of evidence under provisions of FAA until after defendant pled guilty).

29. For a discussion of the problems inherent in police interrogation that can lead to false confessions, see George C. Thomas III & Richard A. Leo, Confessions of Guilt: From Torture to *Miranda* and Beyond 223–25 (2012); Brandon Garrett, *The Substance of False Confessions*, 62 Stan. L. Rev. 1051 (2010); Mark A. Godsey, *Reliability Lost, False Confessions Discovered*, 10 Chap. L. Rev. 623 (2010).

30. 384 U.S. 436 (1966).

31. Charlie Savage, *Debate over Delaying of* Miranda *Warning*, N.Y. Times, Apr. 20, 2013; Joel Achenbach & Robert Barnes, *Authorities Seek Answers in Boston Marathon Bombing*, Wash. Post, Apr. 20, 2013.

32. United States v. Abdulmutallab, 2011 WL 4345243, at *1–2, *5–6 (E.D. Mich. Sept. 16, 2011) (allowing the admission of the unwarned confession as a valid exercise of the public safety exception to *Miranda*).

33. *See* Savage, *supra* note 31.

34. Memorandum from the U.S. Dep't of Justice, Fed. Bureau of Investigation, Custodial Interrogation for Public Safety and Intelligence-Gathering Purposes of Operational Terrorists Inside the United States (Oct. 21, 2010) [hereinafter FBI Public Safety Memo], http://www.nytimes.com/2011/03/25/us/25miranda-text.html.

35. New York v. Quarles, 467 U.S. 649 (1984). For more discussion of the public safety exception in the terrorism context, see Bruce Ching, Mirandizing *Terrorism Suspects? The Public Safety Exception, the Rescue Doctrine, and Implicit Analogies to Self-Defense, Defense of Others, and Battered Woman Syndrome*, 64 Cath. U. L. Rev. 613 (2015), Norman Abrams, *Terrorism Prosecutions in U.S. Federal Court: Exceptions to Constitutional Evidence Rules and the Development of a Cabined Exception for Coerced Confessions*, 4 Harv. Nat'l Sec. J. 58 (2012); Joanna Wright, *Mirandizing Terrorists?: An Empirical Analysis of the Public Safety Exception*, 111 Colum. L. Rev. 1296 (2012).

36. United States v. Khalil, 214 F.3d 111, 121–22 (2d Cir. 2000).

37. *See, e.g.*, David Luban, *Liberalism, Torture, and the Ticking Bomb*, 91 Va. L. Rev. 1425 (2005).

38. Peter Baker, *A Renewed Debate over Suspect Rights*, N.Y. TIMES, May 4, 2010, at A28.

39. Press Release, U.S. Dep't Justice, Office of U.S. Att'y., S. Dist. N.Y., Manhattan U.S. Attorney Announces Guilty Plea of Ahmed Warsame, a Senior Terrorist Leader and Liaison Between Al Shabaab and Al Qaeda in the Arabian Peninsula for Providing Material Support to Both Terrorist Organizations (Mar. 25, 2013), http://www.justice.gov/usao/nys/pressreleases/March13/WarsameUnsealingPR.php.

40. Charlie Savage & Benjamin Weiser, *How the U.S. Is Interrogating a Qaeda Suspect*, N.Y. TIMES, Oct. 8, 2013, at A8.

41. Benjamin Weiser & Michael S. Schmidt, *Qaeda Suspect Facing Trial in New York over Africa Embassy Bombings Dies*, N.Y. TIMES, Jan. 4, 2015, at A9. Adam Goldman, *Video Shows U.S. Abduction of Accused al-Qaeda Terrorist on Trial for Embassy Bombings*, WASH. POST, Feb. 10, 2014.

42. Sari Horwitz, Amy Goldstein & Lynn Bui, *Benghazi Suspect Ahmed Abu Khattala, in D.C., Pleads Not Guilty to Conspiracy Charge*, WASH. POST, June 28, 2014; Michael S. Schmidt, *Holder Decision on Benghazi Case Reverberates*, N.Y. TIMES, Oct. 18, 2014, at A14.

43. FBI Public Safety Memo, *supra* note 34, ¶ 3 (citation omitted).

44. Missouri v. Seibert, 542 U.S. 600, 604 (2004). For further analysis of this issue, see Lee Ross Crain, *The Legality of Deliberate* Miranda *Violations: How Two-Step National Security Interrogations Undermine* Miranda *and Destabilize Fifth Amendment Protections*, 112 MICH. L. REV. 453 (2013).

45. For example, in 2013, U.S. personnel apprehended Nazih Abdul-Hamed al-Ruqai, a suspected Libyan al-Qaeda figure charged in connection with his role in the 1998 East Africa Embassy bombings, outside his house in Tripoli. The FBI proceeded to interrogate him for intelligence purposes for about a week, at which point he was given *Miranda* warnings and then subsequently confessed to his role in the bombings. *See* Benjamin Weiser, *U.S. Asserts Terror Suspect Has Implicated Himself*, N.Y. TIMES, Oct. 23, 2013, at A25.

46. *In re* Terrorist Bombings of U.S. Embassies in East Africa, 552 F.3d 177, 181–85 (2d Cir. 2008).

47. United States v. Bin Laden, 132 F. Supp. 2d 168, 171–72 (S.D.N.Y. 2001).

48. *Id.* at 185–89.

49. *Id.* at 188–89.

50. *In re Terrorist Bombings*, 552 F.3d at 203.

51. *Id.* at 206–09.

52. United States v. Abu Ali (*Abu Ali I*), 528 F.3d 210, 227 (4th Cir. 2008).

53. *See, e.g.*, Dickerson v. United States, 530 U.S. 428, 432–35 (2000) (discussing the history and continuing viability of the voluntariness test); Oregon v. Elstad, 470 U.S. 298, 304–05 (1985); *Abu Ali I*, 528 F.3d at 227, 231 (citing, inter alia, United States v. Yousef, 327 F.3d 56, 145 (2d Cir. 2003)).

54. *See* Wadie E. Said, *Coercing Voluntariness*, 85 IND. L.J. 1, 4–6 (2010) (discussing the history and criticism of the voluntariness test, and highlighting how the test for voluntariness is determined by nebulous standards such as "essentially free and unconstrained choice," and if "a defendant's 'will has been overborne and his capacity for self-determination critically impaired'") (citations omitted).

55. *Yousef*, 327 F.3d at 145–46 (shocks the conscience exception); *Abu Ali I*, 528 F.3d at 227–28 (joint venture exception).

56. 342 U.S. 165 (1952).

57. *See* Said, *supra* note 54, at 7–10 (detailing the criticism of the test and citing *United States v. Karake*, 443 F. Supp. 2d 8, 52–53 nn.73–74 (D.D.C. 2006)).

58. William J. Stuntz, *The Political Constitution of Criminal Justice*, 119 HARV. L. REV. 780, 822 (2006).

59. *See* Said, *supra* note 54, at 11–12 (discussing the history of the joint venture exception and its applicability in both the Fourth and Fifth Amendment contexts); *Abu Ali I*, 528 F.3d at 229–30; *Karake*, 443 F. Supp. 2d at 13 (discussing cases that considered the issue of "active" or "substantial" participation).

60. For this section, the facts and rulings in *Abu Ali* are taken from the lengthier discussion in Said, *supra* note 54, at 16–34; *see also* Wadie E. Said, *The Message and Means of the Modern Terrorism Prosecution*, 21 TRANSNAT'L L. & CONTEMP. PROBS. 175, 181–87 (2012). The basis for the rulings and facts discussed is from *Abu Ali I*, as well as United States v. Abu Ali (*Abu Ali II*), 395 F. Supp. 2d 338, 341, 343–44 (E.D. Va. 2005), and Abu Ali v. Ashcroft (*Abu Ali III*), 350 F. Supp. 2d 28, 33 (D.D.C. 2004).

61. For a critical analysis of the joint venture ruling in *Abu Ali*, see Jenny-Brooke Condon, *Extraterritorial Interrogation: The Porous Border Between Torture and U.S. Criminal Trials*, 60 RUTGERS L. REV. 647 (2008).

62. For more detail on this issue, see AMNESTY INT'L, USA: THE TRIAL OF AHMED ABU ALI—FINDINGS OF AMNESTY INTERNATIONAL'S TRIAL OBSERVATION 4–6 (Dec. 14, 2005), http://www.amnesty.org/en/library/info/AMR51/192/2005/en.

63. U.S. DEP'T OF STATE, COUNTRY REPORTS ON HUMAN RIGHTS PRACTICES FOR 2003: SAUDI ARABIA (Feb. 25, 2004), http://www.state.gov/g/drl/rls/hrrpt/2003/27937.htm.

64. Writing on this same issue, Professor Stephen Vladeck expresses some doubt that had the court considered the reports, it would have changed its opinion on the voluntariness of Abu Ali's confession. *See* Stephen I. Vladeck, *Terrorism Trials and the Article III Courts after* Abu Ali, 88 TEX. L. REV. 1501, 1513 n.82 (2010) ("[I]t is not at all obvious that the district court would have reached a different credibility determination, or would therefore have found Abu Ali's statements to have been involuntarily given.").

65. Neela Bannerjee, *Administration Rebuffed in Ruling on Deportation*, N.Y. TIMES, Jan. 11, 2008.

66. Khouzam v. Ashcroft, 361 F.3d 161, 163, 165, 169, 171 (2d Cir. 2004).

67. Khouzam v. Attorney Gen. of United States, 549 F.3d 235, 239, 259 (3d Cir. 2008).

68. For an extensive discussion of the ruling on Salah's confession, see Said, *supra* note 54, at 34–42.

69. Boim v. Holy Land Found. for Relief & Dev., 511 F.3d 707, 712 (7th Cir. 2007), *vacated, reh'g en banc granted*, 2008 U.S. App. LEXIS, at *1 (7th Cir. June 16, 2008), *modified*, 549 F.3d 685 (7th Cir. 2008). Salah also had the distinction of being the first American citizen to be classified as a "specially designated terrorist" by the Treasury Department's Office of Foreign Assets Control, meaning he could not open a bank account, receive employment, or donate to his mosque without first obtaining approval from the government; after suing the government, he was finally removed from the list in late 2012. Scott Shane, *Man Removed from Terror Suspect List*, N.Y. TIMES, Nov. 8, 2012, at A13; David Cole, *The New McCarthyism: Repeating History in the War on Terrorism*, 38 HARV. C.R.-C.L. L. REV. 1, 28 (2003).

70. United States v. Marzook (*Marzook I*), 435 F. Supp. 2d 708, 777 (N.D. Ill. 2006).

71. United States v. Marzook (*Marzook II*), 412 F. Supp. 2d 913 (N.D. Ill. 2006).

72. *Marzook I*, 435 F. Supp. 2d at 718; *see also* United States v. Salah, 462 F. Supp. 2d 915, 917–18 (N.D. Ill. 2006) (stating that the government admitted that ISA used the following methods during the time period in question: hoods, handcuffs, shackles, handcuffing a detainee to a small chair while hooded, threatening harm to detainee and his family, sleep deprivation, and, under certain circumstances suggesting an imminent threat to human life, slapping).

73. *Marzook I*, 435 F. Supp. 2d at 777.

74. *Karake*, 443 F. Supp. 2d 12–14.

75. *Id.* at 85 n.110.

76. *Id.* at 61.

77. Fed. R. Evid. 401 ("Evidence is relevant if: (a) it has any tendency to make a fact more or less probable than it would be without the evidence; and (b) the fact is of consequence in determining the action.").

78. Fed. R. Evid. 402 ("Irrelevant evidence is not admissible.").

79. Fed. R. Evid. 403.

80. United States v. Jayyousi, 657 F.3d 1085, 1107–08 (11th Cir. 2011) (citing United States v. Merrill, 513 F.3d 1293, 1301 (11th Cir. 2008)); Jennifer L. Mnookin, *Atomism, Holism, and the Judicial Assessment of Evidence*, 60 UCLA L. Rev. 1524, 1557 (2013) ("Rule 403 is thus explicitly designed to favor admissibility; it is, therefore, a low-threshold evidentiary determination, both because it is tilted towards admissibility and because it places the burden of establishing the danger on the party that wishes to exclude."); Edward J. Imwinkelried, *Impoverishing the Trier of Fact: Excluding the Proponent's Expert Testimony Due to the Opponent's Inability to Afford Rebuttal Evidence*, 40 Conn. L. Rev. 317, 336 (2007) ("As one court observed in a case involving expert testimony, in effect exclusion under Rule 403 is a last resort.") (internal citation omitted).

81. *See* Spirit v. Mendelsohn, 552 U.S. 379, 387–88 (2008) ("Relevance and prejudice under Rules 401 and 403 are determined in the context of the facts and arguments in a particular case, and thus are generally not amenable to broad *per se* rules.") (citing Fed. R. Evid. advisory committee's notes).

82. While I was an assistant federal public defender in Florida, I worked on a large terrorism conspiracy case, as already noted. The allegations against all of the defendants were rooted in their activities in North America on behalf of the Palestinian Islamic Jihad, a designated FTO. The government conceded that none of the defendants had ever been involved with planning or committing an act of violence, but that their support for the group constituted a violation of a series of criminal statutes, largely centered on the ban on providing material support to an FTO. Because the group had carried out a series of suicide bus bombings in the Middle East, the FBI wanted to demonstrate the force and impact of the bombings, so it enacted its own demonstration at a test site, blowing up old public buses from the regional transportation authority duly equipped with dummies to substitute for actual riders. One of the dummies was wearing a t-shirt with "John FBI Academy" on it. The FBI also prepared a report on the test bombings, replete with images, and a video recording featuring freeze-frame and slow-motion replays of the bombings for maximum impact. The court deferred ruling until trial on a defense objection that such a presentation to the jury would be prejudicial, a decision that ultimately led to the government's withdrawal of the demonstrative explosion evidence. Where defense counsel clearly thought that such evidence was both irrelevant and prejudicial, the FBI at least considered it relevant

enough to carry out the tests and have the prosecution indicate to the court the intention to produce it as evidence at trial. Clearly, opposing sides in criminal litigation can have diverging and opposing views on what is relevant and prejudicial. *See* United States v. Hatem Naji Fariz, Case 8:03-cr-00077-JSM-TBM, Doc. 982, Motion in Limine of Hatem Naji Fariz to Preclude the Introduction of the Attacks, or Alternatively to Require Order of Proof to Reduce Unnecessary Prejudice Regarding Alleged Attacks, and to Preclude the Introduction of Irrelevant, Prejudicial, and Hearsay Evidence, Request for A Pretrial Hearing, and Memorandum of Law in Support, Apr. 25, 2005; Elaine Silvestrini, *Al-Arian Defense Targets Evidence*, TAMPA TRIBUNE, Apr. 27, 2005; United States v. Hatem Naji Fariz, Case 8:03-cr-00077-JSM-TBM, Doc. 1136, Order on Defendant's Motion in Limine, May 27, 2005.

83. United States v. Salameh, 152 F.3d 88, 110–11 (2d Cir. 1998).

84. FED. R. EVID. 404(b)(1) ("Evidence of a crime, wrong, or other act is not admissible to prove a person's character in order to show that on a particular occasion the person acted in accordance with the character.").

85. *Salameh*, 152 F.3d at 112.

86. United States v. Hammoud, 381 F.3d 316, 326 (4th Cir. 2004), *overruled on other grounds sub nom.* Hammoud v. United States, 543 U.S. 1097 (2005).

87. *Id*. at 340–43.

88. *Id*. (detailing the challenge to the videotape presentation).

89. *Id*. at 341–42 (citing *Salameh*, 152 F.3d at 111).

90. *Id*. at 384 n.16 (Gregory, J., dissenting).

91. The Fourth Circuit found the Supreme Court's decision in *Old Chief v. United States*, which required the government to allow a defendant to stipulate to his status as a felon in a prosecution on being a felon in possession of a weapon, was not applicable to Hammoud's case, in that "the videotapes were admissible to prove facts beyond Hammoud's stipulation." 381 F.3d at 342 n.12 (citing Old Chief v. United States, 519 U.S. 172, 174, 186–87 (1997)).

92. *Hammoud*, 381 F.3d at 327–31.

93. See *United States v. Stewart*, 590 F.3d 93, 98–100, 101–08 (2d Cir. 2009), for the full factual record in the case.

94. *Id*. at 132–33; *see also* Julia Preston, *Tape Ties Bin Laden to Call to Aid Sheik*, N.Y. TIMES, Sept. 8, 2004, at B3.

95. United States v. Sattar, 395 F. Supp. 2d 79, 103–04 (S.D.N.Y. 2005). Federal Rule of Evidence 105 governs the use of limiting instructions. FED. R. EVID. 105 ("When evidence which is admissible as to one party or for one purpose but not admissible as to another party or for another purpose is admitted, the court, upon request, shall restrict the evidence to its proper scope and instruct the jury accordingly.").

96. *Stewart*, 590 F.3d at 132–33.

97. *See* FED. R. EVID. 405(b) ("When a person's character or character trait is an essential element of a charge, claim, or defense, the character or trait may also be proved by relevant specific instances of the person's conduct.").

98. United States v. Siraj, 468 F. Supp. 2d 408, 413 (E.D.N.Y. 2007), *aff'd*, 533 F.3d 99 (2d Cir. 2008).

99. Robin Shulman, *The Informer: Behind the Scenes, or Setting the Stage?*, WASH. POST, May 29, 2007, http://www.washingtonpost.com/wp-dyn/content/article/2007/05/28/AR2007052801401.html; *Siraj*, 468 F. Supp. 2d at 415.

100. *Siraj*, 468 F. Supp. 2d at 414.

101. *Id.* at 419, 422–23.

102. *Id.* at 420.

103. 545 F.3d 139, 145 (2d Cir. 2008).

104. *Id.*

105. *Id.* at 160.

106. *Id.* at 161.

107. *Id.* at 162.

108. *Id.*

109. *Id.*

110. *Id.* at 163.

111. *Id.*

112. *Id.* at 178–79.

113. *See* United States v. Duka, 671 F.3d 329, 50–52 (3d Cir 2011) (finding no Federal Rule of Evidence 403 violation when district court admitted videos of beheadings watched by the defendants as proof of their motive and intent in an alleged plot to attack U.S. military personnel in Fort Dix, N.J.); United States v. Abu-Jihaad, 630 F.3d 102, 133–34 (2d Cir 2010) (same type of ruling concerning "violent, pro-jihadist" videos).

114. Federal Rule of Evidence 702 states:

> A witness who is qualified as an expert by knowledge, skill, experience, training, or education, may testify in the form of opinion or otherwise if:
>
> (a) the expert's scientific, technical, or other specialized knowledge will help the trier of fact to understand the evidence or to determine a fact in issue;
> (b) the testimony is based on sufficient facts or data;
> (c) the testimony is the product of reliable principles and methods; and
> (d) the expert has reliably applied the principles and methods to the facts of the case.

FED. R. EVID. 702.

115. Daubert v. Merrell Dow Pharm., Inc., 509 U.S. 579, 592–93, 597 (1993); FED. R. EVID. 702 advisory committee note.

116. *See* Kumho Tire Co. v. Carmichael, 526 U.S. 137, 156 (1999).

117. *E.g.*, United States v. Defreitas, No. 07-CR-543 (DLI) (SMG), 2011 WL 317964, at *7 (E.D.N.Y. Jan. 31, 2011).

118. *See* FED. R. EVID. 703 ("The facts or data in the particular case upon which an expert bases an opinion or inference may be those perceived by or made known to the expert at or before the hearing. If of a type reasonably relied upon by experts in the particular field in forming opinions or inferences upon the subject, the facts or data need not be admissible in evidence in order for the opinion or inference to be admitted. Facts or data that are otherwise inadmissible shall not be disclosed to the jury by the proponent of the opinion or inference unless the court determines that their probative value in assisting the jury to evaluate the expert's opinion substantially outweighs their prejudicial effect."); Jennifer L. Mnookin, *Expert Evidence and the Confrontation Clause After* Crawford v. Washington, 15 J. L. & POL'Y 791, 803 (2007) ("In short, so long as experts may rely on inadmissible factual matters as the bases for their conclusion, there is an inevitable tension between jury education and adherence to the rest of the rules of evidence.").

119. *See, e.g.*, Wesley Yang, *The Terrorist Search Engine*, N.Y. MAG., Dec. 13, 2010 (referring to Kohlmann as "the Doogie Howser of Terrorism" and discussing Kohlmann's credentials that lead to his certification as an expert witness in over twenty high profile terrorism prosecutions).

120. *See About Evan Kohlmann: Court Testimonies*, FLASHPOINT PARTNERS, https://flashpoint-intel.com/about_evan_kohlmann.php (last visited Aug. 16, 2013) (on file with author) (listing twenty-seven American prosecutions in which Kohlmann has testified as an expert, as well as several prosecutions in various foreign courts); United States v. Abu Ghayth, 2014 WL 978629 (S.D.N.Y. Feb. 28, 2014) ("[Kohlmann] has been qualified to testify in twenty-five federal criminal trials.").

121. United States v. Farhane, 634 F.3d 127, 158–60 (2d Cir. 2011).

122. *See About Evan Kohlmann: Court Testimonies, supra* note 120.

123. Yang, *supra* note 119.

124. United States v. Kassir, No. S204 Cr. 356(JFK), 2009 WL 910767, at *6 (S.D.N.Y. Apr. 2, 2009); Philip Giraldi, *Terrorism Experts on Parade*, ANTIWAR.COM (July 27, 2011, 11:00 PM), http://original.antiwar.com/giraldi/2011/07/27/terrorism-experts-on-parade/.

125. Giraldi, *supra* note 124.

126. NAT'L COMM'N ON TERRORIST ATTACKS UPON THE UNITED STATES, THE 9/11 COMMISSION REPORT 58 n.37 (2004) (citing EVAN F. KOHLMANN, AL-QAIDA'S JIHAD IN EUROPE: THE AFGHAN-BOSNIAN NETWORK (2004)), http://9-11commission.gov/report/911Report.pdf; *see also Kassir*, 2009 WL 910767, at *6 ("[Kohlmann's] book about al Qaeda in Europe is cited in the 9–11 Commission's Report.").

127. Giraldi, *supra* note 124.

128. United States v. Paracha, No. 03 CR 1197(SHS), 2006 WL 12768, at *20 (S.D.N.Y. Jan. 3, 2006) (internal citations omitted).

129. *E.g.*, United States v. Subasic, 568 F. App'x 234, 235 (4th Cir. 2014); United States v. Mostafa, 2014 WL 1744717, at *1–6 (S.D.N.Y. Apr. 23, 2014); United States v. Kaziu, 559 Fed. App'x 32, 38 (2d Cir. 2014); United States v. Abu Ghayth, 2014 WL 978629, at *1 (S.D.N.Y. Feb. 28, 2014); United States v. Hassan, 742 F.3d 104, 129–32 (4th Cir. 2014); United States v. Farhane, 634 F.3d 127, 158–59 (2d Cir. 2011); United States v. Benkahla, 530 F.3d 300, 309 n.2 (4th Cir. 2008); United States v. Abu-Jihaad, 600 F. Supp. 2d 362, 366 n.2 (D. Conn. 2009); *Kassir*, 2009 WL 910767, at *4–7; United States v. Sabir, No. S4 05 Cr. 673 (LAP), 2007 WL 1373184, at *7–9 (S.D.N.Y. May 10, 2007); *Paracha*, 2006 WL 12768, at *18–21.

Research has revealed two instances of Kohlmann's testimony being limited. The first is *United States v. Amawi*, in which the district court denied his proposed testimony as "not relevant to the issues in this case," and that "the limited probative value of his testimony is outweighed very substantially by its very considerable potential for unfair prejudice to the defendants." 541 F. Supp. 2d 945, 949–55 (N.D. Ohio 2008). Kohlmann ultimately was allowed to testify once the government further narrowed the scope of his proposed testimony, and the Sixth Circuit later found no error in allowing his testimony. United States v. Amawi, 695 F.3d 457, 478–79 (6th Cir. 2012); United States v. Amawi, 552 F. Supp. 2d 669, 672 n.2 (N.D. Ohio 2008). The second comes from an unreported decision in the prosecution of Sohiel Omar Kabir, where the district court allowed Kohlmann to testify as an expert regarding al-Qaeda, the Taliban, and the global jihad movement, but not about "homegrown extremism" or the "contemporary extremist" profile. *See* United States v. Kabir, Minute Order Granting in Part Motion to Exclude Testimony of Evan Kohlmann, ED CR 12-00092-VAP (C.D. Ca. July 7, 2014).

130. *See* Maxine D. Goodman, *A Hedgehog on the Witness Stand—What's the Big Idea?: The Challenges of Using* Daubert *to Assess Social Science and Nonscientific Testimony*, 59 AM. U. L. REV. 635, 660–69 (2010) (analyzing five cases in which the government called Kohlmann as an expert) (internal citations omitted).

131. *Id.* at 669.

132. *See, e.g., Farhane*, 634 F.3d at 159 n.32 (noting Kohlmann's expert testimony in previous cases).

133. Goodman, *supra* note 130, at 669.

134. United States v. Aref, 285 F. App'x 784, 789–92 (2d Cir. 2008). For an in-depth discussion of the prosecution and its troubling reliance on an undercover informant, see Wadie Said, *The Terrorist Informant*, 85 WASH. L. REV. 687, 726–28 (2010) (discussing the role of an FBI informant in the terrorism prosecution of Yassin Aref and Mohammed Hossain).

135. Petra Bartosiewicz, *Experts in Terror*, NATION, Feb. 4, 2008, at 20–21.

136. *Id.* at 21; *see also* Tom Mills, *Evan Kohlmann; The Doogie Howser of Terrorism?*, SPINWATCH.ORG (Apr. 29, 2008), http://www.spinwatch.org/index.php/tom-mills/item/521-evan-kohlmann-the-doogie-howser-of-terrorism.

137. *See* Bartosiewicz, *supra* note 135, at 20 ("'The Al Qaeda connection was critical,' Timimi's defense attorney Edward MacMahon Jr. told me. 'If a jury in the US finds any connection between your client and Osama bin Laden, you're going to get convicted. So Kohlmann provides key testimony in the case that the US bombed an Al Qaeda terror camp in Afghanistan in 1998 and there was a member of Lashkar-e-Taiba in the training camp. That was the connection, and when Timimi was telling the [other defendants] to go to Pakistan, what he was really telling them was to go to Al Qaeda. What Kohlmann really did for the prosecutors was to tie it all up in a big bow.' Timimi was found guilty on all counts at the trial, which took place in a courtroom seven miles from the Pentagon, and sentenced to life in prison.").

138. Yang, *supra* note 119 ("'I think no serious academic would ever testify in such a cavalier fashion with such generalizations and quite frankly mumbo-jumbo-style analysis,' [Magnus Ranstorp, the research director of the Center for Asymmetric Threat Studies at the Swedish National Defence College and a widely recognized authority on terrorism] says. 'It takes about 30 seconds to spot that Kohlmann produces junk science in court.'"); *see also* Bartosiewicz, *supra* note 135, at 20 ("Jessica Stern, a professor of public policy at Harvard University who recently published a book based on four years of field interviews with insurgent leaders, says simply siphoning raw data from Internet chat rooms fails to take a complex view of terrorism. 'They are reading what the terrorists say about themselves, and there's lots of disinformation there,' she said of Kohlmann . . . .").

139. Yang, *supra* note 119.

140. United States v. Jayyousi, 657 F.3d 1085, 1098–1101, 1106–08 (11th Cir. 2011).

141. *Id.*

142. *See id.* at 1095 ("In reviewing the intercepted calls in this case, Agent Kavanaugh noticed the use of code words such as "football" and "soccer" for jihad; "tourism" for jihad; "tourist" for mujahideen; "sneakers" for support; "going on the picnic" for travel to jihad; "married" for martyrdom; "trade" for jihad; "open up a market" for opening a group in support of jihad; open up a "branch" for starting a jihad support group; "the first area" for Afghanistan; "school over there to teach football" for a place to train in jihad; "students" for Taliban; "iron" for weapon; "joint venture" for a group of mujahideen; "full sponsorship" for income for room and board

(at training camp); and "open the door" for opportunity to go to jihad"); *see also id.* at 1099 ("Dr. Gunaratna opined that the defendants used code words in some of their communications. When they used the word "tourism," that meant armed jihad; the word "football and/or soccer" meant fighting or combat; the phrase "to be married" referred to going to paradise or martyr-dom; the phrase "first area" meant Pakistan or Afghanistan; the word "screws" meant bullets; the word "eggplant" meant a rocket propelled grenade launcher; and other words denoting fruits and vegetables were used as codes for arms.").

On a separate point, the issue of allowing an FBI agent or law enforcement officer to testify as an expert on a criminal enterprise's use of codes is not without its problems. *See* Brian R. Gallini, *To Serve and Protect? Officers as Expert Witnesses in Federal Drug Prosecutions*, 19 GEO. MASON L. REV. 363 (2012).

143. *See* United States v. Aguilera-Meza, 329 F. App'x 825, 834 (10th Cir. 2009) (find-ing police officer competent to testify as expert where his first language was Spanish and he had worked undercover approximately fifty times using Spanish drug slang); United States v. Verdin-Garcia, 516 F.3d 884, 893 (10th Cir. 2008) (upholding admission of expert testimony on Spanish drug code where translator had familiarity with slang from region of defendant's origin in Mexico).

144. *Jayyousi*, 657 F.3d at 1099–1100, 1107–08.

145. WASH. INST. FOR NEAR EAST POL'Y, *Biography of Matthew Levitt*, http://www.wash-ingtoninstitute.org/experts/view/levitt-matthew (last visited Dec. 3, 2014).

146. United States v. El-Mezain, 664 F.3d 467, 515 (5th Cir. 2011). Despite this ruling, it should be noted that Levitt's objectivity and credentials have been called into question out-side the courtroom. *See* Ken Silverstein, *The Government's Man: How to Read the Resume of a Terrorist Expert*, HARPER'S, June 2012, at 58–59.

147. *El-Mezain*, 664 F.3d at 515.

148. Chris Hack, *Salah on Trial: Expert Testifies About Hamas*, DAILY SOUTHTOWN (Tinley Park, IL), Oct. 25, 2006.

149. United States v. Hayat, 710 F.3d 875, 880 (9th Cir. 2013).

150. *Hayat*, 710 F.3d at 900.

151. *Id.* at 911 (Tashima, J., dissenting) (emphasis in original).

152. FED. R. EVID. 704(b) ("No expert witness testifying with respect to the mental state or condition of a defendant in a criminal case may state an opinion or inference as to whether the defendant did or did not have the mental state or condition constituting an element of the crime charged or of a defense thereto.").

153. *Hayat*, 710 F.3d at 901–02.

154. *Id.* (internal citations omitted).

155. *See* Gallini, *supra* note 142, at 399–411.

156. *Hayat*, 710 F.3d at 910–15 (Tashima, J., dissenting).

157. *Id.* at 914.

158. *Id.*

159. *Id.* The above examples of expert witnesses divining terroristic intent from cul-tural and religious practices fall into what Leti Volpp has criticized generally as "the racial-ized conception of culture." *See* Leti Volpp, *Blaming Culture for Bad Behavior*, 12 YALE J. L. & HUMAN. 89, 89 (2000). Specifically, in this vein scholars have remarked on the phenom-enon of racializing Arabs and Muslims as terrorists, a pattern an expert witness can certainly

exploit, consciously or unconsciously. *See* Muneer I. Ahmad, *Resisting Guantanamo: Rights at the Brink of Dehumanization*, 103 Nw. U. L. Rev. 1683, 1697 (2009); John Tehranian, Whitewashed: America's Invisible Middle Eastern Minority 121 (2009); Susan M. Akram & Kevin R. Johnson, *Race and Civil Rights Pre-September 11, 2001: The Targeting of Arabs and Muslims, in* Civil Rights in Peril: The Targeting of Arabs and Muslims 18 (Elaine C. Hagopian ed., 2004); Leti Volpp, *The Citizen and the Terrorist*, 49 UCLA L. Rev. 1575, 1575–76 (2002).

160. Hayat's expert witness, a professor of Asian studies who knew Urdu and whose area of specialty was Pakistani society and culture, was forbidden from testifying that the supplication was the sort of prayer commonly carried by Pakistanis for protection and good fortune while traveling because she did not know Arabic. 710 F.3d at 902.

161. *Id.* at 914–15 n.15 (Tashima, J., dissenting).

162. *El-Mezain*, 664 F.3d at 490 (5th Cir. 2011). The other, a military officer, testified as a fact witness regarding the seizure of mainly documentary evidence during raids by the Israeli army on several zakat committee offices in the West Bank.

163. Israel Security Agency, *Core Values of the Israel Security Agency*, http://www.shabak.gov.il/English/about/Pages/valuseEn.aspx (last visited Aug. 19, 2013).

164. *El-Mezain*, 664 F.3d at 490.

165. *Id.* at 494.

166. El-Mezain v. United States, 133 S. Ct. 525 (2012).

167. Smith v. Illinois, 390 U.S. 129, 131–32 (1968).

168. *El-Mezain*, 664 F.3d at 491 (citing *Smith*, 390 U.S. at 133–34).

169. Jeffrey Kahn, *What if the Boy Who Cried Wolf Could Testify Under a Pseudonym . . . as an Expert Witness on Canis Lupus*, Concurring Opinions Blog (Dec. 12, 2011, 1:08 PM), http://www.concurringopinions.com/archives/2011/12/what-if-the-boy-who-cried-wolf-coul d-testify-under-a-pseudonym-as-an-expert-witness-on-canis-lupus.html.

170. Emily Ratner, *Anonymous Accusers in the Holy Land: Subverting the Right of Confrontation in the United States' Largest Terrorism-Financing Trial*, 13 Loy. J. Pub. Int. L. 575, 611 (2012).

171. The cases all dealt with the same expert, a Salvadoran police investigator who testified about the gang MS-13. *See* United States v. Argueta, 470 F. App'x 176, 179–80 (4th Cir. 2012); United States v. Ramos-Cruz, 667 F.3d 487, 500–01 (4th Cir. 2012); United States v. Zelaya, 336 F. App'x 355, 357–58 (4th Cir. 2009); United States v. Machado-Erazo, 951 F. Supp. 2d 148, 158 (D.C. Cir. 2013) (noting that in the previous cases the expert "was only offered to provide 'background information about the internal working of MS-13 generally,' not to give factual testimony about any activities undertaken by these specific defendants") (citing *Ramos-Cruz*, 667 F.3d at 501)).

172. *El-Mezain*, 664 F.3d at 492.

CHAPTER 4

1. Deborah Sontag, *A Videotape Offers a Window into a Terror Suspect's Isolation*, N.Y. Times, Dec. 4, 2006, at A1.

2. *See* Lizette Alvarez, *Sentence for Terrorist Is Too Short, Court Rules*, N.Y. Times, Sept. 19, 2011, at A12; Padilla *ex rel.* Newman v. Rumsfeld, 243 F. Supp.2d 42, 48–49 (S.D.N.Y. 2003),

aff'd in part, rev'd in part sub nom. Padilla v. Rumsfeld, 352 F.3d 695 (2d Cir. 2003) (pointing out the government's "disappointing conduct" in the case), *rev'd*, 542 U.S. 426 (2004); Padilla v. Hanft, 432 F.3d 582, 585 (4th Cir. 2005)(describing how the government's actions gave rise to an impression that it wanted to avoid a ruling by the Supreme Court). Both Padilla and his mother were unsuccessful in holding anyone accountable for his treatment in military custody, as their federal lawsuits were dismissed. Padilla v. Yoo, 678 F.3d 748 (9th Cir. 2012); Lebron v. Rumsfeld, 670 F.3d 540 (4th Cir. 2012).

3. United States v. Jayyousi, 657 F.3d 1085, 1111–12 (11th Cir. 2011).

4. Section 2339A reads as follows:

> Whoever provides material support or resources or conceals or disguises the nature, location, source, or ownership of material support or resources, knowing or intending that they are to be used in preparation for, or in carrying out, a violation of . . . [any one of several dozen enumerated crimes] . . . or in preparation for, or in carrying out, the concealment of an escape from the commission of any such violation, or attempts or conspires to do such an act, shall be fined under this title, imprisoned not more than 15 years, or both, and, if the death of any person results, shall be imprisoned for any term of years or for life.

18 U.S.C. § 2339A.

5. *Jayyousi*, 657 F.3d at 1091; Abby Goodnough, *Prosecutors Turn to Padilla for Closing Arguments*, N.Y. TIMES, Aug. 14, 2007, at A18.

6. United States v. Hassoun et al., Case No. 04-60001-CR-COOKE, Superseding Indictment Count 1, Nov. 17, 2005, 2005 WL 5680800 (S.D. Fla.).

7. *Id.*, Counts 4–11.

8. *Jayyousi*, 657 F.3d at 1091–92.

9. Robert M. Chesney, *Beyond Conspiracy? Anticipatory Prosecution and the Challenge of Unaffiliated Terrorism*, 80 S. CAL. L. REV. 425, 459 (2008) ("§ 956 prosecutions also serve as the most common predicate offense for terrorism-related prosecutions under a separate statute, 18 U.S.C. § 2339A"); Aziz Huq, *Forum Choice for Terrorism Suspects*, 61 DUKE L. J. 1415, 1432 n.61 (2012).

10. United States v. Hassoun et al., Case No. 04-60001-CR-COOKE, Superseding Indictment ¶ 1, Nov. 17, 2005, 2005 WL 5680800.

11. United States v. Hassoun et al., Case No. 04-60001-CR-COOKE, Government's Motion to Reconsider Order Granting Defendant Hassoun's Motion for Clarification of Order Regarding "Manner and Means" of Conspiracy, 2006 WL 4710607 (S.D. Fla. Aug. 7, 2006).

12. Letter from Russell R. Killinger, Assistant United States Attorney, to Kenneth Swartz and Jeanne Baker (July 7, 2006) (attached to Defendant Hassoun's Motion for Clarification of Court's Ruling as to What Government Must Particularize Regarding the "Manner and Means" of the Conspiracy, United States v. Hassoun, 04-cr-60001 (July 25, 2006)), cited in Chesney, *supra* note 9, at 472–73.

13. *Jayyousi*, 657 F.3d at 1107–08; Carol J. Williams, *Padilla Jury Sees Video of Bin Laden*, L.A. TIMES, June 27, 2007, articles.latimes.com/2007/jun/27/nation/na-padilla27 ("'Typically in most jurors' minds there is some sense that the video would not have been allowed to be

shown unless there was some good reason for doing so,' said [veteran trial consultant Philip K.] Anthony, head of DecisionQuest in Los Angeles. 'Presenting what most Americans would view as emotional footage of Bin Laden saying what he's going to do to America … I think more often than not that produces a sense of guilt by association.'").

14. *Jayyousi*, 657 F.3d at 1096–97.

15. *See* Brief of Amicus Curiae Scholars et al. in Support of Petitioners with Experience in Terrorism-Related Issues, Holder v. Humanitarian Law Project, 130 S. Ct. 2705 (2010).

16. Chesney, *supra* note 9, at 473 (noting the difference between charging the defendants with an agreement "to engage in conduct that they intended would produce violent acts overseas," which is preferable and much more narrow than what was alleged in the indictment, namely, "unbounded definition of the agreement that would encompass quite literally the entire swath of conduct associated with the global jihad movement no matter how remote from a particular defendant's actions and intentions"); Peter Margulies, *Guantanamo by Other Means: Conspiracy Prosecutions and Law Enforcement Dilemmas After September 11*, 43 GONZ. L. REV. 513, 541 (2008) (arguing that the government's theory of a global jihad movement is a "vague entity [that] should not substitute for proof of an appropriately tailored agreement").

17. Margulies, *supra* note 16, at 540.

18. *Id.* at 540–41.

19. United States v. Chhun, 744 F.3d 1110, 1118–21 (9th Cir. 2014) (upholding Neutrality Act convictions of a man who plotted to overthrow the government of Cambodia and depose its Prime Minister).

20. KENT ROACH, THE 9/11 EFFECT: COMPARATIVE COUNTER-TERRORISM 194 (2011).

21. Adam Liptak, *Padilla Case Offers New Model of Terrorism Trial*, N.Y. TIMES, Aug. 18, 2007.

22. Abby Goodnough & Scott Shane, *Padilla Is Guilty on All Charges in Terror Trial*, N.Y. TIMES, Aug. 17, 2007, at A1.

23. Sheryl Gay Stolberg, *Obama Would Move Some Detainees to U.S.*, N.Y. TIMES, May 22, 2009, at A1.

24. Benjamin Weiser, *A Plea of Not Guilty for Guantanamo Detainee*, N.Y. TIMES, June 10, 2009, at A25.

25. Editorial, *The Ghailani Verdict*, N.Y. TIMES, Nov. 19, 2010, at A30.

26. United States v. Ghailani, 733 F.3d 29, 38–41 (2d Cir. 2013); Benjamin Weiser, *Terrorism Trial May Point Way for 9/11 Cases*, N.Y. TIMES, Nov. 23, 2009, at A1.

27. Benjamin Weiser, *Judge Bars Major Witness from Terrorism Trial*, N.Y. TIMES, Oct. 10, 2010, at A1.

28. *Ghailani*, 733 F.3d at 40–41.

29. *Id.*; Charlie Savage, *Terror Verdict Tests Obama's Strategy on Trials*, N.Y. TIMES, Nov. 18, 2010.

30. Benjamin Weiser, *Former Detainee's Right to Speedy Trial Wasn't Violated, Appeals Panel Rules*, N.Y. TIMES, Oct. 25, 2013, at A21.

31. *Ghailani*, 733 F.3d at 37.

32. He was precluded from bringing his claim under the Speedy Trial Act, as its provisions apply to delays occurring after a defendant's initial appearance before the court. *See* United States v. Ghailani, 751 F. Supp. 2d 515, 526 n.66 (S.D.N.Y. 2010) (citing 18 U.S.C. § 3161(c)(1)).

33. Barker v. Wingo, 407 U.S. 514, 522 (1972) (describing the constitutional right to a "speedy" trial as difficult to define, as it is "amorphous" and "necessarily relative").

34. *Ghailani*, 733 F.3d at 42–43 (internal citations omitted).

35. *Id.* at 43.

36. *Id.* at 46–52.

37. Anthony O'Rourke, *Extrajudicial Detentions and the Speedy Trial Right: Reflections on United States v. Ghailani*, at 14, http://ssrn.com/abstract = 2427934.

38. *Ghailani*, 733 F.3d at 50–51.

39. Michael B. Mukasey, *The Obama Administration and the War on Terror*, 33 HARV. J. L. & PUB. POL'Y 953, 961 (2010).

40. Petra Bartosiewicz, *The Intelligence Factory: How America Makes Its Enemies Disappear*, HARPER'S, Nov. 2009, at 42-51.

41. DEBORAH SCROGGINS, WANTED WOMEN: FAITH, LIES AND THE WAR ON TERROR: THE LIVES OF AYAAN HIRSI ALI AND AAFIA SIDDIQUI 185–89 (2012).

42. *Id.* at 245–53; Bartosiewicz, *supra* note 40; United States v. Paracha, 2006 WL 12768, at *23 (S.D.N.Y. Jan. 3, 2006).

43. These facts are drawn from *United States v. Siddiqui*, 699 F.3d 690, 696–97 (2d Cir. 2012).

44. *Id.* at 696–99, 710.

45. *Id.* at 697.

46. *Id.* at 705–06.

47. C.J. Hughes, *Neuroscientist Denies Trying to Kill Americans*, N.Y. TIMES, Jan. 29, 2010, at A21.

48. Bartosiewicz, *supra* note 40; SCROGGINS, *supra* note 41, at 248; Declan Walsh, *The Mystery of Dr. Aafia Siddiqui*, GUARDIAN, Nov. 23, 2009, http://www.theguardian.com/world/2009/nov/24/aafia-siddiqui-al-qaida.

49. SCROGGINS, *supra* note 41, at 329.

50. United States v. Marzook, 426 F. Supp. 2d 820, 824–26 (N.D. Ill. 2006).

51. United States v. Campa, 529 F.3d 980, 987–88 (11th Cir. 2008).

52. Stephen Kimber, *The Cuban Five Were Fighting Terrorism. Why Did We Put Them in Jail?*, WASH. POST, Oct. 4, 2013

53. *Campa*, 529 F.3d at 989, 991.

54. United States v. Campa, 459 F.3d 1121, 1154–55 (11th Cir. 2006).

55. *Campa*, 529 F.3d at 1018.

56. Abby Goodnough, *U.S. Paid 10 Journalists for Anti-Castro Reports*, N.Y. TIMES, Sept. 9, 2006, at A9.

CHAPTER 5

1. 543 U.S. 220, 245, 260–61 (2005).

2. *Id.* at 244.

3. 552 U.S. 38, 51 (2007).

4. *Id.*

5. See Wadie E. Said, *Sentencing Terrorist Crimes*, 75 OHIO ST. L.J. 477, 493–98 (2014), for examples.

6. *Id.* at 496–98.

7. U.S. Sentencing Comm'n, U.S. Sentencing Guidelines Manual § 3A1.4 (1995).

8. *Id.* (explaining that a convicted defendant is subject to a 12-level enhancement of his Guidelines calculation if the enhancement is applied; if his Guidelines score after the enhancement does not compute to level 32 by itself, the Guidelines should be automatically adjusted upward to level 32).

9. The full definition is as follows:

(5) The term "Federal crime of terrorism" means an offense that—

(A) is calculated to influence or affect the conduct of government by intimidation or coercion, or to retaliate against government conduct; and

(B) is a violation of—

(i) Section 32 (relating to destruction of aircraft or aircraft facilities), 37 (relating to violence at international airports), 81 (relating to arson within special maritime and territorial jurisdiction), 175 or 175b (relating to biological weapons), 175c (relating to variola virus), 229 (relating to chemical weapons), subsection (a), (b), (c), or (d) of Section 351 (relating to congressional, cabinet, and Supreme Court assassination and kidnaping), 831 (relating to nuclear materials), 832 (relating to participation in nuclear and weapons of mass destruction threats to the United States) 842(m) or (n) (relating to plastic explosives), 844(f)(2) or (3) (relating to arson and bombing of Government property risking or causing death), 844(i) (relating to arson and bombing of property used in interstate commerce), 930(c) (relating to killing or attempted killing during an attack on a Federal facility with a dangerous weapon), 956(a)(1) (relating to conspiracy to murder, kidnap, or maim persons abroad), 1030(a)(1) (relating to protection of computers), 1030(a)(5)(A) resulting in damage as defined in 1030(c)(4)(A)(i)(II) through (VI) (relating to protection of computers), 1114 (relating to killing or attempted killing of officers and employees of the United States), 1116 (relating to murder or manslaughter of foreign officials, official guests, or internationally protected persons), 1203 (relating to hostage taking), 1361 (relating to government property or contracts), 1362 (relating to destruction of communication lines, stations, or systems), 1363 (relating to injury to buildings or property within special maritime and territorial jurisdiction of the United States), 1366(a) (relating to destruction of an energy facility), 1751(a), (b), (c), or (d) (relating to Presidential and Presidential staff assassination and kidnaping), 1992 (relating to terrorist attacks and other acts of violence against railroad carriers and against mass transportation systems on land, on water, or through the air), 2155 (relating to destruction of national defense materials, premises, or utilities), 2156 (relating to national defense material, premises, or utilities), 2280 (relating to violence against maritime navigation), 2281 (relating to violence against maritime fixed platforms), 2332 (relating to certain homicides and other violence against United States nationals occurring outside of the United States), 2332a (relating to use of weapons of mass destruction), 2332b (relating to acts of terrorism transcending national boundaries), 2332f (relating to bombing of public places and facilities), 2332g (relating to missile systems designed to destroy aircraft), 2332h (relating to radiological dispersal devices), 2339 (relating to harboring terrorists), 2339A (relating to providing material support to terrorists), 2339B (relating to providing material support to terrorist organizations), 2339C (relating to financing of terrorism), 2339D (relating to military-type training from a foreign terrorist organization), or 2340A (relating to torture) of this title;

(ii)   sections 92 (relating to prohibitions governing atomic weapons) or 236 (relating to sabotage of nuclear facilities or fuel) of the Atomic Energy Act of 1954 (42 U.S.C. 2122 or 2284);

(iii)   section 46502 (relating to aircraft piracy), the second sentence of section 46504 (relating to assault on a flight crew with a dangerous weapon), section 46505(b)(3) or (c) (relating to explosive or incendiary devices, or endangerment of human life by means of weapons, on aircraft), section 46506 if homicide or attempted homicide is involved (relating to application of certain criminal laws to acts on aircraft), or section 60123(b) (relating to destruction of interstate gas or hazardous liquid pipeline facility) of title 49; or

(iv)   section 1010A of the Controlled Substances Import and Export Act (relating to narco-terrorism).

18 U.S.C. § 2332b(g)(5) (2012) (citation omitted).

10. *See* U.S. Sentencing Comm'n, U.S. Sentencing Guidelines Manual § 3A1.4 cmt. n.2 (1995).

11. *See* U.S. Sentencing Comm'n, U.S. Sentencing Guidelines Manual ch. 5, pt. A (2011) (Sentencing Table), www.ussc.gov/Guidelines/2011_Guidelines/Manual_HTML/5a_SenTab.htm.

12. *See* James P. McLoughlin, Jr., *Deconstructing United States Sentencing Guidelines Section 3A1.4: Sentencing Failure in Cases of Financial Support for Foreign Terrorist Organizations*, 28 Law & Ineq. 51, 62–76 (Winter 2010).

13. *See* U.S. Sentencing Comm'n, 1996 Sourcebook of Federal Sentencing Statistics 31 (1997) [hereinafter 1996 Sourcebook]; U.S. Sentencing Comm'n, 1997 Sourcebook of Federal Sentencing Statistics 41 (1998) [hereinafter 1997 Sourcebook]; U.S. Sentencing Comm'n, 1998 Sourcebook of Federal Sentencing Statistics 41 (1999) [hereinafter 1998 Sourcebook]; U.S. Sentencing Comm'n, 1999 Sourcebook of Federal Sentencing Statistics 41 (2000) [hereinafter 1999 Sourcebook]; U.S. Sentencing Comm'n, 2000 Sourcebook of Federal Sentencing Statistics 41 (2001) [hereinafter 2000 Sourcebook]; U.S. Sentencing Comm'n, 2001 Sourcebook of Federal Sentencing Statistics 41 (2002) [hereinafter 2001 Sourcebook]; U.S. Sentencing Comm'n, 2002 Sourcebook of Federal Sentencing Statistics 41 (2003) [hereinafter 2002 Sourcebook]; U.S. Sentencing Comm'n, 2003 Sourcebook of Federal Sentencing Statistics tbl.18 (2004) [hereinafter 2003 Sourcebook]; U.S. Sentencing Comm'n, 2004 Sourcebook of Federal Sentencing Statistics tbl.18 (Pre-*Blakely*) & tbl.18 (Post-*Blakely*) (2005)

[hereinafter 2004 SOURCEBOOK]; U.S. SENTENCING COMM'N, 2005 SOURCEBOOK OF FEDERAL SENTENCING STATISTICS tbl.18 (Pre-*Booker*) & tbl.18 (Post-*Booker*) (2006) [hereinafter 2005 SOURCEBOOK]; U.S. SENTENCING COMM'N, 2006 SOURCEBOOK OF FEDERAL SENTENCING STATISTICS tbl.18 (2007) [hereinafter 2006 SOURCEBOOK]; U.S. SENTENCING COMM'N, 2007 SOURCEBOOK OF FEDERAL SENTENCING STATISTICS tbl.18 (2008) [hereinafter 2007 SOURCEBOOK]; U.S. SENTENCING COMM'N, 2008 SOURCEBOOK OF FEDERAL SENTENCING STATISTICS tbl.18 (2009) [hereinafter 2008 SOURCEBOOK]; U.S. SENTENCING COMM'N, 2009 SOURCEBOOK OF FEDERAL SENTENCING STATISTICS tbl.18 (2010) [hereinafter 2009 SOURCEBOOK]; U.S. SENTENCING COMM'N, 2010 SOURCEBOOK OF FEDERAL SENTENCING STATISTICS tbl.18 (2011) [hereinafter 2010 SOURCEBOOK]; U.S. SENTENCING COMM'N, 2011 SOURCEBOOK OF FEDERAL SENTENCING STATISTICS tbl.18 (2012) [hereinafter 2011 SOURCEBOOK]; U.S. SENTENCING COMM'N, 2012 SOURCEBOOK OF FEDERAL SENTENCING STATISTICS tbl.18 (2013) [hereinafter 2012 SOURCEBOOK]; 2013 SOURCEBOOK OF FEDERAL SENTENCING STATISTICS tbl.18 (2014) [hereinafter 2013 SOURCEBOOK].

14. In fact, the enhancement was applied only nine times in the first six years after its passage, with no instances of its application in four of those years. 1996 SOURCEBOOK; 1997 SOURCEBOOK; 1998 SOURCEBOOK; 1999 SOURCEBOOK; 2000 SOURCEBOOK; 2001 SOURCEBOOK. Between 2002 and 2005, the enhancement was applied only sporadically, pending the outcome of the line of decisions that culminated with the Supreme Court's opinion in *Booker*. 2002 SOURCEBOOK; 2003 SOURCEBOOK; 2004 SOURCEBOOK; 2005 SOURCEBOOK.

15. 2012 SOURCEBOOK tbl.18; 2013 SOURCEBOOK tbl.18.

16. 2013 SOURCEBOOK tbl.18.

17. United States v. Mohamed, 757 F.3d 757, 759–60 (8th Cir. 2014); United States v. Banol-Ramos, 566 F. App'x 40, 41–43 (2d Cir. 2014); United States v. Wright, 747 F.3d 399, 417–19 (6th Cir. 2014); United States v. Kaziu, 559 F. App'x 32, 39–40 (2d Cir. 2014); United States v. Hassan, 742 F.3d 104, 148–51 (4th Cir. 2014); United States v. Thavaraja, 740 F.3d 253, 258–63 (2d Cir. 2014); United States v. Dye, 538 F. App'x 654, 665–66 (6th Cir. 2013); United States v. Ibrahim, 529 F. App'x 59, 63–64 (2d Cir. 2013); United States v. Thomas, 521 F. App'x 741, 743–44 (11th Cir. 2013); United States v. Kadir, 718 F.3d 115, 125–26 (2d Cir. 2013); United States v. Ortiz, 525 F. App'x 41, 43–44 (2d Cir. 2013); United States v. Banol-Ramos, 516 F. App'x 43, 47–50 (2d Cir. 2013); United States v. Siddiqui, 699 F.3d 690, 708–10 (2d Cir. 2012); United States v. Mohammed, 693 F.3d 192, 201–02 (D.C. Cir. 2012); United States v. Salim, 690 F.3d 115, 126–27 (2d Cir. 2012); United States v. Amawi, 695 F.3d 457, 485–90 (6th Cir. 2012); United States v. Chandia (*Chandia I*), 675 F.3d 329, 338–42 (4th Cir. 2012); United States v. El-Mezain, 664 F.3d 467, 571 (5th Cir. 2011); United States v. Assi, 428 F. App'x 570, 570–71 (6th Cir. 2011); United States v. Mason, 410 F. App'x 881, 887 (6th Cir. 2010); United States v. McDavid, 396 F. App'x 365, 372 (9th Cir. 2010); United States v. Chandia (*Chandia II*), 395 F. App'x 53, 60 (4th Cir. 2010) (per curiam); United States v. Awan, 607 F.3d 306, 312–13 (2d Cir. 2010); United States v. Stewart (*Stewart I*), 590 F.3d 93, 136–52 (2d Cir. 2009); United States v. Christianson, 586 F.3d 532, 540 (7th Cir. 2009); United States v. Ashqar, 582 F.3d 819, 821 (7th Cir. 2009); United States v. Cottrell, 312 F. App'x 979, 981–82 (9th Cir. 2009), *amended and superseded by* 333 F. App'x 213, 215 (9th Cir. 2009); *In re* Terrorist Bombings of U.S. Embassies in E. Africa, 552 F.3d 93, 154–55 (2d Cir. 2008); United States v. Salim, 549 F.3d 67, 77–79 (2d Cir. 2008); United States v. Garey, 546 F.3d 1359, 1363 (11th Cir. 2008); United States v. Parr, 545 F.3d 491, 503–04

(7th Cir. 2008); United States v. Schipke, 291 F. App'x 107, 108 (9th Cir. 2008); United States v. Tubbs, 290 F. App'x 66, 68 (9th Cir. 2008); United States v. Benkahla, 530 F.3d 300, 311 (4th Cir. 2008); United States v. Chandia, 514 F.3d 365, 376 (4th Cir. 2008) (*Chandia III*); United States v. Puerta, 249 F. App'x 359, 360 (5th Cir. 2007) (per curiam); United States v. Hale, 448 F.3d 971, 988 (7th Cir. 2006); United States v. Harris, 434 F.3d 767, 774 (5th Cir. 2005); United States v. Cleaver, 163 F. App'x 622, 630 (10th Cir. 2005); United States v. Arnaout, 431 F.3d 994, 1002 (7th Cir. 2005); United States v. Hammoud, 381 F.3d 316, 355 (4th Cir. 2004), *vacated*, 543 U.S. 1097 (2005); United States v. Mandhai, 375 F.3d 1243, 1247–48 (11th Cir. 2004); United States v. Meskini, 319 F.3d 88, 91–92 (2d Cir. 2003); Haouari v. United States, 429 F. Supp. 2d 671, 681 (S.D.N.Y. 2006).

18. U.S. Sentencing Comm'n, 2013 Ann. Rep. ch. 5, A-45 (2013), http://www.ussc.gov/sites/default/files/pdf/research-and-publications/annual-reports-and-sourcebooks/2013/2013_Annual_Report_Chap5_0.pdf.

19. 582 F.3d 819, 821 (7th Cir. 2009); *see also* United States v. Amawi, 695 F.3d 457, 485–90 (6th Cir. 2012) (finding enhancement applicable but upholding a downward variance from life to 240, 144, and 100 months for each defendant, respectively).

20. *Ashqar*, 582 F.3d at 821.

21. *Id.* at 824–25.

22. *Id.* at 821 (observing that the application of the enhancement changed the defendant's Guidelines range from 24 to 30 months to 210 to 262 months, leaving "[t]he district court [to choose] a point roughly in the middle of those extremes, 135 months' imprisonment"); *see also* United States v. Chandia (*Chandia I*), 675 F.3d 329, 333–34, 341–42 (4th Cir. 2012) (choosing a sentence of 180 months from a pre-enhancement Guidelines range of 63 to 78 months or an enhanced Guidelines range of 360 months to life).

23. The *Ashqar* sentencing was problematic in other respects, not discussed here. *See* Said, *supra* note 5, at 513–17 (detailing the flawed legal analysis in the Seventh Circuit's opinion upholding Ashqar's sentence, and indicating that rather than supporting Hamas, he may have been engaging in a type of political protest).

24. *See* 18 U.S.C. § 2332b(g)(5)(B) (2012).

25. United States v. Wright, 747 F.3d 399, 417–19 (6th Cir. 2014) (affirming application of § 3A1.4 to Occupy Cleveland activists convicted of a plot to blow up a bridge in Ohio); United States v. Dye, 538 F. App'x 654, 665–66 (6th Cir. 2013) (affirming application of § 3A1.4 in case involving the firebombing of a local courthouse to disrupt its operations and in retaliation of pending charges against the defendant); United States v. Mason, 410 F. App'x 881, 884, 887 (6th Cir. 2010) (upholding application of § 3A1.4 to Earth Liberation Front defendant for arson convictions that targeted university agriculture department building and commercial logging equipment); United States v. McDavid, 396 F. App'x 365, 367, 372 (9th Cir. 2010) (upholding application of § 3A1.4 to defendant convicted of conspiring to bomb "a federal facility for tree genetics, a federal dam and fish hatchery, and cell phone towers"); United States v. Christianson, 586 F.3d 532, 534, 537–40 (7th Cir. 2009) (upholding application of § 3A1.4 to Earth Liberation Front—"identified by the FBI as a domestic eco-terrorist group"—defendants who pled guilty to destroying government property); United States v. Garey, 546 F.3d 1359, 1363 (11th Cir. 2008) (upholding application of § 3A1.4 for conviction on counts of threatening to use a weapon of mass destruction against federal building); United States v. Schipke, 291 F. App'x 107, 107–08 (9th Cir. 2008) (upholding application of § 3A1.4 and sentence for threatening to use a weapon of mass destruction);

United States v. Tubbs, 290 F. App'x 66, 67–68 (9th Cir. 2008) (upholding application of § 3A1.4 after guilty plea to multiple arsons); United States v. Puerta, 249 F. App'x 359, 359–60 (5th Cir. 2007) (per curiam) (upholding application of § 3A1.4 to material support count and conspiracy to sell cocaine); United States v. Hale, 448 F.3d 971, 974, 988 (7th Cir. 2006) (upholding application of § 3A1.4 for convictions related to plot to kill federal judge); United States v. Harris, 434 F.3d 767, 774 (5th Cir. 2005) (upholding application of § 3A1.4 for convictions stemming from planting a bomb to damage a municipal building); United States v. Cleaver, 163 F. App'x 622, 624, 630 (10th Cir. 2005) (upholding application of § 3A1.4 for convictions arising from attack on IRS office).

26. United States v. Hammoud, 381 F.3d 316, 325–27 (4th Cir. 2004), *vacated*, 543 U.S. 1097 (2005).

27. 381 F.3d at 326.

28. *Id.* at 354–56.

29. *Id.* at 348–53.

30. *Id.* at 356.

31. *Id.* at 361–62 (Motz, J., dissenting) ("The maximum sentence that the district judge could have imposed in this case, had he not made any additional factual findings, was 57 months.").

32. Hammoud v. United States, 543 U.S. 1097 (2005); United States v. Hammoud, 405 F.3d 1034, 1034 (4th Cir. 2005).

33. United States v. Hammoud, 483 F. App'x 865, 867, 873 (4th Cir. 2012).

34. *Id.* at 873 n.10.

35. *Id.*

36. *Hammoud*, 381 F.3d at 384 n.16 (Gregory, J., dissenting) (citations omitted) (emphasis in original).

37. Adam Liptak, *The Year in Ideas; Material Support*, N.Y. TIMES (Dec. 15, 2002), http://www.nytimes.com/2002/12/15/magazine/the-year-in-ideas-material-support.html.

38. *El-Mezain*, 664 F.3d at 484, 490, 579.

39. *See id.* at 570–71.

40. *Id.* at 571. The Fifth Circuit explained its logic with the following paragraph:

> As pointed out by the Government, the trial was replete with evidence to satisfy application of the terrorism enhancement because of the defendants' intent to support Hamas. The Hamas charter clearly delineated the goal of meeting the Palestinian/Israeli conflict with violent jihad and the rejection of peace efforts and compromise solutions. The defendants knew that they were supporting Hamas, as there was voluminous evidence showing their close ties to the Hamas movement. The evidence of statements made by the defendants at the Philadelphia meeting and in wire intercepts throughout the course of the investigation demonstrated the defendants' support for Hamas's goal of disrupting the Oslo accords and the peace process, as well as their agreement with Hamas's goals of fighting Israel. To the extent that the defendants knowingly assisted Hamas, their actions benefitted Hamas's terrorist goals and were calculated to promote a terrorist crime that influenced government.

> *Id.* (citations omitted).

41. In the prosecution, the charging documents referred to zakat committees in the abstract, leaving the impression that all religious-based charity in the West Bank and Gaza Strip fell under the Hamas umbrella, a rather broad statement, to be sure. *See* Superseding Indictment at ¶ 4, United States v. Holy Land Found. for Relief & Dev., No. 3:04-CR-240-G (N.D. Tex. Nov. 30, 2005); Wadie E. Said, *The Material Support Prosecution and Foreign Policy*, 86 IND. L.J. 543, 588 (2011).

42. Said, *supra* note 41, at 586 (noting the issue of nondesignation of the zakat committees).

43. *See id.* at 590–91.

44. *See* Emily Ratner, *Anonymous Accusers in the Holy Land: Subverting the Right of Confrontation in the United States' Largest Terrorism-Financing Trial*, 13 LOY. J. PUB. INT. L. 575, 582, 583–84 (2012) (collecting sources).

45. *El-Mezain*, 664 F.3d at 527.

46. *Id.* at 488; *see also* Ratner, *supra* note 44, at 584–88 (collecting sources).

47. *See* McLoughlin, *supra* note 12, at 109–11; *cf.* Kennedy v. Louisiana, 554 U.S. 407, 437 (2008) (expressly reserving the right to uphold heightened penalties for, inter alia, terrorism, which it described as an "offense[] against the State").

48. For a discussion of this issue, see Said, *supra* note 5, at 512–17.

49. *See, e.g.,* United States v. Ashqar, 582 F.3d 891, 821–22 (7th Cir. 2009).

50. United States v. Abu Ali, 528 F.3d 210, 221–25 (4th Cir. 2008) (*Abu Ali II*); United States v. Abu Ali, 395 F. Supp. 2d 338, 343 (E.D. Va. 2005) (*Abu Ali I*). For a lengthy discussion and criticism of the federal courts' decision to admit the confession in the Abu Ali prosecution, see Wadie E. Said, *Coercing Voluntariness*, 85 IND. L.J. 1, 17–34 (2010).

51. *Abu Ali II*, 528 F.3d at 225.

52. *Id.* at 221.

53. *Id.* at 269–82 (Motz, J., dissenting) (criticizing, inter alia, "the majority's insistence on refusing to defer to the district court's considered judgment").

54. *Id.* at 262–65 (majority opinion).

55. *See id.* at 269–82 (Motz, J., dissenting).

56. *Id.* at 269 (majority opinion) ("While we of course leave the sentencing function to the able offices of the trial court on remand, we trust that any sentence imposed will reflect the full gravity of the situation before us.").

57. *Abu Ali II*, 528 F.3d at 262.

58. *See* United States v. Abu Ali, 410 F. App'x 673, 676–82 (4th Cir. 2011) (*Abu Ali III*).

59. *Abu Ali II*, 528 F.3d at 264–65.

60. *Id.* at 281 (Motz, J., dissenting).

61. *See id.* at 267–68 (majority opinion).

62. *Id.* at 268 (citation omitted).

63. *Id.*

64. United States v. Stewart, 590 F.3d 93, 151 (2d Cir. 2009) (*Stewart I*).

65. *See id.* at 152–63 (Calabresi, J., concurring); *id.* at 163–86 (Walker, J., concurring in part and dissenting in part).

66. *See id.* at 163–86 (Walker, J., concurring in part and dissenting in part).

67. *See id.* at 152–63 (Calabresi, J., concurring).

68. *Id.* at 172–74 (Walker, J., concurring in part and dissenting in part).

69. *Id.* at 154 n.3 (Calabresi, J., concurring).

70. *Stewart I*, 590 F.3d at 176–77 (Walker, J., concurring in part and dissenting in part) (citing United States v. Abu Ali, 528 F.3d 210, 264–65 (4th Cir. 2008) (*Abu Ali II*)).

71. *Stewart I*, 590 F.3d at 155–57 (Calabresi, J., concurring).

72. *Id.* at 156.

73. "Heartland" is a term of art used in the Guidelines to connote the paradigmatic type of conduct that constitutes a specific crime. Only extraordinary conduct or circumstances that render a crime truly unusual could be described as outside the "heartland" and therefore allow for a sentence outside the Guidelines range. *See* UNITED STATES SENTENCING GUIDELINES MANUAL, ch.1, pt. A, at 6 ("The Commission intends the sentencing courts to treat each guideline as carving out a 'heartland,' a set of typical cases embodying the conduct that each guideline describes. When a court finds an atypical case, one to which a particular guideline linguistically applies but where conduct significantly differs from the norm, the court may consider whether a departure is warranted.").

74. *Stewart I*, 590 F.3d at 177–78 (Walker, J., concurring in part and dissenting in part).

75. *See* Tamar R. Birckhead, *The Conviction of Lynne Stewart and the Uncertain Future of the Right to Defend*, 43 AM. CRIM. L. REV. 1, 7 (2006); Benjamin Weiser, *Judge Orders Release of Dying Lawyer Convicted of Aiding Terrorism*, N.Y. TIMES, Jan. 1, 2014, at A15.

76. *See Stewart I*, 590 F.3d at 170 (Walker, J., concurring in part and dissenting in part).

77. *See generally* Birckhead, *supra* note 75, at 1–52 (arguing that post-9/11 Special Administrative Measures (SAMs) represent classic government overreaching that compromises civil liberties and access to courts).

78. *See Stewart I*, 590 F.3d at 177–78.

79. *See* United States v. Jayyousi, 657 F.3d 1085, 1116–17 (11th Cir. 2011).

80. *Id.*

81. *Id.* at 1115–16.

82. *Id.* at 1116.

83. *Id.* at 1117.

84. *Id.* (citing United States v. Meskini, 319 F.3d 88, 92 (2d Cir. 2003)).

85. *Id.* at 1118.

86. *Id.* at 1118.

87. *Id.* ("The district court also improperly relied on the Terry Nichols and Zacarias Moussaoui prosecutions as examples of the types of behavior that warrant a life sentence because the government sought the death penalty in those cases. On remand, we admonish the district court to avoid imposition of a sentence inconsistent with those of similarly situated defendants. It should not draw comparisons to cases involving defendants who were convicted of less serious offenses, pleaded guilty, or who lacked extensive criminal histories, nor should it draw comparisons to cases where the government sought the imposition of the death penalty. *See United States v. Abu Ali*, 528 F.3d 210, 265 (4th Cir. 2008) ('[T]o require a similar infliction of harm before imposing a similar sentence would effectively raise the bar too high. We should not require that a defendant do what . . . Nichols did in order to receive a life sentence.').").

88. *Jayyousi*, 657 F.3d at 1118.

89. *Id.*

90. *Id.* at 1118–19.

91. *See id.* at 1119–35 (Barkett, J., concurring in part and dissenting in part) (dissenting from majority's decisions to allow FBI agent to testify as expert, to permit the admission of

Padilla's non-*Mirandized* statements to law enforcement, and to overturn as substantively unreasonable Padilla's sentence).

92. *Jayyousi*, 657 F.3d at 1131 (quoting Gall v. United States, 552 U.S. 38, 51 (2007)).

93. *Id.* at 1134.

94. *Id.*

95. *Id.* at 1133–34.

96. *Id.* at 1132–33.

97. *Id.* at 1132.

98. *Id.* at 1132 (Barkett, J., concurring in part and dissenting in part).

99. *Id.* at 1117 (majority opinion).

100. *Id.* at 1132–33 (Barkett, J., concurring in part and dissenting in part) (citing United States v. Irey, 612 F.3d 1160, 1213–16 (11th Cir. 2010)).

101. 657 F.3d at 1133 (citing United States v. Meskini, 319 F.3d 88, 92 (2d Cir. 2003)).

102. *Id.* at 1133.

103. *Id.* at 1134.

104. Warren Richey, *The Strange Saga of Jose Padilla: Judge Adds Four Years*, Christian Science Monitor, Sept. 9, 2014.

105. United States v. Ressam, 679 F.3d 1069, 1106 (9th Cir. 2012) (Schroeder, J., dissenting) ("The majority's implicit assumption that terrorism is different, and must be treated differently, thus flies in the face of the congressionally sanctioned structure of sentencing that applies to terrorism as well as all other kinds of federal criminal offenses. Our courts are well equipped to treat each offense and offender individually, and we should not create special sentencing rules and procedures for terrorists").

106. *Meskini*, 319 F.3d at 92.

107. For an example of a sentencing judge making such distinctions, see *United States v. Babar Ahmad & Syed Talha Ahsan*, 3:04CR301(JCH), 3:06CR194, *Sentencing Hearing* at 56 (D. Conn., July 16, 2014) ("So to the extent that the *Meskini* case talks about terrorists . . . I do not agree that anyone who is guilty of material support is in that category of terrorists") (pleading on file with author).

108. U.S. Dep't of Just., *Remarks by Attorney General Holder at the Southern Center for Human Rights Frederick Douglass Awards*, Nov. 13, 2014, http://www.justice.gov/opa/speech/remarks-attorney-general-holder-southern-center-human-rights-frederick-douglass-awards.

109. U.S. Sentencing Commission, *Comment of Honorable Patti B. Saris, Chair, U.S. Sentencing Commission, On Amendment Reducing Drug Guidelines Becoming Effective Tomorrow*, Oct. 31, 2014, http://www.ussc.gov/sites/default/files/pdf/news/press-releases-and-news-advisories/news-advisories/20141031_News_Advisory.pdf.

110. See U.S. Dep't of Just., Legal Resource Guide to the Federal Bureau of Prisons 2014, at 38–39 (2014), http://www.bop.gov/resources/pdfs/legal_guide.pdf [hereinafter BOP Guide].

111. *Id.* at 38; *see also* 28 C.F.R. § 501.2 (authorizing this type of SAM). The Director can authorize the Warden to implement this type of SAM "[u]pon direction of the Attorney General." BOP Guide, *supra* note 110, at 38.

112. BOP Guide, *supra* note 110, at 38.

113. *Id.*

114. *Id.*

115. *Id.* at 39; *see also* 28 C.F.R. § 501.3 (authorizing this type of SAM). As with the previous SAM application, the Director can authorize the Warden to implement this type of SAM "[u]pon direction of the Attorney General." BOP GUIDE, *supra* note 110, at 39.

116. BOP GUIDE, *supra* note 110, at 39.

117. *Id.* at 39.

118. *Id.*

119. United States v. Felipe, 148 F.3d 101, 109–12 (2d Cir. 1998); Benjamin Weiser, *Judge Allows Gang Leader to Talk with Other Infamous Prisoners*, N.Y. TIMES, Mar. 11, 1999, at B1.

120. Atul Gawande, *Hellhole*, NEW YORKER, Mar. 30, 2009; CTR. FOR CONSTITUTIONAL RIGHTS, *Torture: The Use of Solitary Confinement in U.S. Prisons*, ccrjustice.org/solitary-factsheet; *Solitary Watch* website, http://solitarywatch.com/about/.

121. John Schwartz & Benjamin Weiser, *Judge Allows Trial on Terrorist's Challenge to Prison Rules*, N.Y. TIMES, Oct. 4, 2011, at A23.

122. Yousef v. Reno, 254 F.3d 1214 (10th Cir. 2001).

123. *Stewart I*, 590 F.3d at 98–100.

124. Joshua L. Dratel, *Ethical Issues in Defending a Terrorism Case: Stuck in the Middle*, 2 CARDOZO PUB. L. POL'Y & ETHICS J. 65, 104 (2003); Schwartz & Weiser, *supra* note 121 (noting that courts are generally deferential to the authorities in terrorism cases involving SAMs).

125. al-Owhali v. Holder, 687 F.3d 1236, 1239, 1243 (10th Cir. 2012).

126. *Id.* at 1243.

127. Mohammed v. Holder, 47 F. Supp. 3d 1236,1265 (D. Colo. June 17, 2014).

128. Laura Rovner & Jeanne Theoharis, *Preferring Order to Justice*, 61 AM. U. L. REV. 1331, 1367 (2012).

129. *Id.* at 1359–62.

130. *Id.* at 1369–70.

131. *See, e.g.*, Heena Musabji & Christina Abraham, *The Threat to Civil Liberties and Its Effect on Muslims in America*, 1 DEPAUL J. SOC. JUST. 83, 102–08 (2007); Birckhead, *supra* note 75; Chris Ford, *Fear of a Blackened Planet: Pressured by the War on Terror, Courts Ignore the Erosion of the Attorney-Client Privilege and Effective Assistance of Counsel in 28 C.F.R. § 501.3(D) Cases*, 12 WASH. & LEE J. CIVIL RTS. & SOC. JUST. 51 (2006); Sam A. Schmidt & Joshua L. Dratel, *Turning the Tables: Using the Government's Secrecy and Security Arsenal for the Benefit of the Client in Terrorism Prosecutions*, 48 N.Y.L. SCH. L. REV. 69, 70–76 (2004); Marjorie Cohn, *The Evisceration of the Attorney-Client Privilege in the Wake of September 11, 2001*, 71 FORDHAM L. REV. 1233, 1251 (2003); Akhil Reed Amar & Vikram David Amar, *The New Regulation Allowing Federal Agents to Monitor Attorney-Client Conversations: Why It Threatens Fourth Amendment Values*, 34 CONN. L. REV. 1163 (2002).

132. Alana Semuels, *Legal Battle Flares over Dzhokhar Tsarnaev Security Measures*, L.A. TIMES, Nov. 7, 2013. Concerns about monitored attorney-client communications also plague national security cases in general, where the specter of NSA spying on all electronic communications has attorneys concerned that they cannot ensure confidentiality with clients. *See* Dan Froomkin, *Top Journalists and Lawyers: NSA Surveillance Threatens Press Freedoms and Right to Counsel*, INTERCEPT, July 28, 2014, https://firstlook.org/theintercept/2014/07/28/nsa-surveillance-threatens-press-freedom-right-counsel-survey-finds/.

133. Dan Eggen, *Screening of Mail at Federal Prisons Lags*, Wash. Post, Oct. 4, 2006.

134. Dan Eggen, *Facility Holding Terrorism Inmates Limits Communication*, Wash. Post, Feb. 25, 2007.

135. Alia Malek, *Gitmo in the Heartland*, Nation, Mar. 28, 2011, http://www.thenation.com/article/159161/gitmo-heartland.

136. Fed. Bureau of Prisons, U.S. Penitentiary, Terre Haute, CMU Institution Supplement 1 (2006), https://www.aclu.org/files/pdfs/prison/benkahlavbop_institutional-supplement.pdf [hereinafter Terre Haute Institution Supplement]. "The Institution Supplements for both the Terre Haute CMU and the Marion CMU are nearly identical." Aref v. Holder (*Aref I*), 774 F. Supp.2d 147, 153 n.1 (D.D.C. 2011). Thus, like the *Aref* court, the citations here are to the Terre Haute Institution Supplement. *See id.*

137. Terre Haute Institution Supplement, *supra* note 136. "Additionally, the unit contains a range of cells dedicated to segregated housing of those inmates in need of being placed in administrative detention or disciplinary segregation status." *Id.*

138. *Id.* at 1–3. However, privileged attorney-client communications cannot be monitored, and "properly scheduled, unmonitored legal visits" are exempt from the CMU visitation parameters. *Id.* at 2.

139. *Id.* at 2.

140. *Id.*

141. *Id.*

142. *Id.* at 2.

143. *Id.* The rule is subject to the same exception that applies in telephone communications: the inmate and visiting community member may converse in another language via previously scheduled simultaneous translation monitoring. *Id.* at 2–3.

144. Terre Haute Institutional Supplement, *supra* note 136, at 2–4.

145. David M. Shapiro, *How Terror Transformed Federal Prison: Communication Management Units*, 44 Colum. Hum. Rts. L. Rev. 47, 62–68 (2012) (summarizing the differences between regular BOP custody and the CMU).

146. *See Aref I*, 774 F. Supp. 2d at 153; ACLU, *Bureau of Prisons Should Shutter Secretive and Isolated Communications Management Units, Says ACLU* (June 2, 2010), https://www.aclu.org/prisoners-rights/bureau-prisons-should-shutter-secretive-and-isolated-communications-management-unit [hereinafter *ACLU Article*]; Carrie Johnson & Margot Williams, *"Guantanamo North": Inside Secretive U.S. Prisons*, NPR (Mar. 3, 2011), http://www.npr.org/2011/03/03/134168714/guantanamo-north-inside-u-s-secretive-prisons.

147. Lindh v. Warden, Fed. Corr. Inst., Terre Haute, Ind., 2013 WL 139699, at *15–16 (S.D. Ind. Jan. 11, 2013).

148. Lindh v. Warden, Fed. Corr. Inst., Terre Haute, Ind., 2013 WL 3790897, at *3 (S.D. Ind. July 19, 2013).

149. Aref v. Holder, 953 F. Supp. 2d 133 (D.D.C. 2013) (*Aref II*); *Aref I*, *supra* note 136; Ctr. for Constitutional Rights, *Communications Management Units*, July 9, 2014, http://www.ccrjustice.org/files/CCR_CMU_2014Documents-20140709.pdf.

150. *See* Aref v. Holder, Case No. 1:10-cv-00539-BJR, Memorandum of Law in Support of Plaintiffs' Motion for Summary Judgment 8–11, Apr. 23, 2014 (summarizing the lack of

policy and disparate criteria), http://ccrjustice.org/files/Memo%20in%20Support%20of%20
Summary%20Judgment%20Motion.pdf

151. *Aref II*, 953 F. Supp. 2d at 136–37 ("An inmate may be placed in a CMU because

(a) [t]he inmate's current offense(s) of conviction, or offense conduct, included association, communication, or involvement, related to international or domestic
terrorism;

(b) [t]he inmate's current offense(s) of conviction, offense conduct, or activity while
incarcerated, indicates a propensity to encourage, coordinate, facilitate, or otherwise act in furtherance of, illegal activity through communication with persons in
the community;

(c) [t]he inmate has attempted, or indicates a propensity, to contact victims of the
inmate's current offense(s) of conviction;

(d) [t]he inmate committed prohibited activity related to misuse/abuse of approved
communication methods while incarcerated; or

(e) [t]here is any other evidence of a potential threat to the safe, secure, and orderly
operation of prison facilities, or protection of the public, as a result of the inmate's
unmonitored communication with persons in the community").

152. CTR. FOR CONSTITUTIONAL RIGHTS, *supra* note 149; *Aref I*, 774 F. Supp. 2d at 154–56
(reproducing the plaintiffs' CMU designation statements, which were cursory and, in their
view, contained erroneous or disputed information).

153. Kevin Gosztola, *Communication Management Units: BOP's Lack of Process
Allows for Targeting of Muslims, Political Speech*, DISSENTER, Apr. 24, 2014, http://
dissenter.firedoglake.com/2014/04/24/communication-management-un
its-bureau-of-prisons-lack-of-process-permits-targeting-of-muslims-political-speech/

154. Royer v. Fed. Bureau of Prisons, 934 F. Supp.2d 92, 94–95, 99–100 (D.D.C. 2013).

155. Royer v. Fed. Bureau of Prisons, Case No. 10-cv-1196 (RCL), *Memorandum and Order*,
Jan. 15, 2014, http://legaltimes.typepad.com/files/1-15-14-order.pdf.

156. Eggen, *supra* note 134 (the other inmates were a Croatian convicted of violent crimes and
an unidentified Colombian).

157. *Aref v. Holder, supra* note 150, Memorandum of Law in Support of Plaintiffs' Motion
for Summary Judgment 10, http://ccrjustice.org/files/Memo%20in%20Support%20of%20
Summary%20Judgment%20Motion.pdf.

158. *Id.* at 10–11.

159. Malek, *supra* note 135; Christopher S. Stewart, *"Little Gitmo,"* N.Y. MAG., July 11, 2011, http://nymag.
com/news/features/yassin-aref-2011-7/; Annie P. Waldman, *Inside the Kafkaesque World of the US's "Little
Guantanamos,"* VICE MAG., Mar. 20, 2014, http://www.vice.com/read/inside-the-kafkaesque-world-of-
the-uss-little-guantanamos; Molly Crabapple, *The United States Wants the World to Forget These
Prisoners*, CREATIVE TIME REP., July 21, 2014, http://creativetimereports.org/2014/07/21/
molly-crabapple-us-wants-world-to-forget-communications-management- unit-prisoners/.

160. Kevin Gosztola, *Podcast: CCR Senior Attorney Rachel Meeropol on "Truly Kafkaesque"
Bureau of Prisons' Policy for CMUs*, DISSENTER, May 4, 2014, http://dissenter.firedoglake.
com/2014/05/04/podcast-ccr-senior-attorney-rachel-meeropol-on-truly-kafkaesque-bureau-of-
prisons-policy-for-cmus/.

161. *Aref I*, 774 F. Supp.2d at 155.

162. Malek, *supra* note 135.

163. *See, e.g.*, Rezaq v. Nalley, 677 F.3d 1001, 1013–16 (10th Cir. 2012).

CONCLUSION

1. Ashutosh Bhagwat, *Terrorism and Associations*, 63 EMORY L.J. 581, 583, 615 (2014).

2. Benjamin Weiser, *The Drugs and the Robberies Aren't Real, but the Charges Are*, N.Y. TIMES, Dec. 5, 2014 at A26.

3. United States v. Dunlap, 593 Fed. App'x 619, (9th Cir., Dec. 4, 2014) ("While we, like the district court, question the wisdom of the government's expanding use of fake stash house sting operations, we are bound by our court's prior decisions holding that when such sting operations are conducted, as in this case, within the guidelines established by our precedent, they do not violate due process and cross the line into outrageous government conduct").

4. Gabrielle Canon, *I Was There When an Undercover Cop Pulled a Gun on Unarmed Protestors in Oakland. Here's How It Happened*, MOTHER JONES, Dec. 12, 2014, http://www.motherjones.com/mojo/2014/12/undercover-officer-gun-berkeley-oakland-protest.

5. Eric Lichtblau & William M. Arkin, *More Federal Agencies Are Using Undercover Operatives*, N.Y. TIMES, Nov. 16, 2014, at A1.

6. Frances Robles & Julie Hirschfeld Davis, *U.S. Frees Last of the "Cuban Five," Part of a 1990s Spy Ring*, N.Y. TIMES, Dec. 18, 2014, at A18; Marjorie Cohn, *Cuban Five at Heart of US/ Cuba Deal*, COUNTERPUNCH, Dec. 18, 2014, http://www.counterpunch.org/2014/12/18/cuban-five-at-heart-of-us-cuba-deal/.

In a different but related context, in late May 2014, the U.S. government freed five Taliban captives, including two senior leaders, who had been held for many years in military detention at Guantanamo, in exchange for a U.S. serviceman captured and held by the Taliban in Afghanistan. Eric Schmitt & Charlie Savage, *American Soldier Freed by Taliban in Prisoner Trade*, N.Y. TIMES, June 1, 2014, at A1.

7. Mark Mazzetti, *Senate Panel Faults C.I.A. over Brutality and Deceit in Terrorism Investigations*, N.Y. TIMES, Dec. 10, 2014 at A1.

8. Helene Cooper, *127 Prisoners Remain at Guantanamo as U.S. Sends 5 to Kazakhstan*, N.Y. TIMES, Jan. 1, 2015 at A6; *Guantanamo by the Numbers*, HUMAN RIGHTS FIRST (last updated Dec. 11, 2014), http://www.humanrightsfirst.org/sites/default/files/gtmo-by-the-numbers.pdf.

9. Stephen I. Vladeck, *Terrorism Prosecutions and the Problem of Constitutional "Cross-Ruffing,"* 36 CARDOZO L. REV. 101, 102–03 (2014) ("current case law does—and would—allow the government to 'cross-ruff' almost with impunity both prior to a criminal trial and, if the defendant is acquitted or receives a relatively short sentence, after he is no longer subject to confinement as a result," defining "cross-ruffing" as "to use military and law enforcement authorities *together* in a manner that avoids the restrictions that would attach if a detainee were subjected exclusively to one of those paradigms") (emphasis in the original).

Index

DISCARD

CPSIA information can be obtained
at www.ICGtesting.com
Printed in the USA
BVOW08s2323211217
503178BV00002B/4/P

9 780190 296810